Critical Essays on Benjamin Franklin

Melvin H. Buxbaum

G.K. Hall & Co. • Boston, Massachusetts

Library of Congress Cataloging-in-Publication Data
Critical essays on Benjamin Franklin

(Critical essays on American literature)
Includes index.
1. Franklin, Benjamin, 1706-1790. I. Buxbaum, Melvin H. II. Series
E302.6.F8C785 1987 973.3'092'4 87-44
ISBN 0-8161-8699-5 (alk. paper)

This publication is printed on permanent/durable acid-free paper
MANUFACTURED IN THE UNITED STATES OF AMERICA

CRITICAL ESSAYS ON AMERICAN LITERATURE

This series seeks to anthologize the most important criticism on a wide variety of topics and writers in American literature. Our readers will find in various volumes not only a generous selection of reprinted articles and reviews but original essays, bibliographies, manuscript sections, and other materials brought to public attention for the first time. This volume on Benjamin Franklin, certainly one of the most diverse thinkers and writers in American history, contains sections on Literary, Political, Economic, Scientific, and Religious concerns as well as a concluding group of essays containing "Views from Abroad." In addition to an extensive introduction by Melvin H. Buxbaum, which surveys the history of scholarly comment on this work, there are reprinted articles by D. H. Lawrence, Hugh J. Dawson, Alfred Owen Aldridge, and I. Bernard Cohen as well as original essays by Ormond Seavey, William B. Willcox, Tracy Mott and George W. Zinke, and Donald H. Meyer. We are confident that this volume will make a permanent and significant contribution to American literary study.

James Nagel, General Editor

Northeastern University

CONTENTS

INTRODUCTION
Melvin H. Buxbaum 1

Literary Concerns

Fathers and Sons: Franklin's "Memoirs" as Myth and Metaphor
Hugh J. Dawson 19

The Lawrence Attack

Benjamin Franklin [1918] 41
D. H. Lawrence

Benjamin Franklin [1923] 50
D. H. Lawrence

Benjamin Franklin and D. H. Lawrence as Conflicting Modes of Consciousness 60
Ormond Seavey

Political Concerns

Benjamin Franklin and the Nature of American Diplomacy 81
Jonathan R. Dull

Franklin's Last Years in England: The Making of a Rebel 96
William B. Willcox

Economic Concerns

Benjamin Franklin's Economic Thought: A Twentieth Century Appraisal 111
Tracy Mott and George W. Zinke

Scientific Concerns

The Science of Benjamin Franklin 129
I. Bernard Cohen

Religious Concerns

Franklin's Religion 147
Donald H. Meyer

Views from Abroad

[Introduction to *Franklin and His Contemporaries*] 169
Alfred Owen Aldridge

Franklin and the Imperial Court 176
Kimura Ki

Franklin in the American Mirage of the Risorgimento 183
Antonio Pace

Franklin: An Idol of the Times 202
Horst Dippel

INDEX 211

INTRODUCTION

Leonard Woods, in his 1826 *Life of Franklin,* decried the pitiful state of Franklin biography. It was about time, he complained, to overcome the simplistic notions and prejudices that had characterized discussions of the philosopher and provide a fair and probing account of him.[1] Unfortunately, Woods was responding to a tradition of bias and superficiality that was already more than half a century old; and, second, there really was a genuine need to depict Franklin in all his remarkable complexity. He was, after all, a great man and benefactor and deserves serious treatment. Yet it is only fair to observe that Franklin is elusive, having donned many different masks in his public and private lives; therefore, it is hard for a biographer to know just who is the real Benjamin Franklin. And this problem has been exacerbated by the fact that his political activities generally provoked feelings marked by passion and bias rather than fairness and accuracy.
been exacerbated by the fact that his political activities generally provoked feelings marked by passion and bias rather than fairness and accuracy.

In 1764, for example, he led a faction made up of his political allies, who included frequently reluctant Quakers, in an effort to wrest Pennsylvania from its proprietor, Thomas Penn, and bring it under the control of the Crown. The move was immediately challenged by the Presbyterians and Germans as well as by others in the Proprietary Party, all of whom joined in launching a steady and vitriolic attack on Franklin as a politician and man and thereby provided very negative contributions toward Franklin biography. The plan to change the government, one writer charged in *An Answer to the Plot,* was a manifestation of Franklin's well known dangerous ambition. He was quite willing to sacrifice the religious liberties of Presbyterians and Germans so that he could ingratiate himself to the king and secure the appointment as Royal Governor of Pennsylvania.[2] This view of the situation was echoed repeatedly by other typically anonymous authors,[3] and Franklin's defenders, though active, were hard pressed to save his reputation, for he was variously accused of being a tyrant, a traitor to his fellow Pennsylvanians and a bigot.[4] It was in this year that Franklin lost for the only time an election for the Assembly.

It was by no means the last time he was to be attacked, though. His activities in England and France in behalf of the American causes brought upon him the animosity of British and American Tories. With them as with the supporters of Thomas Penn, there was no middle ground, no attempt to moderate anger with judgment. In 1774 the Crown's Solicitor General, Alexander Wedderburn, savaged the sixty-eight-year-old Franklin, calling him a deceitful, malicious incendiary and traitor to a government that had given him honors and profitable positions.[5] Wedderburn's tirade helped to establish his tone of subsequent attacks on Franklin who, throughout the eighteenth century, was portrayed as a plagiarist, a petty, self-seeking politician, a warmonger and as a traitor.[6]

Most of these detractors were caught up in the furor engendered by the War of Independence, but as late as 1797, Jonathan Boucher, An American Tory, chastised Franklin in a sermon entitled "On the Character of Ahitophil" and in his "Appendix to the Two Sermons on Absalom and Ahitophil."[7] The sermons were originally preached in America before the Revolution but published at the later date in *A View of the Causes and Consequences of the American Revolution. . . .* When he first delivered the sermon in 1774, Boucher likened Franklin to Ahitophil, who "acted a busy and important part" in the revolt of Absalom.[8] There was little doubt in Boucher's mind that Franklin had long planned the revolt against the mother country, and twenty-three years later, the minister defended the comparison, charging Franklin with being a demagogue. This so-called patriot had not only initially supported the Stamp Act but had positively "originated" the idea of the tax. It was no great principle that changed his view but rather anger at having been insulted by Alexander Wedderburn. American had therefore little cause to claim that Franklin was even an honorable man, much less a national hero.[9]

The one-sidedness of Franklin's enemies is paralleled by the equally intemperate nature of his friends in America and abroad. If his detractors belittled him unfairly, his supporters often idealized him beyond all reason. The anonymous author of *The Scribbler*, a 1764 pamphlet defending Franklin's effort to make Pennsylvania a royal colony, rebuked those who had charged philosopher with political ambition and hostility toward the Germans and Scot Irish. These people did not appreciate Franklin, did not understand that far from being personally interested in the situation, Franklin was actually a selfless patriot who, as was customary with him, sought only the welfare of the province.[10] Three years later, Jesuit Giuseppe Maria Mazzelarri wrote a poetic account of electricity, *Electricorum libri VI*, and declared that Franklin's outstanding accomplishment in the sciences was even more impressive because he came from so primitive a country as America rather than from cultivated and learned Europe. His success, then, was virtually without positive external influence, deriving instead from his remarkable natural abilities and his intense desire to help mankind. Franklin was thus not only a scientist but hero to all men and a model for other philosophers.[11] In 1777, Jacques Barbeu-Dubourg, writing in his

Calendrier de Philadelphie par l'année M DCC LXXVII, praised the American statesman and moralist for having inculcated into his countrymen the Poor Richard type virtues that provided a healthy contrast to the supercilious manners of Europeans. To Dubourg, Franklin was the noblest of savages, a natural man whose life suggested the promise of the future.

This sentiment was widespread in France, which searched for living proof of Rousseau's theory concerning the goodness of natural man. Jean Le Rond d'Alembert, in fact, expresed the view poetically in 1779 in "Vers sur M. Franklin." Inspired by Turgot's famous epigram—he seized the lightning from the sky, and the sceptre from tyrants—Alembert extolled Franklin for his numerous virtues generally, but he could not resist calling particular attention to his subject's unaffected simplicity, matchless humanity and courage. Alembert was genuinely worried, though, that his tribute failed to do justice to Franklin's qualities and achievements.[12]

It was common for Franklin to be acclaimed extravagantly for what he was and what he had done. Many of his contemporaries paid homage to him for his brilliance, honesty, humanitarianism, modesty (which is more than Franklin himself admitted to in his *Autobiography*), wisdom and patriotism, all of which made him seem not only a larger-than-life sage, but a gift of God to men, a true liberator in every way. Jean Jacques Leroux des Tillets, in his 1779 *Dialogue entre Pasquin et Marphorio*, made Franklin the spirit of science, destroying whatever is false science. French readers were treated by Leroux des Tillets to an American who was not only a philosopher, but an all-knowing magician who could do no wrong.[13] That same year Franklin was praised by Aimé Ambroise Joseph Feutry who, drawing upon Athens for his inspiration and symbolism, declared that Franklin was "le Solon du nouvel hémisphere,"[14] Perhaps the most idealized treatment in the eighteenth century occurred in the *Almanach des muses* for 1785. Here we are told that to find a parallel to the universally admired Franklin, one had to turn to Greek mythology, for the American is surely nothing less than modern Nestor.[15] Franklin's death in 1790 added nothing significant to the achievement of a balanced view of him, and so the entire century is dominated by perceptions and treatments that are either unreasonably negative or impossibly idealized.

One would expect, though, that by 1826, the year of Woods's complaint, enough time would have elapsed to permit a more judicious assessment of this complex and remarkable man; however, this was not the case. Early in the century, parson Weems began his continuations of Franklin's life until by 1818 he substituted his fanciful biography for the philosopher's own account, which was, because of its earthy qualities, presumably less appealing and salable to early nineteenth-century readers. What we have in Weems's life is an idealized Franklin of the kind his fondest admirers, especially the French, created during the Revolutionary War and afterwards. But the man who described himself as George Washington's parson also made Franklin a pious Christian at the end. For Weems, describing his subject's last illness, says that Franklin kept in front of him and delighted in a picture of Christ on the cross. All's well that ends well! Weems clearly believed that America was not yet ready to accept a confirmed deist as a national hero, or at least not to pay for reading about one.[16]

The two major points in Weems's biography, that of Franklin as a Poor Richard success model and as a Christian at the end, persisted throughout the nineteenth century and even beyond. That these are misperceptions and as such are unfair to Franklin and to readers seems not to have mattered or, perhaps, not to have been well understood by the last century. He is therefore depicted by Federico Giunti, Bartolomeo Aquarone, and other Italian writers as a middle-class Socrates and a worthy model for their countrymen to follow if they would improve their lot in life and bring prosperity to the Italy of the Risorgimento.[17] Other Europeans and also Americans, responding to the rapid and extreme changes brought about by industrialization and capitalism, urged their contemporaries to accept willingly these changes by ignoring Franklin's complexity, altruism, and concerns about unwarranted concentrations of wealth and presented him simply as a spokesman for capitalism and its values.[18] At a time when workers were desperately poor, horribly exploited, and understandably hostile toward their work and their employers, they were told not very helpfully to consider that the lives of St. Augustine and Franklin proved workers possessed the potential for dignity, if only they would put forth the effort to succeed.[19] Their condition was not very different from Franklin's, they were told, and so they could attain what he did by practicing his well publicized virtues.[20] If workers and their families were suffering, the fault lay not in astonishingly rapid industrial growth, in unbridled capitalism, or with Robber Barons, but apparently with the workers themselves! One could hardly find a more certain way of making Franklin an irrelevant bore.

The second major fabrication in Weems's narative is that Franklin died a pious Christian. Charles Hulbert repeated the story as early as 1820 and embellished it. His Franklin is a closet Christian who, on his deathbed, advises a young man to make the study of the Bible the serious work of his life.[21] It is true that Franklin wore many masks and permitted the French to think him a virtuous Quaker. Yet the exigencies of political fundraising aside, he never hid his deism. In fact, he had an opportunity for a dramatic deathbed conversion which would have made him more palatable in certain quarters. His old acquaintance and fellow scientist, the Reverend Ezra Stiles, had expressed concern over Franklin's rejection of Christianity and hoped for an eleventh hour change of heart. Instead, Franklin's reply reaffirms his deism:

> I believe in one God, the creator of the universe, That he governs it by his Providence. That he ought to be worshipped. That the most acceptable service we render to him is doing good to his other children. That

> the soul of man is immortal, and will be treated with justice in another life respecting its conduct in this. These I take to be the fundamental points in all sound religion, and I regard them as you do in whatever sect I meet with them.[22]

Franklin, then, cannot be held responsible for the many attempts of such authors as Freeman Hunt, John Nicholas Norton, and William Makepeace Thayer to render him Christianized and sanitized.[23]

Other apologists cannot quite make him a pious convert, but they do what they can to make him Christian enough to be a bona fide American hero. The Duyckinck brothers wrote that although Franklin lapsed into deism, his New England background kept him truly pious and nearly religious all his life and thus saved him from going the way of Tom Paine and the French.[24] Thomas Hughes and John Torrey Morse tried to convince their readers that Franklin was actually a Unitarian Christian or a fundamental rather than sectarian Christian with Anglican leanings, not at all a deist and far more a conventional Christian than had been realized with regard to his worship and morality.[25] Even James Parton, whose life of Franklin is still the most complete, fell prey to the Christianizing impulse.[26] He thus joins other defenders of Franklin who, though interesting for historical and cultural reasons, do little to help us understand the man adequately.

Franklin's detractors are once again as guilty of simplism, inaccuracy, prejudice, and distortion as are his friends. If his supporters ignore unpleasant realities, his opponents find serious faults where there were none. To a number of them, Franklin is a man devoid of religious or moral principles or even a hint of spirituality. Early in the nineteenth century Joseph Dennie in *The Port Folio* saw this supposed flaw as the basis for continuing old Tory and Federalist attacks on the too democratic and lowbrow Franklin. Among the charges leveled at him by *The Port Folio* were that he was an extreme republican or even Jacobin whose immoral deism and "pitiful system of Economics" had degraded the American character. Little else, however, could be expected of one who was a mere plagiarist and rejected Christianity and opposed established churches.[27]

Dennie was unsparing in his criticism of Franklin, but it remained for the Reverend Hugh M'Neile to damn him. In 1841 he delivered a lecture that was supposed to honor Franklin's memory, but the minister confidently asserted that any tribute would have to be confined to his subject's good deeds and his opposition to slavery. As important and commendable as these things were, they were inadequate, for Franklin "knew not God" and was consequently "spotted with guilt—and dumb, absolutely dumb, as to the pardon of that guilt."[28] Thirteen years later an anonymous author also feared that Franklin had been merely a worldly man and had been damned.[29] If it was distressing to read such superficial and biased nonsense at midcentury, what can be said when in 1896 we read the same sort of thing? And it comes not from some anonymous hack or from a zealot with an axe to grind, but from so normally an astute and honest critic as Brander Matthews, one of the few men of his time who realized that Mark Twain was not just another Artemus Ward. Yet, Matthews laments, Franklin was incapable of faith because he was without the slightest degree of spirituality.[30]

His foes seem as intent on diminishing Franklin as his admirers are to idealize him. He is accused of being a plagiarist,[31] and a mere utilitarian.[32] Moreover, as one agitator for women's suffrage charged, Franklin was a terrible husband and father to leave Debby Franklin and his two children while he fiddled around with politics in England. Debby Franklin, we are told, was left alone to see her small children through all the dangerous childhood diseases. William Duane pointed out that when Franklin left on his first mission to England late in 1757, William Franklin was 26 and Sally 14; however, it is the perception of Franklin as a poor husband and father, not the facts, that reigns here.[33]

Franklin had been so abused by both his friends and enemies, had been made to seem such a morality-spouting hypocrite, vulgarian, and bore that the time was ripe for Mark Twain to act and satirize him as the bane of normal boys throughout the world.[34] F. B. Greene in 1880 and Harry B. Weiss in 1935 also parodied the Poor Richardisms which they took to represent the true and complete Franklin and hoped to rid the world of the adages and of the kind of mind that produced them.[35] Still another critic, Donald G. Mitchell, believed he discovered the reasons for Franklin's moral deficiencies and crudities: he had grown up without the ameliorating influence of refined ladies. To be sure, as long as he remained in America or even in England his impulse to coarseness was controlled. How could it be otherwise? But France was his undoing. There all the vulgarity in his nature and writings were allowed to surface, for in France, no one cared![36] At the end of the century, Henry S. Pancoast found the source of Franklin's trouble elsewhere. Admitting that Franklin did have literary and personal merit, he was nevertheless far too practical, materialistic, and limited in his vision to represent the true American character, and it was a serious error to think of him as typically American. He actually represented instead the English character.[37] Sidney George Fisher, in 1898, thought balance required that Franklin be demythologized and presented as the earthy man he was; however, he so self-consciously tries to compensate for the Weems-like accounts of Franklin that he too is guilty of negative distortion.[38] Obviously, then, detractors of Franklin, like his admirers, failed to produce a balanced account of his life and career which did justice to his complexity, astonishing versatility, and genius but which also considered his limitations and faults. Nineteenth-century readers were not much closer to balanced understanding of Franklin than their eighteenth-century counterparts.

The twentieth century has made some headway in achieving such a perception. Through many specialized studies we have come to see him more accurately. Still, our success has been quite limited. For one thing, too many modern commentators have perpetuated the absurd notion that Franklin is at bottom just plain folks in America, a representative of the qualities we all have by virtue of being born Americans. Paul Elmer More supported this view in 1900, declaring: "In his shrewdness, versatility, self-reliance, wit, and also in his lack of the deeper reverence and imagination, he . . . more than any other man who has yet lived, represents the American character."[39] A few years later, William Peterfield Trent echoed this view,[40] and another observer, Nathan Haskell Dole, added the surprising opinion that Franklin was a typical American also because he became wealthy and famous.[41] The point has continued to be made to our own day, even by well known scholars who should know better.[42]

The religious issue, if not as prominent as in the nineteenth century, is still nevertheless a factor in modern perceptions of Franklin. While M. M. Mangasarian, an admirer of the statesman, declared flatly that Franklin was much too intelligent and rational a man to be a Christian,[43] the more common judgment is that he was in fact a good Christian, an opinion expressed as late as 1958,[44] or that although he was not a Christian or believer in any conventional sense, he did uphold sound religious and moral principles[45] which effectively made him religious.

Perhaps the single most important issue in shaping the modern understanding of Franklin derives from how one sees him with respect to his economic opinions. Max Weber has conditioned a good many people to see Franklin as Poor Richard, the embodiment of the capitalist thrust inherent in all Calvinists and Yankees.[46] This belief disturbed Edward Everett Hale, who argued that the philosopher was not the ancestor of Scrooge but actually had far broader views of economics than Weber and his many followers realized.[47]

Neither Hale's article nor even a book-length study of Franklin's economics effected the desired change in perception.[48] This most complex and elusive of all the founders was still identified with men like Rockefeller, Carnegie, and Theodore Roosevelt as well as with Poor Richard and the maxims.[49] A decidedly unobjective defender of Franklin, William Guggenheim, asserted that if the sage had been alive in 1929, he would try to convince the Russian people to give up their "Bolshevik tendency" in favor of capitalism[50] and thus presumably improve relations between the Soviet Union and the United States. Later, William E. Lingelbach tried to win justice for Franklin as an economic thinker by pointing out errors in Weber's discussion,[51] but his success was very limited.

The image of Franklin as the forerunner of modern capitalists persisted through the Great Depression. The maxims of Poor Richard were thought to be Franklin's most considered views and to contain the solutions for the problems of unemployment, the depressed stock market, and business failures.[52] An anonymous author, writing in the alumni magazine of the University of Pennsylvania in 1937, attempted to help improve the situation by suggesting that Americans reaffirm their commitment to thrift. The impact on the economy of such a move would be very positive, and there was no more meaningful way to begin than by replacing the likeness of Lincoln on the penny with that of Franklin.[53] A. Whitney Griswold saw a silver lining in the gloomy clouds of 1934 and reminded his countrymen that such diverse ancestors as Cotton Mather, Timothy Dwight, and Franklin all believe, in their own ways, that "God desired Americans to be rich."[54] How much this expression of hope strained the piety and faith of the hungry is unknown. Russell Duane more sensibly offered an economic program. Franklin, he said, would solve our economic problems by venturing briefly into socialist reforms and then returning as soon as possible to rugged individualist free enterprise.[55]

The difficulty with such discussions in general is that they tend to corroborate Weber, ignoring his reductive approach to experience and his simplistic, if shrewd and imaginative, rendering of the American character and of Franklin. Weber and his disciples never considered the full range of Franklin's economic thought and normally limit their reading to the *Autobiography,* the almanacs and, at best, a few other pieces. Such notable scholars as Dixon Wecter and I. Bernard Cohen have cautioned that Franklin is no mere prototype of the modern capitalist,[56] and other modern students of American culture have bewailed the impoverishment of Franklin's complexity and the virtual seizure of him by the Babbitts of the world,[57] but the old image remains well entrenched.[58] It is as embarrassing as it is amusing that they should have felt comfortable in making him one of them. In 1929, for example, he was not only elected the Patron Saint of the American Society of heating and Ventilating Engineers,[59] but was memorialized by a friendly versifier in the following way:

> In leisure time he'd hang around
> Where women, wine and wit abound
> Among the noted seen and water dodgers,
> He'd flip many a merry jest
> With Texas Guinan and Mae West;
> His favoite pal would doubtless be Will Rogers.[60]

This is a degree of egalitarianism Franklin would have found disquieting. Moreover, it is an indication of how incompletely we perceive "Dr. Franklin," as he was nearly always called from 1759 to the end of his life. Another one of his self-styled pals provides a certain but not unusually extreme instance of the corner tavern mentality so often identified with Franklin. This is Joseph Bolton Loughry who, in 1943, wrote a long narrative poem titled *Ben Franklin and His Ass Return to Boston*. The inspiration that informs the poem is the play on the word *Ass*. Mercifully, I offer as an example of this tribute only one stanza, assuring you that it is as good and revealing as any other:

Poor Richard's ghost ascends here;
The tale of his ass ends here;
The dénoument, delayed o'erlong,
Arrives. They must depart.
As their brave spirits rise now
To mansions in the skies, now
Be this our prayer: May they both share
A glorious *himmelfahrt*.[61]

The very nature of such commentary not only reveals distorted views of Franklin but leads to other unfair perceptions. We must consider the famous criticisms of D. H. Lawrence, William Carlos Williams, and Charles Angoff in light of the long tradition of inadequate and inaccurate commentary on Franklin made by supporters and detractors alike.

Lawrence sees Franklin as the Antichrist of imagination and spirituality, the pattern, shallow dummy American from whom all other such democratic dummies originate. Lawrence mistakes the mask of the *Autobiography*, the placid character who moves effortlessly from one success to another, never getting any deeper into himself than an investigation of his finances, for the real man.[62] Williams thinks of Franklin in even more negative terms as the representative of vulgarity and meanness of spirit and mind that have set Americans against the beauty, nobility, and mystery of the continent.[63] And, of course, Angoff sees Franklin as the embodiment of everything that is wrong with capitalist, vulgar, provincial, and fanatically practical America.[64] All these notions of Franklin derive not only from very inadequate reading on the part of three men, but at least as much from 200 years of such reading and from a predisposition to make him less or better than he was.

In the middle 1950s Perry Miller and Richard D. Miles[65] tried to encourage modern scholars to do better by this great man, but from Van Doren's biography in 1938[66] to the present the results have been disappointing. Van Doren did succeed in showing serious readers that Franklin does not belong to "the dry, prim people," and this is no small achievement. Yet the biography, in spite of its great length and 1,200 endnotes, is finally superficial and biased. Before he began to write, Van Doren determined that his subject was a good and great man, one of the best who had ever lived, and that such a man's story should be presented, in so far as possible, from his own perspective. Basically, therefore, the point of view adopted is Franklin's, a technique leading to shallowness and inaccuracy.[67] It also creates a Franklin who is almost genetically benevolent, selfless, and wise. Unfortunately, this "harmonious human multitude,"as Van Doren calls him, is larger than life, always above events, even some of the most important in history. He almost never experiences the psychic tug and pull we all feel when faced with unhappy or difficult choices. The years before the Revolution show him to be worried and saddened, to be sure, but here too he is made almost entirely self-contained, calm and above the uproar, even when he is the center of the uproar. For all his good humor, then, Franklin suffers a diminution of humanness and depth. Yet Van Doren's is fullest and, in fact, the standard modern biography of Franklin.

The next attempt at a major biography of Franklin occurred twenty-seven years after Van Doren's life and six years after the definitive *Papers of Benjamin Franklin* began to be published. Alfred Owen Aldridge, recognizing how superficially and incorrectly Franklin had been perceived, tried to correct the situation. He points out that the same personality and character traits leading to Franklin's success also caused him considerable distress. On this point, Aldridge gets beyond Van Doren. Of value too is his discussion of Franklin's deteriorating relationship with his son, though the conclusions reached here are questionable. It might also have been necessary to remind readers that Franklin never intended his *Way to Wealth* to be taken as a serious moral work but for the most part the rest of the book neither adds much to our understanding of Franklin nor makes a more accurate perception of him possible.[68]

Like Van Doren, Aldridge begins with an admitted bias in Franklin's favor, saying he will not "draw attention to feet of clay." What he does do is gloss over or ignore his subject's faults and limitations. This problem and Aldridge's inability to penetrate the surface of Franklin disturbed Richard B. Morris, who reviewed the book. He complained that Aldridge had taken much space to say little. While he had scored a few new points on minor facets of Franklin's career, he had shown he "has neither the depth nor imaginative insight" to deal effectively with the philosopher, much less to comprehend him and portray him adequately. Franklin proved "too elusive, too complicated, and too grandiose" for Aldridge's abilities.[69]

Subsequent biographical attempts at understanding and revealing Franklin have fared little better. In 1966 Ralph L. Ketcham wrote an introduction to the philosopher's life intended for undergraduates and general readers.[70] It is a balanced account that tries to see Franklin in light of his time and place. Ketcham did not try to penetrate Franklin's mind and personality, but simply calls attention to his obvious qualities, which include benevolence, wisdom, and enlightened humanism.

A more ambitious effort appeared five years later, in Thomas Fleming's *The Man Who Dared Lightning*.[71] Yet it is a curiously limited book. Fleming decided that the story of Franklin's rise in life through hard work, steadfast application, and outstanding public relations was irrelevant in prosperous contemporary America. He therefore begins the story with the kite experiment and carries through the nearly forty years that remained to his subject. Fleming does very well in offering a provocative, if finally speculative, account of Franklin's relationship with William; yet, he does not understand that William developed his aristocratic tastes from his father, who also sought eagerly to use powerful British connections to advance himself. Moreover, though this book makes extensive use of manuscript and published sources, there is little new offered about Franklin, who is portrayed essentially as he has been since the days of Parton.

In a study that is only part biography, Claude-Anne Lopez and Eugenia W. Herbert explore Franklin the private man, especially in terms of his relations with women.[72] Though Franklin is careful in the *Autobiography* and in letters to justify his conduct toward his family, the authors show clearly that he was not nearly the son, brother, husband, and father one could have expected him to be. Unfortunately, there is no effort here to relate the information presented to broader concerns. Lopez and Herbert are probably correct in offering us a Franklin who was both the moralist of the thirteen virtues and the man who, as Jefferson wrote to Madison on 14 February 1783, went into a frenzy when with an attractive woman; however, what does this paradox have to do with Franklin as politician, philosopher, statesman, and writer? What should we infer about him as a man from the charming and gracefully written anecdotes? The authors, though, had no intention of addressing such matters, and we must accept the book on its own terms.

The year of the Bicentennial brought us a biography of Franklin. David Freeman Hawke's interesting popular narrative ends the story with the Declaration of Independence. Looking through the wealth of manuscript material dealing with the crucial years of Franklin's life in France, Hawke "knew I was in over my head," and decided readers could learn enough to judge his subject even in an abbreviated account.[73] Hawke's candor is appealing and there are good things in his book. Nevertheless, his lack of in-depth knowledge is evident throughout. To cite just a few examples: he asserts that the local Masonic lodge in Phildelphia "welcomed" Franklin as a member;[74] in truth, however, Franklin, using his *Pennsylvania Gazette* as a weapon bludgeoned his way into membership in a group that felt itself above him. Even before 1731, the year he became a member, Franklin determined to enter higher realms of Philadelphia society. In discussing the printer's well-known defense of the Reverend Mr. Samuel Hemphill, Hawke attributes the vicious pamphlets ostensibly written in behalf of Hemphill to Franklin's "religious passion."[75] This is hardly the case, as Hemphill was preaching the kind of cool, moralistic, and rationalistic sermons Franklin enjoyed. Religious passion led to bigotry, and Franklin had accused Hemphill's detractors of just such a failing that inevitably led to the immoral abuse of power. Later, Hawke says that Franklin's despairing letters on conditions in Pennsylvania after the Paxton riots indicate his distress.[76] This is certainly true, but Franklin had not lost control (a point Hawke is fond of making in support of his contention that Franklin had human feelings). In fact, the letters were part of his carefully developed plan to make Pennsylvania a royal colony. They were designed to pave the way for the change. And Hawke's limited understanding of Franklin is also revealed in his failure to recognized the importance of the Cockpit affair in his becoming a revolutionary. In fact, on the report that Franklin vowed to make Wedderburn's "master a LITTLE KING" because of the abuse, Hawke writes: "Only those certain they comprehend the manner of the man know whether Franklin could have made such a remark."[77] But this comment comes on the 327th page of the book, a point at which a biographer should be prepared to make sound inferences about the character and personality of his subject.

A year after Hawke's book, Arthur Bernon Tourtellot's *Benjamin Franklin* was published.[78] This work deals with Franklin's Boston years only, since the author was determined to get at the nature of Franklin's genius and to understand the role his New England background played in the development of that genius. He does neither, in spite of a great deal of information, much of it of marginal relevance to his subject. Though he uses some secondary source material, Tourtellot innocently seems to assume that he is the only person who has written on Franklin's Puritan heritage.

As recently as 1983 there appeared another widely publicized biography, Ronald W. Clark's *Benjamin Franklin*.[79] A popular writer on scientific matters, Clark has actually produced a career study rather than a biography. Though his treatment of Franklin as a scientist is sound, the book shares the basic problem of all the biographies discussed here: it does not enlarge our understanding of the inner Franklin. Those authors who have attempted to get beneath the surface and see Franklin both as a unique individual and as a man of his century, as colonial and cosmopolite, as the unusually complex and elusive figure, have been unsuccessful in a good cause. The complaint Morris made about Aldridge's book could easily be made about any of its successors.

Eighteenth-century accounts of Franklin, then, were shallow and biased and therefore led to inaccurate perceptions of him. The nineteenth century added to our knowledge of him but even more significantly to our misunderstanding. While in the present century we have had a number of excellent specialized studies of Franklin, we have yet to get at his greatness and humanness, at anything like the full man. Until we do, though, we cannot understand completely his achievements as a diplomat and as a writer. It is unfortunately necessary, then, to repeat the call made 160 years ago by Leonard Woods: the time is ripe for a balanced and sophisticated study of Franklin, one that will be eminently readable and reach a wide audience. It is my hope that this collection will aid in the effort in two ways. The organization and selection of essays are intended to define for new students important areas of interest dealing with Franklin's career and personal qualities. For the initiated and relative novices alike, the essays offer valuable insights so that we can better understand his place in history and the degree to which he is relevant to our own time.

It is my very sad task to conclude by noting that two contributors to this volume, George Zinke and Bill Willcox, have died. George served for many years as a professor of economics at the University of Colorado in

Boulder, where colleagues and students knew that here was a man of vision who in one way or another was forever teaching and learning. He was so stimulated by his work on the Franklin essay that even as he lay seriously ill in the hospital, he continued to read and discuss Franklin, economics, and other matters with the enthusiasm that characterized his attitude toward life. Bill Willcox, of course, served for many years as the editor of the *Papers of Benjamin Franklin*. His scholarly excellence and dedication are immediately apparent in the volumes for which he was chiefly responsible. He carried on his work in spite of considerable pain as long as he possibly could, for he, like George Zinke, was positively Franklinian in his commitment to things important and useful. They will both be missed.

MELVIN H. BUXBAUM

Notes

1. Leonard Woods, *The Life of Benjamin Franklin . . .* (London: Hunt and Clarke, 1826).

2. *An Answer to the Plot* [Philadelphia: Anthony Armbruster, 1764], broadside.

3. John Dickinson and others, "The Reasons on Which Were Founded the Protest Offered by Certain Members of the Assembly to That Body Concerning the Sending of Mr. Franklin As Assistant to Our Agent There," *Pennsylvania Journal,* 1 Nov. 1764; [William Smith,] *An Answer to Mr. Franklin's Remarks on a Late Protest* (Philadelphia: William Bradford); [Ludwig Weiss? 1764,] *Getreue Warnung gegen die Löckvogel, samt einer Antwort auf die andere Anrede an die deutsche Freihalter der Stadt und County von Philadelphia* (Philadelphia: [Heinrich Miller, 1764]); [Hugh Williamson,] *The Plain Dealer: Numb. II . . .* (Philadelphia: [Andrew Steuart, 1764]); [Hugh Williamson,] *The Plain Dealer: or Remarks on Quaker Politicks in Pennsylvania. Numb. III* (Philadelphia: [William Dunlap, 1764]); Hugh Williamson, *What Is Sauce for the Goose Is Also Sauce for the Gander* ([Philadelphia:] Anthony Armbruster, 1764); *To the Freeholders and Electors of the City and County of Philadelphia* [Philadelphia: Bradford? 1764].

4. *An die Freyhalter und Einwoheb der Stadt und County Philadelphia, Deutscher Nation* (Philadelphia), 1–4; A *Broadside Directed Againast Benjamin Franklin, Candidate for the Assembly, by German Freeholders of Philadelphia County in 1764* [Philadelphia, 1764].

5. [Alexander] Wedderburn, [Speech] "At the Council Chamber, Saturday, Jan. 29, 1774," *The Letters of Governor Hutchinson and Lieut. Governor Oliver, &c, Printed at Boston*. [Edited by Israel Mauduit,] 2d ed. (London: Printed for J. Wilkie, 1774), 82–121.

6. *Letter to Benjamin Franklin LL.D., Fellow of the Royal Society. In Which His Pretensions to the Title of Natural Philosopher are Considered* (London: Printed for J. Bew, 1776), 1–24; Richard Tickell, *La casette verte de Monsieur de Sartine, trouvée chez Mademoiselle du Thé* (5th ed.? The Hague: Wisherfield, 1779), 1–71; "Life and Character of Dr. Franklin," *Political Magazine and Parliamentary Naval, Military, and Literary Journal* 4 (October 1780):[631]–33; H. S., "A Plagiarism of Dr. Franklin," *Gentleman's Magazine* 51 (November 1781):514–15; Bennet Allen, "Characters of Some of the Leading Men in the Present American Rebellion: Benjamin Franklin," *Political Magazine and Parliamentary, Naval, Military, and Literary Journal* 3 (July 1782):446; "Anecdotal Notices of Dr. Franklin," *Boston Magazine* 1 (May 1784):294; Review of *A Poem Addressed to the Armies of the United States of America*. By David Humphries [Humphreys] Esq.[,] Colonel in the Service of the United States, and Aide-de-Camp to His Excellency[,] the Commander in Chief," *English Review*, April 1785,

312–14; An Englishman Who Loves His Country, pseud., "Thoughts on the Character of Dr. Franklin," *Gentleman's Magazine* 61, pt. 1, no. 5 (May 1791):413–14.

7. Jonathan Boucher, "On the Character of Ahitophel" and "Appendix to the Two Sermons on Absalom and Ahitophel," *A View of the Causes and Consequences of the American Revolution; In Thirteen Discourses, Preached in North America Between the Years 1763 and 1775; With an Historical Preface* . . . (London: Printed for G. G. & J. Robinson, 1797), 407–34, 435–49.

8. Jonathan Boucher, *A View of the Causes and Consequences of the American Revolution* (London: Printed for C. G. & J. Robinson, 1797), 404.

9. Ibid., 445.

10. *The Scribbler: Being a Letter From a Gentleman* [Philadelphia: Anthony Armbruster, 1764], 1–24.

11. Giuseppe Maria Mazzolari, *Electricorum libri VI* (Rome: Slomoni, 1767). Cited in Antonia Pace, *Benjmin Franklin and Italy* (Philadelphia: American Philosophical Society, 1958), 350–51, nos. 32, 34, 35.

12. [Jean Le Rond] d'Alembert, "Vers sur M. Franklin," *Almanach littéraire*, n.p., 1779, 110.

13. Jean Jacques Leroux des Tillets, *Dialogue entre Pasquin et Marphorio*, n.p., 1779, 1–16.

14. Aimé Ambroise Joseph Feutry, "In-Pomptu à M. Benjamin Franklin. 22 mars 1778," *Nouveaux oposcules* . . . (Paris: Chez les libraires qui vendent des nouveautes, 1779), 94.

15. De P., "Epître a madame la Bàronne de Bourdic sur ses relations avec le Docteur Franklin," *Almanach des muses* (Paris: Delalain, 1785), 222–25.

16. Mason Locke Weems, *Life of Benjamin Franklin. With Many Choice Anecdotes and Admirable Sayings of This Great Man, Never Before Published by Any of his Biographers* (3d ed., Hagerstown, Md.: Printed for the author, 1818), 1–337.

17. Federico Giunti, "Preface," *Saggi di morale e d'economia . . . di Benjamino Franklin* . . ., vol. 1 (Pisa: Nistri, 1830); Silvestro Centofanti, *Antologia* (Florence, 1831), 41, no. 2:112–18; "Life of Benjamin Franklin," *The Working Man's Companion; Containing the Results of Machinery, Cottage Evenings, and the Rights of Industry, Addressed to Working-Men* (American ed., New York: Leavitt & Allen, 1831), 130–47; Antonietta Tomasini, *Intorno alla educazione domestica: considerazioni* (Milan: Stella, 1835). Cited in Pace, *Franklin and Italy*, 228–30; Cesare Cantù, *Benjamin Franklin*. Cited in Pace, 427, no. 149 and pp. 231–32, 261–66; Bartolomeo Aquarone, *Beniamino Franklin* . . . (Siena: Moschini, 1864), 1–25.

18. [Jacob Abbott,] *Franklin, the Apprentice Boy* (New York: Harper & Brother, 1855), 21, 26, 65, 76–78, 107, 130, 137–38, 159–60; Henry D. Gilpin, *The Character of Franklin* (Philadelphia: King & Baird, 1857), 1–50; Hugh Stowell Brown, *Twelve Lectures to the Men of Liverpool* (Liverpool: Gabriel Thomson, 1858), 4–12; E. A. Duyckinck and G. L. Duyckinck, "Benjamin Franklin," *American Portrait Gallery* (New York, 1862), 9–26; Richard Hildebrand, *Benjamin Franklin als Nationalökonom* (Jena: Friedrich Mauke, 1863), 1–61; P. H. Hugenholtz, *Benjamin Franklin* (Amsterdam: G. L. Funke, 1871), 1–24; Armand Bly, *L'arte de fair sa fortune de l'acquérir de l'augmenter, de la science du Bonhomme Richard* (Paris: Se vend chez l'auteur, 1877), 1–16; William M. Thayer, *From Boyhood to Manhood: The Life of Benjamin Franklin* (New York: Hurst & Co., 1889), passim.

19. A. De Vara [A. Ravà, pseud.], "Considerazioni generali-Sentenze di Franklin e di S. Agostino—La dignita dell'operaio, etc.," *Consigli agli operai* (Milan: Tipografia Editrice Lombarda, 1872), 7–18, passim. In Pace, *Franklin and Italy*, 304, 434, no. 254.

20. Pace, *Franklin and Italy*, 304, 434, no. 254.

21. C. Hulbert, "Dr. Franklin's Death-Bed Advice Respecting the Bible," *Biographical Sketches* . . . (London: G. & W. B. Whittaker, for C. Hulbert, 1820), A-6, 89–90.

22. Albert Henry Smyth, ed., *The Writings of Benjamin Franklin*. (New York: Macmillan Co., 1907), 83–85.

23. Freeman Hunt, "Franklin a Christian," *American Anecdotes. Original and Select*, vol. 2 (Boston: Putnam & Hunt, 1830), 257–58; John N[icholas] Norton, *Life of Doctor Franklin*, Frankfort, Ky., 1861), passim; Thayer, passim.

24. E. A. Duyckinck and G. L. Duyckinck, "Benjamin Franklin," *Cyclopaedia of American Literature* . . ., vol. 1 (New York: Charles Scribner, 1866), 104–10.

25. Thomas Hughes, "English Views of Franklin," *Lippincott's Magazine* 24 (July 1879):1–14; John Torrey Morse, Jr., *Benjamin Franklin* (Boston: Houghton Mifflin and Co., 1889), passim; "Benjamin Franklin," *Record of Unitarian Worthies* (London: ca. 1870), 193–94.

26. James Parton, *Life and Times of Benjamin Franklin*, vol. 2 (Boston: Houghton Mifflin Co., 1882), 618–19.

27. See *The Port Folio* of 14 February 1801, 53–54; 23 May 1801, 165; 16 June 1804, 187; 19 July 1806, 29–30; October 1819, 313–29; September 1820, 249–50.

28. Hugh M'Neile, *A Lecture on the Life of Dr. Franklin* (Liverpool: Mitchell, Heaton and Mitchell, 1841), 1–46.

29. "The Philadelphia Printer," *Leisure Hour* 3, no. 154 (7 December 1854): 772–75; no. 155 (14 December 1854): 788–91; no. 156 (21 December 1854):804–7.

30. Brander Matthews, "Benjamin Franklin," *Introduction to the Study of American Literature* (New York: American Book Co., 1896), 21–39.

31. In addition to such charges made in *The Port Folio*, see also John Davis, *Travels of Four Years and One Half in the United States of America* . . . (London, 1803), 209–18, and "Franklin and His (Supposed) Parable on Persecution," *Literary and Theological Review* 3, no. 9 (March 1836): 51–56.

32. "Dr. Franklin," *North American Review* 7, no. 21 (September 1818):[289]–323; C. A. Sainte-Bevue, "Franklin," *Causeries du Lundi*, 2d ed. vol. 7, Paris: Garnier Freres, 1853), [117]–45; Herman Melville, *Israel Potter: His Fifty Years of Exile* (New York: G. P. Putnam & Co., 1855), 63–105; "Benjamin Franklin," *London Quarterly Review* 23, no. 46 (January 1865): 483–514.

33. [William Duane,] *Remarks Upon a Speech Delivered by Mrs. E. Cady Stanton! During the Summer of 1870* (Philadelphia: Merrihew & Son, [1870]), 1–7.

34. Mark Twain, "The Late Benjamin Franklin," *Mark Twain's Sketches New and Old* (Hartford: American Publishing Co., 1870), 275–78.

35. [F. B. Greene,] *The Benjamin Franklin Primer* (Boston: Boston School Co., 1880), 1–24; Harry B. Weiss, "The Benjamin Franklin Primer. A Primer Parody," *American Book Collector* 6 (1935): 137–38.

36. Donald G. Mitchell, "Benjamin Franklin," *American Lands and Letters* . . . (New York: Charles Scribner's Sons, 1897), 98–112.

37. Henry S. Pancoast, "Benjamin Franklin (1706–1790)," *An Introduction to American Literature* (New York, [ca. 1898]), 80–92.

38. Sydney George Fisher, *The True Benjamin Franklin* (Philadelphia: J. B. Lippincott, [1898]), passim.

39. Paul Elmer More, *Benjamin Franklin* (Boston: Houghton Mifflin Co., [1900]), passim.

40. William Peterfield Trent, *A History of American Literature*, 12th ed. (London: William Heinemann, 1903), 98–130.

41. Nathan Haskell Dole, Intorduction to *Autobiography of Benjamin Franklin* (New York: Thomas Y. Crowell & Co., 1903), v–xxxix.

42. R. Kayser, "Benjamin Franklin und der Amerikanismus," *Preuszische Jahrbücher*

153 (September 1913): [465]—78; Emma Lillian Dana, "Benjamin Franklin, 'the First Great American,'" *Makers of America . . .* (New York, 1915), 5–38; Daniel G. Hoffman, "The American Hero: His Masquerade," *Form and Fable in American Fiction* (New York: Oxford University Press, 1961), 37–41; John G. Cawelti, *Apostles of the Self-Made Man* (Chicago: University of Chicago Press, [1965]), 9–24; Paul W. Schmidtchen, "No Mere Dabbler He," *Hobbies* 72, no. 6 (August 1967): 104.

43. M. M. Mangasarian, *The Religion of Washington, Jefferson and Franklin* [Chicago, 1907?], 14–18.

44. John S. C. Abbott, *Benjamin Franklin* (New York: The University Society, 1876), passim; Vilmos Gyory, *Franklin, Benjamin, egy igaz polgár élete* (Budapest: A Luther-tarsasagkiadasa, 1927), 166–72, passim; Louis C. Washburn, *Benjamin Franklin's Religion* (Philadelphia: Patriot's Sanctuary, [1928]), 1–14; Albert Hyma, *The Religious Views of Benjamin Franklin* (Ann Arbor: George Wehr Publishing Co., 1958), 1–47.

45. Charles K. Edmunds, "The Character of Benjamin Franklin," *Benjamin Franklin. A Character Sketch* (Milwaukee: H. G. Campbell Publishing Co., 1903), 125–39; Oliver Huckel, "The Religious Side of Benjamin Franklin," *Old Penn Weekly Review* 9, no. 30 (20 May 1911): 939–44; Wayne Whipple, *The Story of Young Benjamin Franklin* (Philadelphia: Henry Altemus Co., 1916), S. Parkes Cadman, "Franklin, the Religious Man," *The Amazing Benjamin Franklin*, ed. and comp. Henry J. Smythe, Jr. (New York: Frederick A. Stokes Co.), 94–100.

46. Max Weber, *The Protestant Ethic and the Spirit of Capitalism*, trans. Talcott Parsons (New York: Charles Scribners Sons, 1958), 47–78.

47. Edward Everett Hale, "Franklin As Philosopher and Moralist," *Independent* 60, no. 2980 (11 January 1906): 89–93.

48. Erika Seipp, *Benjamin Franklins Religion und Ethik* (Giessen, 1932), 1–44.

49. W. Espeu Albig, "Franklin the Patron Saint of Thrift," *Amazing Benjamin Franklin*, 41–46; [Jacob Abbott,] *Benjamin Franklin*, passim; Gilpin, *Character of Franklin*, passim; Hugh Stowell Brown, *Twelve Lectures*, 4–12; E. A. Duyckinck and G. L. Duyckinck, *American Portrait Gallery*, 16–19, passim; Hildebrand, *Nationalökonom*, passim; Hugenholtz, *Franklin*, 6–8, 13–17; Bly, *L'arte*, 1–16; Thayer, *Boyhood*, passim; Eugene Daire and G. De Molinari, "Notice sur Franklin," *Melanges d'economie politique*, vol. 1 (Paris: Guillaumin et Cie, 1847), 623–30; Xavier Treney, "Franklin," *Extraits des economistes des XVIIIe et XIX siecles*, "Bibliotheque de l'enseignement secondaire special," (Paris: Quentin, A. Picard & Kaan), 65–73; Shmarya Loeb Hurwitz, *Lebensbeschreibung von Benjamin Franklin und die bafryying von Amerika* (Warsaw: Progress Publishing Co., 1901), passim; "Benjamin Franklin," *Stories of Great Men* (Young Folks Library of American Literature; New York: Educational Publishing Co., 1901), 133–57.

50. William Guggenheim, "Franklin and Our Relations with Russia," *Benjamin Franklin Gazette*, January 1929, 1.

51. William E. Lingelbach, "American Democracy and European Interpreters," *Pennsylvania Magazine of History and Biography* 61, no. 1 (1937); 21–22.

52. "Franklin-Conscious," *Benjamin Franklin Gazette* 3, no. 4 (May 1937): 8; "Philatelic Exhibition," *Benjamin Franklin Gazette* 3, no. 6 (May 1939): 13; John De Meyer, *Benjamin Franklin Calls on the President* (New York: Ives Washburn, 1939).

53. "A Franklin Penny," *General Magazine and Historical Chronicle* 39 no. 4 (July 1937); 454–55.

54. A. Whitney Griswold, "Three Puritans on Prosperity," *New England Quarterly* 7, no. 3 (September 1934).

55. Russell Duane, "How Franklin Would Solve Our Two Major Problems," *Benjamin Franklin Gazette*, May 1933, 3–4, 8–9.

56. Dixon Wecter, "Poor Richard: The Boy Who Made Good," *The Hero in America, a Chronicle of Hero-Worship* (New York: Charles Scribner's Sons, 1941), 50–80; I. Bernard Cohen, *Benjamin Franklin: His Contribution to the American Tradition* (Indianapolis: Bobbs-Merrill Co., 1953).

57. See generally such discussions of Franklin as the following: Verner W. Crane, *Benjamin Franklin and a Rising People* (Boston: Little, Brown and Co., [1954]); Theodore Hornberger, *Benjamin Franklin* (Minneapolis: University of Minnesota Press, 1962); Ralph L. Ketcham, *Benjamin Franklin* (New York: Washington Square Press, 1966); Alfred Owen Aldridge, *Benjamin Franklin and Nature's God* (Durham: Duke University Press, 1967); Melvin H. Buxbaum, *Benjamin Franklin and the Zealous Presbyterians* (University Park: Pennsylvania State University Press, 1975).

58. Of the great many examples, see the following: "Franklin Thrift Bonds," *Benjamin Franklin Gazette* 4, no. 1 (February 1943): 10; Frederick B. Tolles, "Benjamin Franklin's Business Mentors: The Philadelphia Quaker Merchants," *William and Mary Quarterly*, 3d ser., 4, no. 1 (July 1947): 60–69; William S. Grampp, "The Political Economy of Poor Richard," *Journal of Political Economy* 55, no. 2 (April 1947): 132–41; Seiichiro Minabe, "Benjamin Franklin and Modern Capitalism," *Socio-Economic History* 18, no. 6 (1953): 47–60; Irvin G. Wyllie, *The Self-Made Man in America: The Myth of Rags to Riches* (New Brunswick: Rutgers University Press, 1954); Harold A. Larrabee, ""Poor Richard in an Age of Plenty," *Harper's Magazine* 212, no. 1268 (Jan. 1956): 64–68; Marion L. Musante, "Franklin, the Businessman, First Great Apostle of Free and Competitive Economy . . .," *Journal of the Franklin Institute* 261, no. 1 (1956): 133–42; Herman Jaffee, "Benjamin Franklin: Salesman," *American Salesman* 1, no. 6 (February 1956):13–18.

59. Paul F. Anderson, "Franklin, Our Patron Saint," *The Amazing Benjamin Franklin*, 84–88.

60. Earl H. Emmons, *Odeography of B. Franklin* (New York: Ayerdale Press, 1929).

61. James B. Loughry, *Ben Franklin and His Ass Return to Boston* [Manomet, Mass., ca. 1943].

62. D. H. Lawrence, "Benjamin Franklin," *Studies in Classic American Literature* (New York: Thomas Seltzer, 1923), 13–21.

63. William Carlos Williams, "Poor Richard," *In the American Grain* (New York: Albert & Charles Bone, 1925), 144–57.

64. Charles Angoff, "Benjamin Franklin," *A Literary History of the American People* (2 vols. in 1; New York: Alfred A. Knopf, 1931), 2:295–310.

65. Perry Miller, "The Place of Franklin in American Thought," United States Information Service, Benjamin Franklin Anniversary [Washington: United States Government Printing Office, 1956]; Richard D. Miles, "The American Image of Benjamin Franklin," *American Quarterly* 9, no. 2, pt. 1 (Summer 1957):117–43.

66. Carl Van Doren, *Benjamin Franklin* (New York: Viking Press, 1938).

67. Van Doren accepts as gospel nearly every substantive point in the *Autobiography*. He does not analyze Franklin's relationships with the various religious groups in Massachusetts, Pennsylvania, and New Jersey; nor does he approach in a scholarly way, or even with minimal curiosity, Franklin's role in the division of the Quaker Party in the mid-1750s. The same superficiality or neglect is true of Van Doren's treatment of Franklin's efforts to make Pennsylvania a Crown colony, of Franklin's land speculations in England, and of his relationships with the other commissioners in France.

68. Alfred Owen Aldridge, *Benjamin Franklin, Philosopher and Man* (Philadelphia: J. B. Lippincott Co., 1965), passim.

69. Richard B. Morris, Review of Aldridge's *Benjamin Franklin, Philosopher and Man*, *Saturday Review* 48, no. 46 (13 November 1965):63.

70. Ralph L. Ketcham, *Benjamin Franklin*, Great American Thinker Series (New York: Washington Square Press, 1965).

71. Thomas Fleming, *The Man Who Dared Lightning: A New Look at Benjamin Franklin* (New York: William Morrow & Co., 1971).

72. Claude-Anne Lopez and Eugenia W. Herbert, *The Private Franklin: The Man and His Family* (New York: W. W. Norton & Co., 1975).

73. David Freeman Hawke, *Franklin* (New York: Harper & Row, 1976), ix.

74. Ibid., 44.

75. Ibid., 53–54.

76. Ibid., 210.

77. Ibid., 327.

78. Arthur Bernon Tourtellot, *Benjamin Franklin* (Garden City: Doubleday & Co., 1977).

79. Ronald W. Clark, *Benjamin Franklin* (New York: Random House, 1983).

Literary Concerns

Fathers and Sons: Franklin's "Memoirs" as Myth and Metaphor

Hugh J. Dawson*

During his 1771 vacation at the country home of his friend Jonathan Shipley, Bishop of St. Asaph, Benjamin Franklin began writing the story of his life. At Twyford or sometime later on his tour of Britain and Ireland, he outlined the ambitious chronicle he projected but would never complete. In 1784—when seventy-eight years old, suffering from gout and the stone, and uncertain of again seeing the earlier manuscript that was then in Philadelphia—he fashioned a provisional conclusion to the narrative of his early life that had been abruptly broken off thirteen years before. Letters from Abel James and Benjamin Vaughan acted as a bridge to Part II, in which the events sketched in the 1771 outline were rearranged to provide the "Memoirs" with an appropriate climax. A marginal note in the manuscript, often misread as opening onto the later resumption of his narrative, marks the finished account of his formative years, to which the "Art of Virtue" provides a retrospective commentary. Although he was able to add other sections in 1788 and the winter of 1789–90, the first two parts of the *Autobiography* possess a self-sufficiency that is, in fact, the only rounded unity that Franklin's story has ever had.[1]

Identification of Franklin's independent "Memoirs," like an X-ray's revelation of an earlier portrait beneath a museum masterpiece, refocuses critical attention. The relationships of parts, the reciprocity of theme and design shift before the reader's eyes. Previously unsuspected patterns emerge when the integrity of the two-part text is recognized. An implicit theme of the 1771 narrative is seen to have been taken up thirteen years later in such a way that the political dimension Franklin's story had acquired by 1784 and the inclusion of his "Art of Virtue" mirrored his earlier, psychologically crucial self-measurement against Josiah Franklin and his surrogates. As Franklin confronted his real and symbolic children in the "Memoirs," his understanding of his past was refracted by the sense of America's urgent present and anxious future.

Youth and Age were personae that greatly appealed to Franklin; one

*Reprinted by permission from *Early American Literature* 14, no. 3 (Winter 1979/80): [269]–92.

thinks of his "Advice to a Young Man," "Advice to a Young Tradesman, written by an Old One," and *Poor Richard*. But unlike the stock figures of these dialogues, the personalities of the father-presences in the "Memoirs" are complex and troubling. The father in any male autobiographer's mind is a shifting multiple image: it combines the faces of many fathers past—obscured by the son's feelings of guilt for what he has done and thought and become—with the face he as a father would show to those who follow him, something known to be a mask and perceived by the autobiographer only reflectedly. The discovery of identity, as we often hear, comes only in the resolution of the tension between what others would have the individual be and what he feels he must become. It is the working through of this process that gives the "Memoirs," which were begun as Franklin's report as a father to his son William and later readdressed to his "Posterity," their coherence and special meaning.[2]

In the person of Josiah Franklin and his surrogates, the image of the father is a continual presence in Part I. When Franklin says in the first paragraph that he would show the "conducing Means" by which he has "emerg'd from the Poverty & Obscurity in which [he] was born & bred, to a State of Affluence & some Degree of Reputation in the World," he is describing a pattern that begins long before his raggle-taggle entry into Philadelphia, even earlier than his abortive apprenticeships and flight from Boston. "Poverty & Obscurity" had been the lot of his family long before his birth.[3] Indeed, they had been the fate of the many antecedent generations in whose line Part I records his need to locate himself even as he testifies to his own very different fortunes.[4] Later he will tell of his break with Josiah Franklin, but first he must recall for his son his researching of their forebears and the visits the two of them had made in the summer of 1758 to the ancestral homes in Ecton, Banbury, and Birmingham. Thus, at the very beginning of his book, Franklin presents himself tracing whatever of the family's past could be discovered from the weathered gravestones and faded parish registers of England. At Ecton, he says, he found an account of their ancestors' births, marriages, and deaths dating from 1555. A search that seems to have been prompted by nothing more than genealogical curiosity opens onto two generations of deprivation, and his discoveries become a preamble to all that follows. "By that Register," he writes, "I perceiv'd that I was the youngest Son of the youngest Son for 5 Generations back." This citing of his family's past may at first seem to serve merely to emphasize Franklin's climb from low estate, but the reader cannot miss the quiet force with which he indicts history to explain the "Poverty & Obscurity" that were his birthright. The search for ancestors had revealed how the law of primogeniture had worked through five generations to deny him resources and favor.[5]

The family had been transplanted to the New World when Josiah Franklin, as silk dryer, migrated from Banbury to set up as a tallow chandler in Boston. There, when the father was in his late forties, Benjamin was born. The reader of the "Memoirs" is introduced very early to the male elders who preceded Benjamin—the great-great-grandfather, two grandfathers, and several uncles after whom he hd been taught to model himself.[6] Naturally, however, Josiah Franklin becomes the focus of his son's attention. The book tells of the father's many gifts—his ingenuity, his ear for music, his warmth as a host and conversationalist, his "sound understanding, and solid Judgment in prudential Matters, both in private & publick Affairs"—and laments the straitened family circumstances that kept him from becoming a leader in the affairs of church and colony. If the reader—and sometimes young Benjamin—detects a fault, it is the middle-aged father's tendency to press the boy into a life that is dictated by his own designs and that promises to make good his own missed opportunities. "I was put to the Grammar School at Eight Years of Age," Franklin writes; "My Father intending to devote me as the Tithe of his Sons to the Service of the Church."[7] But within a year the boy was withdrawn from the grammar school. Shortly thereafter he would hear Josiah Franklin blame the financial necessities that bore upon the family for precluding a college education for his son and mock the "mean Living many so educated were afterwards able to obtain." While still young, Franklin could read in his father's derision the reaction of a proud man to history's having foreclosed opportunities to him. If Josiah chided his son for writing poetry and said that "Verse-makers were always Beggars," the boy was alert to the envy beneath the ridicule.[8]

When ten years old, Franklin was put to work in his father's soap and tallow shop. But by the time he was twelve he had shown such a dislike for the work that he was reassigned to his cousin's cutlery trade. Growing fearful that the boy would make good on his threats to run away to sea, his father capitalized on Benjamin's bookish inclinations and apprenticed him to his older son James's print shop. The five years that followed were severely strained by quarrels between the brothers. On those occasions when their disputes were referred to the father, his judgment was generally in the younger son's favor. Nevertheless, in the everyday differences of the print shop, Benjamin was invariably forced to yield. It was not only as the master tradesman to whom Benjamin had been bound that James stood in loco parentis. Since the apprenticeship had been arranged at the father's insistence, it is not surprising that James—nine years older, his majority attained, and responsible for boarding his apprentices as well as supervising their work—arrogated the paternal authority to himself. Twice complaining of the beatings James administered to him and feeling caught in a confusion of roles, the young Benjamin felt a need for fatherly understanding that can still be heard in the "Memoirs": "Tho' a Brother, he considered himself as my Master, & me as his Apprentice; and accordingly expected the same Services from me as he would from another; while I thought he demean'd me too much in some he requir'd of me, who from a Brother expected more Indulgence."[9]

Richard Morris has made passing reference to this clash of personalities as an adolescent psychological crisis of the sort Erik Erikson finds in the lives of Luther and Gandhi. The *Autobiography,* he says, "reveals a sixteen-year-old rebelling against sibling rivalry and the authority of his household, using a variety of devices to maintain his individuality and sense of self-importance."[10] Morris might have added that sibling rivalry is an element in the behavioral pattern Freud described as the oedipal rebellion against the father. Especially since the terms of apprenticeship had displaced onto the brother the role of the father, Josiah Franklin should be seen as the real target of much of Benjamin's hostility toward James.

When their antagonism persisted, the young apprentice decided to break with his brother. Finding Boston's printing opportunities closed to him, he made plans to go to New York only to discover his father siding with James and intent upon preventing his leaving. His escape was thus a flight from two threatening father-figures who were yet relatives for whom, Franklin makes it clear, he always bore a loving regard.[11]

The years that followed, when Franklin was proving himself in the world, were marked by a series of encounters with surrogate fathers. In the short glimpses of William Bradford, who sent him from New York to Philadelphia, and the Quaker who on his first day in Philadelphia directed him from the disreputable "Sign of the Three Mariners" to the "Crooked Billet," the reader recognizes the first two in a long series of chance acquaintances and older fellow-subjects who showed the young tradesman paternal solicitude or proved to be false fathers against whom he found he must assert his integrity.[12]

After a year away from home, Franklin won the favor of Sir William Keith, who—with what seemed godfatherly generosity—offered to establish him in business. Decked out in fine clothes and displaying his new wealth, Franklin made his return to Boston in pointed contrast with his ragamuffin arrival in Philadelphia. His father, although happy that Benjamin had drawn the attention of Pennsylvania's baronet-governor, believed his son was still too young for such responsibilities. When Sir William later showed himself faithless in his promises, the young Franklin could only muse with the special hurt of filial disappointment, "What shall we think of a Governor's playing such pitiful Tricks, & imposing so grossly on a poor ignorant Boy!"[13]

If the colonial governor finally proved false in spite of his imposing figure, Benjamin's telling of the episode reveals his further disappointment with Josiah Franklin. A subsequently canceled passage indicates that his father's true reason for not aiding Benjamin was to be found in his confession that "he had advanc'd too much already to my Brother James."[14]

The Philadelphia years were a time during which Franklin felt a gathering sense of himself. The "Memoirs" look back on the period, as they do to his first stay in London, recalling the "dangerous Time of Youth & the hazardous Situations I was sometimes in among Strangers, remote from the Eye & Advice of my Father."[15] Experience would show that men like Samuel Keimer were unworthy of his trust. Some who seemed fatherly, like Simon Meredith, would end by embarrassing him. However, even more plainly than Sir William Wyndham in London, Meredith made what was meant and perceived as an adoptive gesture in return for Franklin's good influence on his son. As a struggling printer, he gained the "Patronage" of Andrew Hamilton, and later, the invaluable sponsorship of Thomas Denham, who took him as his protégé and made him his legatee. It is Denham who is memorialized as one who "counsell'd me as a Father, having a sincere Regard for me: I respected & lov'd him."[16]

Again and again, Franklin is grateful to men who have enlarged his world. Those who allowed him the use of their libraries—Matthew Adams, Governor Burnet, and John Wilcox—appear as paternalistic benefactors readmitting him to the world of books to which Josiah Franklin had first introduced him. When he was about to publish an irreligious pamphlet he would later regret, his fatherly employer Samuel Palmer tried to dissuade him. Through men as socially eminent as he wished his father could have been, he gained entry to a new society; William Lyons introduced him to Bernard Mandeville, and he reports having had hopes of meeting Sir Isaac Newton through Dr. Henry Pemberton. When he stretches history in telling of his reception by Sir Hans Sloane, his purpose is only to improve the familiar scene in which his youthful self demonstrates his merit before an aging patron.[17]

Franklin splits the good and bad features of the father between Isaac Decow, the Surveyor General of Pennsylvania, and the dour merchant Samuel Mickle. Decow, whose industrious ways Franklin would imitate "was a shrewd sagacious old Man, who told me that he began for himself when young by wheeling Clay for the Brickmakers, learnt to write after he was of Age, carry'd the Chain for Surveyors, who taught him Surveying, and he had now by his Industry acquir'd a good Estate." The fearful and unventuresome Mickle, however, had so retreated from life as to become a caricature of Death. The paragraph that rehearses his doom-saying is the reader's only meeting with the lugubrious merchant, and he stands to the reader's eye as he did to Franklin's own as an epitome of the older generation's pessimism. Indeed, one is surprised to discover that at the time the twenty-two-year-old Franklin met him in 1728 Mickle, whom the "Memoirs" call "an elderly Man," was only about thirty-four. He delivers a doleful forecast heavy with the elders' gloomy mind-set and is the antithesis of Isaac Decow, by then well past seventy but proof of what the self-actualizing man might make of his future.[18]

The "Memoirs" that Franklin had undertaken with the intention of "gratifying the Suppos'd Curiosity of [his] Son" and perhaps others of his family, were by 1784 "intended for the Publick,"[19] The letters from James and Vaughan not only urged him to make his story known to a larger audience, but their stress upon its advantage to the "Minds of Youth" made their inclusion a means of transition from narrative to exemplum. In hoping that he would "shew . . . how much is to be done, *both to sons and fathers,*" they opened onto the vindication and symbolic reconciliation with Josiah Franklin that form the climax of the "Memoirs."[20]

Although it is not known just when in 1784 Franklin wrote part II, his letters of late 1783 and the following year are filled with expressions of care for those he treated as sons.[21] He writes from Passy to Polly Hewson and Benjamin West of his feeling an old man's longing to see their families, especially their sons who were his godsons. At the same time, in letters to Thomas Mifflin, Henry Laurens, Charles Thomson, and John Jay, he is busily engaged in seeking preferment—"some Employ that may probably be permanent"—for his favorite grandson, William Temple Franklin. Although Franklin often managed to overlook Temple's wastrel ways, he grew anxious as his twenty-two-year-old grandson set out to visit London in the summer of 1784. He wrote William Franklin of his trust that the father would "prudently avoid introducing him to Company, that it may be improper for him to be seen with."[22] One cannot miss the echo of Franklin's own London dalliances during his "dangerous Time of Youth."[23] Nor could it have escaped the autobiographer's attention that his irresponsible and jobless grandson was very nearly arrived at the age at which his own story of resolution and success had broken off.

Another grandson, Benjamin Franklin Bache, had also come under Franklin's care. In 1783–84, the grandfather imitated the decision Josiah Franklin had mde sixty-five years earlier and placed his teen-age charge under the tutelage of printers and font-casters. One of the period's leading artisans, Philippe-Denys Pierres, was brought to the press Franklin had established at Passy, and in 1785 François-Ambrois Didot was engaged to instruct young Benny in casting type.[24]

While Franklin could not have missed the variations on his earlier life story being lived out by his grandsons, nothing would so have recalled his troubled relations with his father as his estrangement from his son William, which reached a crisis in 1784. William had been colonial governor of New Jersey at the time of the Revolution. After siding with the Loyalists, he had been held prisoner for a time in Connecticut and in 1782 was sent to England a broken man.[25] Although Patience Wright and others reported William's poor health and sought help for him, Franklin was unyielding. Before and after the Treaty of Paris, he regarded the Loyalists with scorn; he argued that the king owed them nothing and the Americans even less. John Adams described him at the peace negotiations as "very staunch against the Tories, more decided a great deal on this Point than Mr. Jay or my self."[26] On July 22, 1784, William wrote from London to ask a meeting with his father. His loyalty to the king had been a matter of conscience. Even after suffering the mistreatment meted out to the Loyalists, he would support the king again.[27] The father's reply was cool. He would receive William in good time. Meanwhile, he insisted that family bonds should be stronger than political commitments.

> You conceived, you say, that your Duty to your King and Regard for your Country requir'd this. I ought not to blame you for differing in Sentiment with me in Public Affairs. We are Men, all subject to Errors. Our Opinions are not in our own Power; they are form'd and govern'd much by Circumstances, that are often as inexplicable as they are irresistible. Your Situation was such that few would have censured your remaining Neuter, *tho' there are Natural Duties which precede political ones, and cannot be extinguish'd by them.*[28]

Franklin may already have foreseen the strained reunion that took place when he stopped in England en route to Philadelphia the following summer. Certainly the estrangement from William could scarcely have had a more ironic contrast than Franklin's reported regard of Thomas Paine as "his adopted political son."[29]

In the note preceding the letters from his friends inserted before Part II, Franklin explains that the "Affairs of the Revolution occasion'd the Interruption."[30] The requests of James and Vaughan, his uncertainty that he would ever resume the longer story he had outlined, and the memories of his early years, which had been stirred by the activities of his son and grandsons—all these, together with some leisure time and his changed circumstances following the signing of the peace treaty, resulted in the philosophical capstone with which he tentatively concluded the "Memoirs." Turning to advantage the stress that his correspondents had placed upon his providing an example *"both to sons and fathers,"* the second part not only crowns the earlier narrative, but—in its pairing of Franklin's father and wife, its contrast of his own practice with the Presbyterian minister's preaching, its orderly lists and tabulations leading to his discussion of the thirteen virtues' ironic closure—it possesses a complex internal symmetry.[31]

The plan to attain moral perfection, which has become the most famous section of the *Autobiography*, is extraneous to the capstone function of Part II. Having joined the two parts by means of the letters and his report of the founding of the Philadelphia Library Company, Franklin summarizes the rewards of his study, frugality, and industry in paired passages—one a statement of his public success, the other a testimonial to his domestic happiness; the first inspired by the advice of his father and bearing out a quotation from Solomon, the other made possibly by his wife's devotion and exemplifying the truth of an old English proverb. From the perspective of Passy, Franklin could look back upon the breaking off of Part I at the threshold of his adulthood as providing the frame for the story of his years of growth. Josiah and Deborah Franklin, who mark the beginning and ending of the 1771 narrative, are reintroduced into the capstone's setpiece. If his gratitude to his wife seems no more than dutiful, Franklin's literal improvement of his father's hopes is unexampled:

> My Father having among his Instructions to me when a Boy, frequently repeated a Proverb of Solomon, *"Seest thou a Man diligent in his*

> *calling, he shall stand before Kings, he shall not stand before mean Men.*" I from thence consider'd Industry as a Means of obtaining Wealth and Distinction, which encourag'd me, tho' I did not think that I should ever literally stand before Kings, which however has since happened.—for I have stood before five, & even had the honour of sitting down with one, the King of Denmark, to Dinner.[32]

Solomon's proverb, together with the religious thoughts that shortly follow it, anticipates the Great Judgment when all Franklin's virtues and errata would be revealed. The symbolic fathers—Solomon, the crowned heads of the Old World, and the Great King of the next—are convened with Josiah Franklin to witness how a prophecy that the father could only have regarded as a scriptural locution both marks the real distance the son has come and harmonizes his adolescent rebellion with the Divine Plan.[33] The quotation from the Bible and his stress upon his "Calling"might have satisfied his father's shade that the son had been right to go his own way. But to clinch his argument, Franklin offers a sketch of a tedious Presbyterian minister, implicitly the failure he might have been had he become the "Tithe of his [father's] Sons to the Service of the Church." Always careful not to mock others' beliefs, Franklin merely mentions the minister's emphasis on piety rather than practical virtue, but the juxtaposition of the propagator of dogma and platitudes with his own empiricist's habit of testing all claims by experience has its own force. As evidence of his liberal spirit, he offers an epitome of his beliefs, mentions his financial support of many churches, and tells of the private liturgy he has observed since 1728.[34] To these details he appends his ideas on the "Art of Virtue"—describing the "little Book" he has always carried with him, its precepts, its periodic examinations of conscience, and his self-discipline for moral improvement.[35]

Franklin had grown up knowing the last great Puritans. He remembered running errands for Increase Mather and hearing him preach. In a nostalgic letter of May 1784, he recalls the most famous of his surrogate fathers and tells of seeking Cotton Mather's advice on his first return to Boston.[36] The elder Mather had denounced just the independence Franklin would show:

> It is from Pride that young men are not willing to be under Government: Children will not be ruled by their Parents, nor Servants by their Masters, and the reason is that they are ruled by the Pride of their own hearts. An inordinate affectation of liberty, is the sin which reigns in Youth commonly. Whats said concerning the Young Prodigal is a description of the spirit which useth to prevail in Unconverted Young Men. He was not willing to continue in his Fathers Family, nor to be under his Fathers inspection and government, but would be gone into far Countries. Luke.12,13. Do we not fear just so in many Young men amongst our selves? Nothing will serve them, but to be going far from their fathers house, that so they may without control walk in the way of their

> heart and after the sight of their own eyes. An humble and dutiful respect to their Parents would make them think themselves happy in being near them.[37]

The younger Mather spoke to the same pride exhibited by Boston's youth: "Let the admonitions of your *Parents*, never be forgotten with you. Treasure up their Admonitions." The influence of the elders should continue even into adulthood: "*Obey* your *Parents* Conscientiously. Yea, though you should be as much above twenty as *Isaac* was when his Father bad him Ly down upon his Altar, yet I say, *Obey* them Conscientiously." Looking ahead to the accounting to be made to parents on the Last Day, he described the disobedient youth as a parricide:

> How can you find it in your *Hearts* to shorten the *Lives* of those, through whom you your selves have Derived your *Lives?* You do this when you chafe, and Cut, and Wast the Hearts of your *Parents*, by the Heart breaking Sight, of your Ungodliness, and make them e'n *Weary of their Lives?* I Remember, that the Apostle *Paul*, reckoning up the Transgressors of the *Ten Commandments*, the Transgressors of the *Fourth* Commandment, he calls, *The Profane;* but the Transgressors of the *Fifth* Commandment, he calls, in I Tim.I.9. *Murtherers of Fathers, and Murtherers of Mothers*. It seems, by breaking of the *Fifth* Commandment, you will break the *Sixth* also; yea, by being Undutiful Children, you will become the worst sort of *Murtherers*.[38]

As if warning the young Franklin, Cotton Mather cautioned those who played with thoughts of becoming runaways to the sea: "Oh! That the Young Men, who follow the *Sea*, and most of all, they that without a good Cause and Call run away to the *Sea*, would very particularly consider of it!"[39]

Again and again in the late Puritan jeremiads, Franklin could have heard such denunciations of the ingratitude of children and the frequently reiterated parallelism of the disobedience of children and the rejection of God.[40] Recurrently in Part I, Josiah Franklin and the figure of God appear together. It is in the library of the father who intended him for the ministry that young Benjamin does his first readings in theology. He draws charges of atheism just as he is breaking with his father. He recalls the religious instruction of his parents before telling of his conversion to Deism, and the reader feels his sense of the Divine Accuser as he regrets the absence of his inhibitory father when he strayed among the fleshpots of distant cities. When in 1784 he quotes Solomon and explains the religion of doing good that he has practiced instead of becoming a tiresome minister, he is both a son vindicating himself to Josiah Franklin and an old man rehearsing exculpatory testimony before God of the "Diligence" with which he has lived out his self-discovered creed. Thus the mythic pattern of the "Memoirs" is cyclical; the Prodigal Son who was lost has returned, but to explain the lessons learned in making good.[41]

Readers have long recognized Franklin's sense that his personal history was the story of his people in microcosm. As though feeling his experiences to possess a salvific value, he assumes, in Sacvan Bercovitch's words, "an identity representative of the rising nation. . . . and the 'essential' Franklin is the *exemplum* of corporate selfhood, ascending from dependence to dominance. It was surely to hint at this soteriological *exemplum* that Franklin included in the work Benjamin Vaughan's letter hailing Franklin as the epitome 'of *a rising people*.' " Charles Sanford reads the *Autobiography* as a "great moral fable, . . . a work of imagination which, by incorporating the 'race' consciousness of a people, achieves the level of folk myth."[42] However, because they work from the apparently formless four-part *Autobiography*, Bercovitch and Sanford miss the close congruence of the personal testament of 1784 with contemporary political concerns.

As early as 1751, in "Observations Concerning the Increase of Mankind," Franklin identified himself with the legislators and inventors who "may properly be called *Fathers* of their Nation."[43] Memories of his furtive departure from Boston—"I was sensible that if I attempted to go openly, Means would be used to prevent me"—are detectable in his 1773 argument against a proposed Parliamentry prohibition of emigration to America; it would "make a prison of the Island for this confinement of free Englishmen, who naturally love Liberty, and would probably by the very Restraint be more stimulated to break thro' it."[44] Nine years later he would again attack those who would "make a prison of England, to confine men for no other crime but that of being useful and industrious, and to discourage the learning of the useful mechanical arts, by declaring that as soon as a man is master of his business he shall lose his liberty and become a prisoner for life."[45] Within months of his writing the second part of his "Memoirs," he recapitulated his story in describing the American opportunities open to "Artisans of all the necessary and useful kinds. . . . If they are poor, they begin first as Servants or Journeymen; and if they are sober, industrious, and frugal, they soon become Masters, establish themselves in Business, marry, raise Families, and become respectable Citizens." If he had become the representative American, it was because the free environment favored just those moral precepts he had lived by:

> The almost general Mediocrity of Fortune that prevails in America obliging its People to follow some Business for subsistence, those Vices, that arise usually from Idleness, are in a great measure prevented. Industry and constant Employment are great preservatives of the Morals and Virtue of a Nation. Hence bad Examples to Youth are more rare in America, which must be a comfortable Consideration to Parents. To this may be truly added, that serious Religion, under its various Denominations, is not only tolerated, but respected and practised. Atheism is unknown there; Infidelity rare and secret; so that persons may live to a great Age in that Country, without having their Piety shocked by meeting with ei-

> ther an Atheist or an Infidel. And the Divine Being seems to have manifested his Approbation of the mutual Forbearance and Kindness with which the different Sects treat each other, by the remarkable Prosperity with which He has been pleased to favour the whole Country.[46]

In the medieval-Renaissance world picture inherited by the American colonists, men lived within a series of concentric spheres—family, church, state, and cosmos—each paternalistically governed. From James I, Hobbes, and works like Sir Robert Filmer's *Patriarcha,* there had derived a legitimation of monarchy so heavy with the imagery of fatherhood that by the time of the Revolution the representation of father-king, parent-England, and children-colonies had become, among both Americans and Englishmen, the most popular cluster of metaphors in political discourse.[47]

> Over and over again—in letters, diaries, newspapers, pamphlets, proclamations, and formal debates—they likened the empire to a family, a family in which England enjoyed the rights and duties of parental authority over the colonies while the colonies enjoyed the corresponding rights and duties of children. No other formulation of the ties that bound the empire was employed so frequently or so deliberately or so consistently through every phase of the imperial controversy. Indeed, no other formulation of those ties came nearly so close to being the very *lingua franca* of the Revolution.[48]

Not surprisingly, these images of the king as "father" and of England as the "mother-" or "parent-country" are commonplaces of Franklin's public and private writings.[49]

In 1784 Franklin wrote from Passy amidst what Vaughan's letter called "the immense revolution of the present period." The American Revolution was over; those of France and other countries lay ahead. Franklin had been engaged in negotiating the peace, in coming to new terms with the father-king and parent-country. He explained that the "Affairs of the Revolution occasion'd the Interruption" in his story.[50] They had also brought a changed sense of himself. Just as within his family he had become the father-figure in others' reenactments of his youth, so his public role had been transformed. As much as he had abhorred their violence, he had been the conciliatory senior brother in absentia of the Sons of Liberty; now he had become the eldest of the Founding Fathers. As long ago as 1776, Arthur Lee had described him to Lord Shelburne as America's *"Pater Patriae."*[51] Now James urged him to write for the "American Youth" and Vaughn looked forward to his story's "effects upon your vast and rising country, as well as upon England and upon Europe." In words directed not so much to the autobiographer himself as to Franklin the representative of his people, Vaughan describes the "Memoirs" as presenting "a table of the internal circumstances of your country" for "all that has happened to you is also connected with the detail of the manners and situation of *a rising people.*" As the story of both the man and his recently independent country, the book would "shew that you are ashamed of no origin; a thing the more important, as you prove how little necessary all origin is to happiness, virtue, or greatness." The letter, which was dated January 31, 1783, alludes unmistakably to Franklin's interrogation in the Stamp Act debates which almost exactly seventeen years earlier had proved so important to the nascent American identity; the "Memoirs" would "prove yourself as one who from your infancy have loved justice, liberty and concord, in a way that has made it natural and consistent for you to have acted, as we have seen you act in the last seventeen years." In the post-Revolutionary rapprochement, the book would have an invaluable function: "Let Englishmen be made not only to respect, but even to love you. When they think well of individuals in your native country, they will go nearer to thinking well of your country; and when your countrymen see themselves well thought of by Englishmen, they will go nearer to thinking well of England."[52]

The inclusion of his friends' letters, a curiosity in the *Autobiography*, was central to the unity achieved in the "Memoirs." Structurally, they bridged the dissimilar first and second parts. By urging publication of the story, they enabled Franklin to abandon the epistolary form of 1771 and incorporate his ideas on virtue in a unified reflection upon the meaning of his early years. In their deference to his sagacity, they unwittingly reintroduced the old man absent since the first pages written at Twyford. Most important, they drew the parallel between his own and his country's fortunes which he could not discreetly declare in his own voice. If nothing else, Franklin's having been found wanting in "Humility" would seem to have precluded his stating the analogy himself.[53] However, he had pointed up the latent political correspondences in his gloss to the account of his apprenticeship to his brother James: "I fancy his harsh & tyrranical Treatment of me might be a means of impressing me with that Aversion to arbitrary Power that has stuck to me thro' my whole Life."[54] In the aftermath of the Revolution, Abel James urged "kind, humane and benevolent Ben Franklin" to resume his story in order to "promote a greater spirit of Industry and early Attention to Business, Frugality and Temperance with the American Youth."[55] When Vaughan made the otherwise implicit analogy explicit, incorporation of the letters converted the "Memoirs' " exemplum into political metaphor; Franklin's need to be reconciled with his father found its psychological parallel in the independent country's desire for recognition and the restoration of good feelings with the monarch it had rejected.

To explain the inclusion of his friends' letters as in part motivated by Franklin's wish to appropriate Vaughan's analogy is not to argue that he wrote with anything approaching full consciousness of the "Memoirs"' patterns of father-figures. Rather, when the ever common-sensical autobiographer discounts the "several little family Anecdotes of no importance to others," the modern reader may suspect he does not know how much he has told. For Franklin to have admitted the full congruence of the political anxieties of 1784 with his family history would have been to recognize that he and all Americans had been "Murtherers." Instead, like the Second Continental Congress, he was able to rationalize his actions as obedience to a higher law i.e., Solomon's injunction to be diligent that Josiah Franklin had himself endorsed. After the Revolution that gave America its own standing before kings, Franklin's story was "intended for the Publick" and would resonate for the larger audience that would, at a deep level, identify its achievement and guilt with his.[56]

Although discussion of the "Art of Virtue" occupies more than half of Part II, it is formally as anomalous as the letters from James and Vaughan, being an appendage supplied in response to the latter's request for Franklin's long-deferred manual of conduct.[57] As long as the independent structure of the "Memoirs" went unrecognized, the importance of the symbolic reconciliation as the climax to the 1771 narrative was overshadowed by the regimen of self-perfection. Within the self-sufficient design of 1784, however, the "Art of Virtue" is structurally a sort of coda in which the themes of the preceding narrative and reconciliation movements are given varied but confirmatory restatement.

No less than the earlier sections, the summary of the "Art of Virtue" is heavy with the presence of Franklin's idealized father. It was, after all, Josiah Franklin whose mealtime conversations had first "turn'd [his son's] Attention to what was good, just, & prudent in the Conduct of Life."[58] The neurotic erasures and fresh starts on the ivory pages of Franklin's book are classic testimony to his need to arraign himself before the internalized father's "Eye & Advice," an anxiety the son has plainly secretly enjoyed.[59] In its eighteenth-century cognate meaning, "virtue" still referred to that mature masculinity a son would demonstrate to his father; what the *Oxford English Dictionary* defines as "the possession or display of manly qualities; manly excellence, manliness."[60] The need to prove mastery and dominance appears in Franklin's strategy against himself: "My Intention being to acquire the *Habitude* of all these Virtues, I judg'd it would be well not to distract my Attention by attempting the whole at once, but to fix it on one of them at a time, and when I should be Master of that, then to proceed to another, and so on till I should have gone thro' the thirteen." As if to underscore the successful resolution of the uncertainties that had plagued his adolescence, Franklin the son and Franklin the father become figural representations in the coda's contrast of youth and age. In the motto copied from Addison's *Cato,* in the passage quoted from Thomson's poem *The Seasons,* and in the "little Prayer, which was prefix'd to [his] Tables of Examination," Franklin is three times the suppliant or dependent son. He prays to the "Father of Light and Life," and in the petition of his own framing, he asks, "O Powerful Goodness! bountiful Father! merciful Guide! Increase in me that Wisdom which discovers my truest Interests; Strengthen my Resolutions to perform what that Wisdom dictates. Accept my kind Offices to thy other Children, as the only Return in my Power for thy continual

Favours to me." As the stern paterfamilias, he rebukes his wife's extravagance, and the voice of the patriarch is heard when he recalls his daily examinations and feels "it may be well my Posterity should be informed, that to this little Artifice, with the Blessing of God, their Ancestor ow'd the constant Felicity of his Life down to his 79th Year."[61]

Franklin's ethic was itself a break with the past. An early letter to his parents, meant to be reassuring, did not disguise the fact that he no longer shared the faith of his father and the Mathers.[62] His hope was not in the sainthood of the elect but in "the Virtuous and good Men of all Nations." Experience, not theology, sanctioned his practice. The conversion experience had been succeeded by the commitment to good works, and the church, by the voluntary association. In Franklin's list of precepts, the theological and cardinal virtues of Christianity all but disappear. "Tranquility" replaces anxious faith. Rules for social conduct—silence in conversation, order in business, cleanliness in one's person—become primary concerns. Instead of absolutes, Franklin urges discretion ("Avoid Extreams") or settles for ambiguity ("Rarely use Venery but for Health or Offspring"). Temporal felicity is the sufficient reward of virtue: "Vicious Actions are not hurtful because they are forbidden, but forbidden because they are hurtful, the Nature of Man alone consider'd. . . . It was therefore every one's Interest to be virtuous, who wish'd to be happy even in this World."[63]

Although the "Art of Virtue" makes no explicit postcolonial political statement, Franklin's moral emphases coincided with the thinking of his people. Having repudiated institutions they felt lived by luxury, Americans required an indigenous order founded in simplicity and industry. Gordon Wood and other historians have described Americans' consuming anxiety over public and private virtue in the years following the Revolution.[64]

> Since the elimination of a king reduced the traditional restraints of force and fear, the citizens of a republic had to exhibit an extraordinary morality of self-control in order to secure an orderly and just society. Classical republicanism stipulated that public virtue, or disciplined devotion to the public good, could not exist without private virtue, exhibited in the character traits of temperance, frugality, and rigorous self-restraint. . . . In America this classical conception of virtue—as consistently intense, disinterested self-abnegation—gradually merged into a more modern meaning that emphasized the productive industry of the active citizen.[65]

The realization of new possibilities would come only when free men lived by moral principles. "In the conventional usage of the day, *virtue* meant the voluntary observance of the recognized standards of right conduct, while *independence* implied exemption from all external moral control or support." For both Franklin and his country, morality and freedom were mutually reinforcing. "Full mastery of self . . . required that a man have both virtue—freedom from one's own passions—and independence—freedom from the passions and/or control of others."[66] Franklin's "Art of Virtue" was aimed at more than his individual improvement. From its inception, the "bold and arduous Project of arriving at moral Perfection" had had a social dimension. But the demands of a busy life had prevented his implementing a program "that required the whole Man to execute." From Passy he could only allude to this "*great extensive* Project," but in Philadelphia he would resume by making use of early memoranda to describe the "united Party for Virtue" he still hoped might grow from others' imitation of his regimen to take the lead in public reform.[67]

Franklin's growing realization that America must break with the parent country had been as protracted as his decision to leave Boston.[68] But by transcending the expectations to which the society of his fathers would have confined him, he—like America—had achieved "Affluence & Independance." The old order that had denied wealth and office to Josiah Franklin finds its contrast in the new possibilities that have allowed the son and representative American to improve upon his father's station: "To *Industry* and *Frugality* [the son ascribed] early Easiness of his Circumstances, & Acquisition of his Fortune, with all that Knowledge which enabled him to be an useful Citizen, and obtain'd for him some Degree of Reputation among the Learned. To *Sincerity & Justice* the Confidence of his Country, and the honourable Employs it conferr'd upon him."[69] That Franklin speaks of himself as a "Citizen" rather than a subject and describes his charge as having been from his "Country" rather than the colonies he had formerly represented are measures of his new consciousness.

Jack Greene has remarked upon the early Americans' obstacles to accepting their good fortune:

> From a psychological point of view, the most difficult problem faced by the Europeans, even after several generations, was learning how to live with prosperity. Coming out of a society of scarcity, where people actually died of hunger, where whole populations had lived in perpetual poverty not just for one generation but for hundreds of years, they had a hard time learning how to be comfortable with prosperity and the more relaxed form of life it permitted, how not to feel guilty or anxious because they had things so good.[70]

Franklin, although free of John Adams' horror of luxury, showed his deep ambivalence toward it in a letter of July 26, 1784.[71] At about the same time he revealed his divided conscience in the "Memoirs." Prosperity was not to be simply enjoyed; it should be instrumental to further, multiplying virtue. Their Philadelphia home had been a model of austerity until Deborah Franklin presented him with a china bowl and silver spoon. Although he professes Puritan-Quaker simplicity—"Mark how Luxury will enter Families, and make a Progress, in Spite of Principle"—Franklin writes with greater pride than irony in concluding his telling of the episode: "This was the first Appearance of Plate & China in our House, which afterwards in a

Course of years as our Wealth encreas'd augmented gradually to several Hundred Pounds in Value." The origins of Franklin's uneasy acceptance of prosperity can be traced to his father's insistence upon "steady Industry and a prudent Parsimony,"and the indifference "to the Victuals on the Table, whether it was well or ill drest" that he taught his family. As so often in his story, Franklin reveals his guilty ambivalence at having disobeyed his father in the process of surpassing him.[72]

In the summer of 1788 Franklin was secure in Philadelphia. In August, a month after official announcement of the Constitution's adoption, he took up his *Autobiography*.[73] The earlier outgoing personality returns as he reverts to telling of his public career. Although Josiah Franklin lived until his son was about forty, his disappearance from the story after Benjamin's middle twenties is not surprising. The essential working through of the rivalry with the father, with its agonizing self-measurements, was past. In Part III the autobiographer's resumption of his narration coincided with young Franklin's shift of attention from his private concerns to the public assertion of himself characteristic of one his age.

> The end of adolescence sees a relaxation of the intensified concentration on self-development often visible in the late teens and early twenties. Psychoanalysts speak here of the waning of adolescent narcissism—a displacement of the individual's own inner life from the center of the world. . . . As Peter Blos concludes: "Infantile conflicts are not removed at the close of adolescence, but they are rendered specific, they become ego-syntonic, i.e., they become integrated within the adult self-representations." The result is a new mental formation that "perpetuates familiar, antecedent trends within the adult personality," while orienting the individual toward significant external objects in a new way.[74]

In Philadelphia Franklin wrote with the aid of surviving letters and notes that recalled his attitudes and outlook in the early 1730's. Beginning by telling of the intended public dimension of his project for virtue, Part III chronicles the successes that followed from the release and concentration of his adult energies. With time the practice of his private discipline was abandoned. Its disuse reflected his growing away from the strictures of the internalized parent and the priority of new, mature concerns: "After a while I went thro' one Course [of self-examination] only in a Year, and afterwards only one in several Years, till at length I omitted them entirely, being employed in Voyages & Business abroad with a Multiplicity of Affairs, that interfered, but I always carried my little Book with me."[75] The father lingering in the mind remained objectified in the cherished, talismanic physical presence of the book.

Although Franklin's relations with his father were often conflicted, he knew Josiah's personality and example to have been enabling rather than destructive. The "Memoirs" tell how the father had himself felt obliged to leave his parents and homeland. Benjamin reincarnates his father's "mechanical Genius," aptitude for learning, and musical gifts. Both were spirited conversationalists and keen students of public affairs. Benjamin's library study "repair'd in some Degree the loss of the learned Education my Father once intended for me." He knew the signs of Josiah's approbation essential to his growth. The father who more often favored him in arbitrating his disputes with his brother would have recognized the superiority of the Silence Dogood letters and admired Benjamin's management of the *New England Courant*. For his part, young Franklin could understand why his father, a conservative product of the old order, had tried to hold him in Boston and later rejected Governor Keith's offer. Even in his disappointment, he was heartened: "My Father, tho' he did not approve Sir William's Proposition was yet pleas'd that I had been able to obtain so advantageous a Character from a person of such Note where I resided, and that I had been so industrious & careful as to equip my self so handsomely in so short a time." The runaway of a year earlier was given his father's consent to return to Philadelphia. He left with "some small Gifts as Tokens of his & my Mother's Love, when I embark'd for New-York, now with their Approval & their Blessing."[76] The need to seal that approbation and the desire to invest the story of his personal rebellion with new meaning gave form to the "Memoirs" of Franklin's old age.

Notes

1. "Memoirs"—the term by which Franklin referred to his story in his letters—is used in this article to refer to the two-part account of his early years. *Autobiography* refers to the four-part book that tells of his life to 1759. For evidence of the independent unity of the first two parts, see Hugh J. Dawson, "Franklin's 'Memoirs' in 1784: The Design of the *Autobiography,* Parts I and II," *Early American Literature,* 12 (1977–78), 286–93.

2. Although Franklin's addressing his story to his son has usually been discounted as a rhetorical posture, two statements written late in life indicate that the first part had been intended for William Franklin. An August 16, 1786, letter to Matthew Carey explains that Part I had been "written to my Son, and intended only as Information to my Family" (*The Writings of Benjamin Franklin,* ed. Albert H. Smyth [New York, 1906], IX, 533–34). As late as 1788 Franklin added to the manuscript of the *Autobiography* a subsequently cancelled statement that he had written the narrative of his early years with the intention "of gratifying the Suppos'd Curiosity of my Son" (*Benjamin Franklin's Memoirs: Parallel Text Edition,* ed. Max Farrand [Berkeley and Los Angeles, 1949], p. 184 n.). See also Dawson, "Franklin's 'Memoirs,' " p. 292 n. 8.

3. *Parallel Text,* p. 2. Charles Sanford, *The Quest for Paradise: Europe and the American Moral Imagination* (Urbana, Ill, 1961), pp. 123–24, cites this passage as providing the *Autobiography*'s "central organizing theme" and argues that Franklin's entry into Philadelphia serves as the principal reference point for his explanation of his life. I would argue that, while most of Sanford's citations are appropriate to this scene, Franklin's measurements of his success in *Parallel Text,* pp. 2, 82, and 302 are as clearly to be taken as referring to his condition at birth.

4. There is considerable evidence outside the *Autobiography* showing Franklin's concern with his forefathers' identity and the family's social standing. The only letter from his father to him of which there is record is in answer to a request for an account of his genealogy

(*The Papers of Benjamin Franklin*, ed. Leonard W. Labaree et al. [New Haven, 1959–], II, 229–32). In 1764, Franklin's candidacy in the Pennsylvania election was bedeviled by references to his common origins and taunts about his fathering of William Franklin. See J. Philip Gleason, "A Scurrilous Colonial Election and Franklin's Reputation," *William and Mary Quarterly*, 3d Ser., 18 (1961), 68–84; and Alfred Owen Aldridge, *Benjamin Franklin: Philosopher & Man* (Philadelphia and New York, 1965), pp. 166–67. We know of his efforts—unavailing as they proved—to keep his son and grandson from repeating this last erratum (see, for example, *Writings*, IX, 254). In presenting Benjamin Franklin Bache to Voltaire, Franklin, who was so acutely aware of history's having denied his father an education, seems to have wanted to impress upon his grandson the possibilities that were now his heritage. See A. Owen Aldridge, *Franklin and His French Contemporaries* (New York, 1957), pp. 9–11; and Aldridge, "Benjamin Franklin and the Philosophes," *Studies in Voltaire and the Eighteenth Century* (Geneva, 1963), XXIV, 43–48.

5. *Parallel Text*, pp. 4–10. In a letter of July 31, 1758, Franklin had written of his genealogical discoveries: "I am the youngest Son of the youngest Son of the youngest Son of the youngest Son for five Generations; whereby I find that had there originally been any Estate in the Family none could have stood a worse chance for it." In an effusion of vanity, he added what he promptly crossed out: ". . . but by God's Blessing on my own Industry I find I have far'd as well or done tolerably as most of them" (*Papers*, VIII, 118).

6. *Parallel Text*, pp. 8, 14–18. On July 11, 1771, Franklin had by chance purchased some old pamphlets once owned by his namesake and favorite uncle. These seem to have turned his mind to the family's past just prior to his stay at Twyford. See also *Papers*, XVIII, 175–76.

7. *Parallel Text*, pp. 16–24.

8. *Parallel Text*, pp. 18–20, 32. Farrand notes that the manuscript has "generally" written above "always," which is crossed out in pencil (*Parallel Text*, p. 32 n.). He gives no explanation for printing the cancelled word. The Labaree edition prints "generally" without comment (*The Autobiography of Benjamin Franklin*, ed. Leonard W. Labaree et al. [New Haven, 1964], p. 60).

9. *Parallel Text*, pp. 46–48.

10. *Seven Who Shaped Our Destiny: The Founding Fathers as Revolutionaries* (New York, 1973), pp. 7–8. See also Paul W. Conner, *Poor Richard's Politicks: Benjamin Franklin and His New American Order* (New York, 1965), p. 211; Kenneth S. Lynn, *A Divided People* (Westport, Conn., 1977), pp. 49–52. For a long, insightful psychological study of Franklin, see Richard L. Bushman, "On the Uses of Psychology: Conflict and Conciliation in Benjamin Franklin," *History and Theory*, 5 (1966), 225–40.

11. Historians of the New England colonial family would argue that Franklin's ambivalence toward his father was a not uncharacteristic response to the child-rearing practices of the period. See John E. Walzer, "A Period of Ambivalence: Eighteenth-Century American Childhood," in *The History of Childhood*, ed. Lloyd de Mause (New York, 1974), pp.351–82; David Flaherty, *Privacy in Colonial New England* (Charlottesville, Va., 1972), pp. 55–59; Emory Elliot, *Power and the Pulpit in Puritan New England* (Princeton, 1975), pp. 16–87; Edmund S. Morgan, *The Puritan Family: Religion and Domestic Relations in Seventeenth-Century New England* (New York, 1966), pp. 65–86; and Philip Greven, *The Protestant Temperament: Patterns of Child-Rearing, Religious Experience and the Self in Early America* (New York, 1977).

12. *Parallel Text*, pp. 52–54, 64. On Franklin's first arrival in Philadelphia, see Alfred Owen Aldridge, "The First Published Memoir of Franklin," *William and Mary Quarterly*, 3d Ser., 24 (1967), 624–28.

13. *Parallel Text*, pp. 72–76, 106.

14. *Parallel Text*, p. 76 n.

15. *Parallel Text*, p. 148.

16. On Keimer, *Parallel Text*, pp. 88–92, 138, 142, 174; on Meredith, *Parallel Text*, pp. 132–40, 164–66; on Wyndham, *Parallel Text*, pp. 126–28; on Hamilton, *Parallel Text*, pp. 164, 172; on Denham, *Parallel Text*, pp. 104, 124–26, 130–32.

17. *Parallel Text*, pp. 32, 82, 108–10. While not all the father-figures who appear in the "Memoirs" are named in the copy of the 1771 outline from which Franklin worked in writing Part II, the surrogate character of the unnamed figures was inherent in the episodes indicated in his notes and incorporated in the text. Because the process by which any male adolescent measures his personality against father-figures is most often experienced only subconsciously, Franklin need not have recognized the surrogate identity he assigned these elders.

18. On Decow, *Parallel Text*, p. 144; on Mickle, *Parallel Text*, pp. 150–52. See also J. A. Leo Lemay, "Benjamin Franklin," in *Major Writers of Early American Literature*, ed. Everett Emerson (Madison, Wis., 1972), p. 239.

19. *Parallel Text*, p. 184 n.

20. *Autobiography*, pp. 134, 136. Italics in original.

21. Since Franklin describes himself as being in his seventy-ninth year, Part II was not written before his birthday, January 17, 1784 (*Parallel Text*, p. 230).

22. *Writings*, IX, 140–44, 211–15, 251–52, 254, 257–58.

23. *Parallel Text*, p. 148.

24. *Writings*, IX, 47–48, 279; Aldridge, *Benjamin Franklin*, p. 346; Carl Van Doren, *Benjamin Franklin* (Cleveland and New York, 1948), p. 722; Claude-Anne Lopez and Eugenia W. Herbert, *The Private Franklin: The Man and His Family* (New York, 1975), p. 288; Luther S. Livingston, *Franklin and His Press at Passy* (New York, 1914), pp. 74, 177.

25. The only full biography of Franklin's son is William E. Mariboe, "The Life of William Franklin, 1730 (1)–1813: '*Pro Rege et Patria*,' " Diss. University of Pennsylvania 1962. See also Catherine Fennelly, "William Franklin of New Jersey," *William and Mary Quarterly*, 3d Ser., 6 (1949), 361–82; Willard S. Randall, "William Franklin: The Making of a Conservative," in *The Loyalist Americans: A Focus on Greater New York*, ed. Robert A. East and Jacob Judd (Tarrytown, N.Y., 1975), pp. 56–73; and Lynn, *A Divided People*, pp. 21–22, 40.

26. *Writings*, VIII, 621–27, 650–51; IX, 175, 347–51, 556; Mariboe, pp. 553–54; Lopez and Herbert, pp. 224–25, 250–51; Van Doren, p. 691; Richard Morris, *The Peacemakers* (New York, 1963), pp. 375, 418–19; Mary Beth Norton, *The British-Americans: The Loyalist Exiles in England 1774–1789* (Boston, 1972), pp. 173–80; Herbert E. Klinglehofer, "Matthew Ridley's Diary during the Peace Negotiations of 1782," *William and Mary Quarterly*, 3d Ser., 20 (1963), 132.

27. William Franklin to Benjamin Franklin, July 22–August 6, 1784. This letter is in the library of the American Philosophical Society. Parts are quoted in Lopez and Herbert, pp. 252–53; and Mariboe, pp. 562–63.

28. Writings, IX, 252–54. Apart from the inherent doubtfulness of its claim that family relations should be of greater force than political conscience, Franklin's argument has a self-contradicting ex post facto character. Eleven years earlier, in a letter of October 6, 1773, he had counseled William on his service as colonial governor: "You are a thorough government man, which I do not wonder at, nor do I aim at converting you. I only wish you to act uprightly and steadily, avoiding that duplicity, which in Hutchinson, adds contempt to indignation. If you can promote the prosperity of your people, and leave them happier than you found them, whatever your political principles are your memory will be honored" (*Writings*, VI, 144–45). Mariboe and Fennelly emphasize the governor's commitment to principle. Franklin, however, was not above playing upon his son's unhappy financial situation in order to gain his resignation. He repeatedly reminded William that continuing in the inadequately paid governorship prevented his paying personal debts due the father. At the same time, William knew himself to be suspect in many British and Loyalist eyes because he was his father's

son (Mariboe, pp. 395–441, 474–75; Fennelly, p. 369; and Lopez and Herbert, pp. 239–52). These suspicions are mentioned in the ms. letter, William Franklin to Benjamin Franklin, July 22–August 6, 1784 and in a reported letter, William Franklin to Benjamin Franklin, June 8, 1771 (*The Complete Works of Benjamin Franklin*, ed. John Bigelow [New York, 1887], IX, 44).

29. For the reunion and Franklin's equivalent disinheritance of William, see *Writings*, X, 469, 493–510; Lopez and Herbert, pp. 279, 305; Van Doren, pp. 726, 761; Aldridge, *Benjamin Franklin*, pp. 375, 400. On Franklin and Paine, see the journal of John Hall printed in Moncure David Conway, *The Life of Thomas Paine* (New York, 1892), II, 468.

30. *Parallel Text*, p. 184.

31. *Autobiography*, pp. 134, 136.

32. *Parallel Text*, p. 204. Franklin had borrowed from the same verse (Proverbs 22:29) in composing his father's epitaph. See *Parallel Text*, p. 26; and *Papers*, VII, 229–30.

33. Franklin's anxieties here echo central themes of two favorite readings mentioned in Part I. Like Bunyan's Christian, he has reached his "Heavenly City," but he suffers nagging feelings of guilt, similar to those of Robinson Crusoe, for having departed from the course in life indicated for him by his father. Charles Sanford stresses the importance of Bunyan for Franklin and reads the *Autobiography* as a secular analogue of *The Pilgrim's Progress* (*The Quest for Paradise*, pp. 122–25). When Franklin first mentions Bunyan and Defoe together, reference is made to Defoe's *Essay upon Projects*. When he later recalls his "old favourite Author Bunyan's Pilgrim's Progress," he also speaks of "De foe in his Cruso" (*Parallel Text*, pp. 30, 54).

34. *Parallel Text*, pp. 18, 206–10; *Papers*, I, 101–9. Franklin's Presbyterian minister was the Rev. Samuel Hemphill. See Merton A. Christensen, "Franklin on the Hemphill Trial: Deism versus Presbyterian Orthodoxy," *William and Mary Quarterly*, 3d Ser., 10 (1953), 422–40.

35. *Parallel Text*, pp. 210–36. See also *Parallel Text*, p. 128; and *Papers*, I, 99–100.

36. *Writings*, VI, 86–88; IX, 208–10.

37. Increase Mather, "Solemn Advice to Young Men, not to Walk in the Ways of their Heart . . ." (Boston, 1695), pp. 20–21. For the relations of fathers and sons as treated in New England sermons generally, see Elliott, *Power and the Pulpit*.

38. Cotton Mather, "Help for Distressed Parents Or, Counsels and Comforts for Godly Parents Afflicted with Ungodly Children: . . ." (Boston, 1695), pp. 46, 60–61, 62. See also Cotton Mather, "A Family Well-Ordered" (Boston, 1699), pp. 38–79.

39. Cotton Mather, "Repeated Warnings, Another Essay to Warn Young People against Rebellion That Must Be Repented Of" (Boston, 1712), p. 2.

40. Richard Slotkin, "Narratives of Negro Crime in New England, 1675–1800," *American Quarterly*, 25 (1973), 7–9.

41. *Parallel Text*, pp. 28–30, 52, 144–48. Meyer Abrams has identified the wanderings of the Prodigal Son as providing the archetypal Christian *peregrinatio* in *Natural Supernaturalism: Tradition and Revolution in Romantic Literature* (New York, 1971), pp. 165–68. See also Michael Walzer, *The Revolution of the Saints: A Study in the Origins of Radical Politics* (New York, 1968), pp. 197–98.

42. Bercovitch, *The Puritan Origins of the American Self* (New Haven, 1975), pp. 143, 185, 234; Sanford, *The Quest for Paradise*, pp. 122, 123.

43. *Papers*, IV, 231.

44. *Papers*, XX, 526.

45. *Writings*, VIII, 306.

46. *Writings*, VIII, 606, 608, 613–14. Smyth assigns this essay to September 1782 (*Writings*, VIII, 603), but Van Doren argues that it cannot have been written before the last

months of 1783 (*Benjamin Franklin,* p. 704). Verner W. Crane follows William Temple Franklin in fixing its date as early 1784 ("Franklin's 'The Internal State of America' [1786]," *William and Mary Quarterly,* 3d Ser., 15 [1958], 219).

47. Edwin G. Burrows and Michael Wallace, "The American Revolution: The Ideology and Psychology of National Liberation," *Perspectives in American History,* 6 (1972), 165–306; Winthrop D. Jordan, "Familial Politics: Thomas Paine and the Killing of the King, 1776," *Journal of American History,* 60 (1973), 294–308; Bruce Mazlish, "Leadership in the American Revolution: The Psychological Dimension," in *Leadership in the American Revolution* (Washington, D.C., 1974), pp. 112–33; Peter Laslett, "Sir Robert Filmer: The Man versus the Whig Myth," *William and Mary Quarterly,* 3d Ser., 5 (1948), 523–46; John W. Robbins, "The Political Thought of Sir Robert Filmer," Diss. Johns Hopkins University 1973; Gordon J. Schochet, *Patriarchalism in Political Thought: The Authoritarian Family and Political Speculation and Attitudes in Seventeenth-Century England* (Oxford, 1975); Bernard Bailyn, *The Ideological Origins of the American Revolution* (Cambridge, Mass., 1967), pp. 310–19; Jack P. Greene, "An Uneasy Connection," in *Essays on the American Revolution,* ed. Stephen G. Kurtz and James H. Hutson (New York, 1973), pp. 32–80; R. W. K. Hinton, "Husbands, Fathers and Conquerors," *Political Studies,* 15 (1967), 291–300, and 16 (1968), 55–67; Michael Walzer, *Regicide and Revolution: Speeches at the Trial of Louis XVI* (Cambridge, 1974), pp. 25–26; Walzer, *The Revolution of the Saints,* pp. 149, 183–98; Greven, *The Protestant Temperament,* p. 398 n. 8. Freud himself notes the psychological correspondence of fathers and kings in his *Introductory Lectures in Psychoanalysis* in *The Standard Edition of the Complete Psychological Works of Sigmund Freud,* ed. and trans. James Strachey (London, 1961), XV, 153, 159.

48. Burrows and Wallace, p. 168.

49. See, for example, *Papers,* IV, 229; *Writings,* VI, 273, 290, 311, 415, 419, 458–60; VII, 85–86; *Benjamin Franklin's Letters to the Press,* ed. Verner W. Crane (Chapel Hill, N.C., 1950).

50. *Autobiography,* p. 139; *Parallel Text,* p. 184.

51. *The Revolutionary Diplomatic Correspondence of the United States,* ed. Francis Wharton (Washington, D.C., 1889), II, 239. Stanley Elkins and Eric McKitrick have sketched the effect of the Revolution on the younger American leaders in "The Founding Fathers: Young Men of the Revolution," *Political Science Quarterly,* 76 (1961), 203–6. In his own way, Franklin seems to have shared in this generational change, of which Douglass Adair has written that "the Founding Fathers, in a very true sense, are thus children of the Revolution, men who are transformed in the making of it" (*Frame and the Founding Fathers: Essays by Douglass Adair,* ed. Trevor Colbourn [New York, 1974], p. 7).

52. *Autobiography,* pp. 134–40. For Franklin's examination before the House of Commons, see *Papers,* XIII, 124–62.

53. *Parallel Text,* pp. 234–36.

54. *Parallel Text,* p. 48 n.

55. *Autobiography,* p. 134. On Franklin's story as metaphor of America, see Conner, *Poor Richard's Politicks,* pp. 12–15; and Earl Fendelman, "Toward Walden Pond: The American Voice in Autobiography," *Canadian Review of American Studies,* 8 (1977), 17.

56. *Parallel Text,* p. 184.

57. *Autobiography,* pp. 135, 138.

58. *Parallel Text,* p. 24.

59. *Parallel Text,* pp. 148, 226.

60. Vaughan's letter (*Autobiography,* p. 135) says Franklin's story would attract to America "settlers of virtuous and manly minds."

61. *Parallel Text,* pp. 214, 220–22, 206, 230.

62. *Papers,* II, 202–4.

63. *Parallel Text,* pp. 238, 212–14, 232. Franklin's expectation of virtue's earthly reward had been stated earlier at p. 148. See also *Papers,* I, 101–09.

64. Wood's classic study of the early republic's concern with virtue is *The Creation of the American Republic, 1776–1789* (Chapel Hill, N.C., 1969). Perry Miller, Edmund Morgan, Bernard Bailyn, J. G. A. Pocock, and Jack P. Greene have also written of eighteenth-century Americans' sense of the interdependence of private and public morality.

65. Drew R. McCoy, "Benjamin Franklin's Vision of a Republican Political Economy for America," *William and Mary Quarterly,* 3d Ser., 35 (1978), 618–19.

66. Greene, "An Uneasy Connection," pp. 59–60.

67. *Parallel Text,* pp. 210, 232, 236–42. According to William Temple Franklin, his grandfather's book was marked "Sunday, 1st July, 1733" (*Memoirs of the Life and Writings of Benjamin Franklin, LL.D. F.R.S. . . .* [London, 1818], p. 90 n.). The reading notes incorporated in the *Autobiography* (*Parallel Text,* pp. 236–38) were dated May 9, 1731. The plan may have derived from the notes Franklin made on his 1726 voyage from Gravesend to Philadelphia, only part of which have survived (*Parallel Text,* p. 128; and *Papers,* I, 99–100; IX, 104–5, 374–75; XII, 162).

68. See Yehoshua Arieli, *Individualism and Nationalism in American Ideology* (Cambridge, Mass., 1964), pp. 45–48; and Jack P. Greene, "The Alienation of Benjamin Franklin—British American," *Journal of the Royal Society for the Encouragement of the Arts, Manufactures and Commerce,* 124 (1976), 52–73.

69. *Parallel Text,* pp. 216, 230.

70. Greene in conversation in John A. Garraty, *Interpreting American History: Conversations with Historians* (New York, 1970), I, 54. See also Greene, "Search for Identity: An Interpretation of Selected Patterns of Social Response in Eighteenth-Century America," *Journal of Social History,* 3 (1970), 219; and Fred Weinstein and Gerald M. Platt, *The Wish to Be Free: Society, Psyche and Value Change* (Berkeley and Los Angeles, 1969), pp. 201–2.

71. *Writings,* IX, 240–48. See also Conner, *Poor Richard's Politicks,* especially pp. 21–107; Lewis J. Carey, *Franklin's Economic Views* (New York, 1928); Alfred Owen Aldridge, "Franklin as Demographer," *Journal of Economic History,* 9 (May 1949), 25–44.

72. *Parallel Text,* pp. 214–16, 204–06, 78, 24. Franklin expresses his republican suspicions of silver plate in the July 26, 1784, letter cited in note 71 above; *Writings,* IX, 242–43.

73. *Parallel Text,* p. 236. Adoption of the Constitution had been officially announced on July 2, 1788. It is of interest that Franklin signed his will on July 17. His two grandsons were very generously treated. William Temple Franklin received the remission of his debts to the grandfather and rights to Franklin's extensive land claims in Georgia. Besides what would pass to him from his parents' inheritance, Benjamin Franklin Bache was left all Franklin's type and other printing equipment in Philadelphia. The will's gestures to William Franklin were quite different. Three years after their reunion in Southampton, Franklin could only bring himself to forgive his son's outstanding debts and will him the books already in his possession together with the family's nearly valueless lands in Nova Scotia. "The part he acted against me in the late war, which is of public notoriety, will account for my leaving him no more of an estate he endeavoured to deprive me of" (*Writings,* X, 493–510).

74. Jerrold Seigel, *Marx's Fate: The Shape of a Life* (Princeton, 1978), p. 180. The passages quoted by Seigel are from Blos, *On Adolescence* (New York, 1962), pp. 134–35.

75. *Parallel Text,* p. 226.

76. *Parallel Text,* pp. 16, 22–24, 204, 44–50, 76–78.

The Lawrence Attack

Benjamin Franklin [1918]

D. H. Lawrence*

The idea of the perfectibility of man, which was such an inspiration in Europe, to Rousseau and Godwin and Shelley, all those idealists of the eighteenth and early nineteenth century, was actually fulfilled in America before the ideal was promulgated in Europe. If we sift the descriptions of the "Perfect Man," and accept the chief features of this ideal being, keeping only to what is possible, we shall find we have the abstract of a character such as Benjamin Franklin's.

A man whose passions are the obedient servants of his mind, a man whose sole ambition is to live for the bettering and advancement of his fellows, a man of such complete natural benevolence that the interests of self never obtrude in his works or his desires—such was to be the Perfect Man of the future, in the Millennium of the world. And such a man was Benjamin Franklin, in the actual America.

Therefore it is necessary to look very closely at the character of this Franklin. The magicians knew, at least imaginatively, what it was to create a being out of the intense *will* of the soul. And Mary Shelley, in the midst of the idealists, gives the dark side to the ideal being, showing us Frankenstein's monster.

The ideal being was man created by man. And so was the supreme monster. For man is not a creator. According to the early creed, the only power that the Almighty Creator could *not* confer upon His created being, not even upon the Son, was this same power of creation. Man by his own presence conveys the mystery and magnificence of creation. But yet man has no power over the creative mystery. He cannot *make* life—and he never will.

This we must accept, as one of the terms of our being. We know we cannot make and unmake the stars or the sun in heaven. We can only be at one, or at variance with them. And we should have the dignity of our own nature, and know that we cannot ordain the creative issues, neither in ourselves nor beyond ourselves. The ultimate choice is not ours. The creative mystery precedes us.

*Reprinted from the *English Review* 27 (July–December 1918): [397]–408.

This has been the fallacy of our age—the assumption that we, of our own will, and by our own precept and prescription, can create the perfect being and the perfect age. The truth is, that we *have* the faculty to form and distort even our own natures, and the natures of our fellow men. But we can *create* nothing. And the thing we can make of our own natures, by our own will, is at the most a pure mechanism, an automaton. So that if on the one hand Benjamin Franklin is the perfect human being of Godwin, on the other hand he is a monster, not exactly as the monster in *Frankenstein*, but for the same reason, viz., that he is the production or fabrication of the human will, which projects itself upon a living being, and automatises that being according to a given precept.

It is necessary to insist for ever that the source of creation is central within the human soul, and the issue from that source proceeds without any choice or knowledge on our part. The creative gesture, or emanation, for ever precedes the conscious realisation of this gesture. We are moved, we *are*, and then, thirdly, we *know*. Afterwards, fourthly, after we know, we can *will*. And when we *will*, then we can proceed to make or construct or fabricate—even our own characters. But we can never construct or fabricate or even change our own *being*, because we have our being in the central creative mystery, which is the pure present, and the pure Presence, of the soul—present beyond all knowing or willing. Knowing and willing are external, they are as it were the reflex or *afterwards* of being.

Fairly early in life Franklin drew up creed, which, he intended, "should satisfy the professors of every religion, but which should shock none." It has six articles.

"That there is One God, who made all things."

"That He governs the world by His Providence."

"That He ought to be worshipped with adoration, prayer, and thanksgiving."

"But that the most acceptable service of God is doing good to man."

"That the Soul is immortal."

"And that God will certainly reward virtue and punish vice, either here or hereafter."

Here we have a God who is a maker and an employer, whose one business is to look after the smooth running of the established creation, particularly the human part of it—Benjamin is not afraid to "but" the Lord his impertinent "buts"—who makes each man responsible for the working of the established system; and who reserves for Himself the right of granting a kind of immortal pension, in the after-life, to His praiseworthy mechanics of creation, or of condemning the unworthy to a kind of eternal workhouse.

Such a God is, of course, only the inventor and director of the universe, and not a God at all. In order to shock none of the professors of any religion, Benjamin left out all the qualities of the Godhead, utterly dispensed with the mystery of creation. The universe once set up, it has only to be kept running. For this purpose it has an efficient manager in Providence. Providence sees that the business of the universe—that great and complicated factory of revolving worlds—is kept profitably going. The output of human life increases with each generation, and there is a corresponding increase in the necessities of life. Providence is then entirely successful, and the earthly business is a paying concern.

Such is the open, flagrant statement which America makes, a hundred and fifty years after the religious arrival of the Pilgrim Fathers. The process of the will-to-control has worked so swiftly, in its activity of mystic destructive metabolism, that in a hundred and fifty years it has reduced the living being to this automatic entity.

The religious truth is the same now as it ever has been: that preceding all our knowledge or will or effort is the central creative mystery, out of which issues the strange and for ever unaccountable emanation of creation: that the universe is a bush which burns for ever with the Presence, consuming itself and yet never consumed; it burns with new flowers and with crumpling leaves that fall to ash; for ever new flowers on the way out of the mystic centre of creation which is within the bush—central and omnipresent; for ever old leaves falling. We cannot know where the quick of next year's roses lies, within the tree. In what part, root or stem or branch, is to be found the presence of next year's apples? We cannot answer. And yet we know that they are within the living body of the tree, nowhere and everywhere.

So, within the living body of the universe, and within the living soul of man, central and omnipresent, in the fingers and lips and eyes and feet, as in the heart and bowels, and in the marshes as in the stars, lies the Presence, never to be located, yet never to be doubted, because it is *always* evident to our living soul, the Presence from which issues the first fine-shaken impulse and prompting of new being, eternal creation which is always Now. All time is central within this ever-present creative Now.

Central is the mystery of Now, the creative mystery, what we have called the Godhead. It pulses for ever, in the motion of creation, drawing all things towards itself. And the running waves, as they travel towards the perfect centre of the revealed, now are buds, and infants, and children; further back, they are seed-scales and moving seed-leaves, and caterpillars; and further back, they are sun and water and the elements moving towards the centre of pure Now, of perfect creative Presence. And in the outflow, the waves travel back. And the first waves are the people with hair tinged with grey, and flowers passing into fruit, and leaves passing into water and fire and mould, and the elements ebbing asunder into the great chaos, and further than the great chaos into the infinite. The reality of realities is the rose in flower, the man and woman in maturity, the bird in song, the snake in brindled colour, the tiger in his stripes. In these, past and present and future are at one, the perfect Now. This is wholeness and pure creation. So there is a ripple and shimmer of the universe, ripples of futurity running towards the Now, out of the infinite, and ripples of age and the autumn, glimmering back towards the infinite. And rocking at all times on the shimmer are the perfect lotus flowers of immanent Now, the lovely beings of consummation.

The quick of wholeness lies in this gleaming Now. But the whole of wholeness lies in the ebbing haste of child-faced futurity, the consummation of presence, and the lapse of sunset-coloured old age. This is completeness, the childish haste towards the consummation, the perfect revelation, the pure Presence, when we are fully a flower and present, the great *adsum* of our being, and then the slow retreat of becoming old.

There is, however, the false Now, as well as the mystic Now. Perpetual youth, or perpetual maturity, this is the false Now—as roses that never fall are false roses. The remaining steady, fixed, this is the false Now. And as the consummation into the whole infinite is the antithesis of pure Presence, so is Eternity the antithesis of the mystic Present, the great Now. For eternity is but the sum of the whole past and the whole future, the complete *outside* or negation of being.

In Europe the desire to become infinite, one with the All, was the adolescent desire to know everything and to be everything. The mystic passion for infinitude is the ultimate of all our passion for love, oneness, equality. It is all an adolescent process. It is a process which comes to a conclusion, and out of which mankind must issue, as the individual man issues from his period of loving and seeking, into the assured magnificence of maturity. This experience of infinitude, oneness with the all, is the ultimate communion wherein the individual is merged into wholeness with all things, through love. But it is no goal. The individual must emerge from this bath of love, as from the baths of blood in the old religions, initiated, fulfilled, entering on the great state of independent maturity.

In America, however, the state of oneness was soon reached. The Pilgrim Fathers soon killed off in their people the spontaneous impulses and appetites of the self. By a stern discipline and a fanatic system of repression, they subdued every passion into rigid control. And they did it quickly. England lapsed again into exuberance and self-indulgence. She produced her Congreves and Addisons and Smolletts, and Robert Burns. But America moved on in one line of inexorable repression.

Now there are two kinds of oneness among mankind. First there is that ecstatic sense, religious and mystic, of uplifting into union with all men, through love. This experience we all know, more or less. But, secondly, there is the hard, practical state of being at one with all men, through suppression and elimination of those things which make differences—passions, prides, impulses of the self which cause disparity between one being and another. Now it seems as if, in America, this negative, destructive form of oneness predominated from the first, a oneness attained by destroying all incompatible elements in each individual, leaving the pattern or standard man.

So that whilst Europe was still impulsively struggling on towards a consummation of love, expressed in Shelley or Verlaine or Swinburne or Tolstoi, a struggle for the mystic state of communion in being, America, much quicker and more decisive, was cutting down every human being towards a common standard, aiming at a homogeneous oneness through elimination of incommutable factors or elements, establishing a standardised humanity, machine-perfect.

This process of strangling off the impulses took place in Europe as in America. Spontaneous movement distinguishes one individual from another. If we remove the spontaneous or impulsive factor, and substitute deliberate purposiveness, we can have a homogeneous humanity, acting in unison. Hence the ideal Reason of the eighteenth century.

So man has a great satisfaction, at a certain period in his development, in seizing control of his own life-motion, and making himself master of his own fate. The desire is so strong it tends to become a lust. It became a lust in the French and in the American. Jean Jacques Rousseau had a fundamental lust for fingering and knowing and directing every impulse, as it was born. He intercepted every one of his feelings as it arose, caught it with his consciousness and his will, then liberated it again, so that he might watch it act within the narrow field of his own observation and permission.

All this was part of the process of oneing, the process of forming a deliberate, self-conscious, self-determined humanity which, in the acceptance of a common idea of equality and fraternity, should be quite homogeneous, unified, ultimately dispassionate, rational, utilitarian. The only difference was that whilst the European ideal remained one of mystic, exalted consciousness of oneness, the ideal in America was a practical unison for the producing of the means of life.

Rousseau analysed his feelings, got them into control in order to luxuriate in their workings. He enjoyed a mental voluptuousness in watching and following the turn of his self-permitted sensations and emotions, as one might watch a wild creature tamed and entrapped and confined in a small space. Franklin, on the other hand, had his voluptuous pleasure in subduing and reducing all his feelings and emotions and desires to the material benefit of mankind.

To seize life within his own will, and control it by precept from his own consciousness, made him as happy as it now makes us sick. With us it is a sick, helpless process. We perceive at last that if we cannot act direct and spontaneous from the centre of creative mystery which is in us, we are nothing. It is no good any more giving us choice—our free will is of no use to us if we no longer have anything to choose. It only remains for us now, in the purest sense, to choose not-to-choose.

Franklin, however, proceeded with joy to seize the life-issues, to get everything into his own choice and will. His God was no longer a creative mystery—He was a reasonable Providence or Producer. And man, being made in the image of God, he too is at his highest a little Providence or Producer of the means of life. Production is the criterion of Godliness, which leads us to the plausible self-righteous, altruistic materialism of our modern world. The difference between production and creation is the difference between existence and being, function and flowering, mechanical force and life itself.

Franklin proceeded to automatise himself, to subdue life so that it should work automatically to his will. Like Rousseau, he makes a confession of his life. But he is purely self-congratulatory. He tells us in detail how he worked out the process of reducing himself to a deliberate entity. This deliberate entity, this self-determined man, is the very Son of Man, man made by the power of the human will, a virtuous Frankenstein monster.

Almost scientifically, Franklin broke the impulses in himself. He drew up a list of virtues, established a set of fixed principles—strictly machine-principles—and by these he proceeded to control his every motion. The modern virtue is machine-principle, meaning the endless repetition of certain sanctioned motions. The old *virtus* meant just the opposite, the very impulse itself, the creative gesture, drifting out incalculable from human hands.

Franklin's list of virtues is as follows:—

1

TEMPERANCE

Eat not to fulness; drink not to elevation.

2

SILENCE

Speak not but what may benefit others or yourself; avoid trifling conversation.

3

ORDER

Let all your things have their places; let each part of your business have its time.

4

RESOLUTION

Resolve to perform what you ought; perform without fail what you resolve.

5

FRUGALITY

Make no expense but to do good to others or yourself—*i.e.*, waste nothing.

6

INDUSTRY

Lose no time, be always employed in something useful; cut off all unnecessary action.

7

SINCERITY

Use no hurtful deceit; think innocently and justly, and, if you speak, speak accordingly.

8

JUSTICE

Wrong done by doing injuries, or omitting the benefits that are your duty.

9

MODERATION

Avoid extremes, forbear resenting injuries so much as you think they deserve.

10

CLEANLINESS

Tolerate no uncleanliness in body, clothes, or habitation.

11

TRANQUILLITY

Be not disturbed at trifles, or at accident common or unavoidable.

12

CHASTITY

Rarely use venery but for health and offspring, never to dullness, weakness, or the injury of your own or another's peace or reputation.

13

HUMILITY

Imitate Jesus and Socrates.

The last clause or item, of humility, Franklin added because a Quaker friend told him he was generally considered proud. Truly he had something to be proud of.

He practised these virtues with ardour and diligence. He drew up a table, giving each of the virtues a column to itself, and having the date, like a calendar, down the side. And every day he put a mark against himself for every lapse of virtue. Unfortunately, he does not give us his marked chart—we might have an even closer view of his character had he done so. He only tells us that the black column was that of "Order." In every other virtue he had considerable proficiency. But he *could not* make himself tidy and neat in his business and in his surroundings, not even to the end of his days. So he tells us.

This is his one weakness, his Achilles heel. Had he not had this harmless failing, he would have been the very Frankenstein of virtue. There is something slightly pathetic, slightly ridiculous, and, if we look closer, a little monstrous, about the snuff-coloured doctor. He worked so diligently and seriously. He was so alive, full of inquisitive interest and eager activity. He had his club for discussing philosophic questions, he made his printing business prosper, he had the streets of Philadelphia swept and lighted, he invented his electric appliances, he was such a straight-principled member of all the important Councils of Philadelphia—then of the American Colonies themselves. He defended himself with such sturdy, snuff-coloured honesty in England, and against his enemies in America, and in France. He wrestled with such indomitable integrity with the French Court, a little, indomitable, amazingly clever and astute, and at the same time amazingly disingenuous, virtuous man, winning from the fine and decadent French such respect, and such huge sums of money to help the Americans in their struggle for Independence. It is a wonderful little snuff-coloured figure, so admirable, so *clever,* a little pathetic, and, somewhere, ridiculous and detestable.

He is like a child, so serious and earnest. And he is like a little old man, even when he is young, so deliberate and reasoned. It is difficult to say which he is—a child or a little old man. But when we come to grips he is neither. In his actuality he is a dreadful automaton, a mechanism. He is a printer, and a philosopher, and an inventor, and a scientist, and a patriot, and a writer of "Poor Richard" jokes for the calendar, and he is virtuous and scrupulous and of perfect integrity. But he is never a man. It did not seem to matter at all to him that he himself was an intrinsic being. He saw himself as a little unit in the vast total of society. All he wanted was to run well, as a perfect little wheel within the whole.

The beauty of incomparable *being* was nothing to him. The inestimable splendidness of a man who is purely himself, distinct and incommutable, a thing of pure, present reality, this meant nothing to Benjamin. He liked comeliness, cleanliness, healthiness, and profusion of the means of life. He could never see that the only riches of the earth is in free, whole, incomparable beings, each man mystically himself, and distinct, mystically distinguished. To him, men were like coin to be counted up, coin interchangeable.

He was, perhaps, the most admirable little automaton the world has ever seen, the invention of the human will, working according to good principles. So far as affairs went, he was admirable. As far as life goes, he is monstrous.

If we look in the little almanacks or booklets that are printed in England, in out-of-the-way corners, even to-day, we shall find humorous, trite paragraphs, where "Poor Richard" is the speaker, and which are little object-lessons to one or another of the "virtues"—economy, or frugality, or modesty. Franklin wrote these almanacks when he was still a young man—more than a hundred and fifty years ago—and they are still printed, now as then, for the poor and vulgar to profit by. They are always trite and, in a measure, humorous, and always shrewd, and always flagrantly material. Franklin had his humour, but it was always of the "don't-put-all-your-eggsin-one-basket" sort. It always derided the spontaneous, impulsive, or extravagant element in man, and showed the triumph of cautious, calculated, virtuous behaviour. Whatever else man must be, he must be deliberate. He must live entirely from his consciousness and his will. Once he lives from his consciousness and his will, it will follow as a matter of course that he lives according to the given precepts, because that is both easiest and most profitable.

We do, perhaps, get a glimpse of a really wondering young Franklin, where he has still the living faculty for beholding with instinct the world around him—when he was a printer's workman, in London, for a short time. But the glimpse is soon over. He is back in America, and is all American, a very model of a man, as if a machine had made him.

He was so dreadfully all-of-a-piece, his attitude is always so consistent and urbane. He has to go to the frontiers of his State, to settle some disturbance among the Indians. And on this occasion he writes:—

> We found they had made a great bonfire in the middle of the square; they were all drunk, men and women quarrelling and fighting. Their dark-coloured bodies, half naked, seen only by the gloomy light of the bonfire, running after and beating one another with fire-brands, accompanied by their horrid yellings, formed a scene the most resembling our ideas of hell that could be well imagined. There was no appeasing the tumult, and we retired to our lodging. At midnight a number of them came thundering at our door, demanding more rum, of which we took no notice.
>
> The next day, sensible they had misbehaved in giving us that disturbance, they sent three of their counsellors to make their apology. The orator acknowledged the fault, but laid it upon the rum, and then endeavoured to excuse the rum by saying: "The Great Spirit, who made all things, made everything for some use; and whatever he designed anything for, that use it should always be put to. Now, when he made rum, he said: "Let this be for the Indians to get drunk with." And it must be so."
>
> And, indeed, if it be the design of Providence to extirpate these savages in order to make room for the cultivators of the earth, it seems not improbable that rum may be the appointed means. It has already annihilated all the tribes who formerly inhabited all the sea coast—

This, from the good doctor, with such suave complacency, is a little disenchanting. But this is what a Providence must lead to. A Providence is a Provider for the universe, and the business of the provider is to get rid of every waster, even if this waster happen to be part of the self-same created universe. When man sets out to have all things his own way he is bound to run up against a great many men. Even to establish the ideal of equality he has to reckon with the men who do really feel the force of inequality. And then equality sharpens his axe. He becomes a great leveller, cutting off all tall men's heads. For no man must be taller than Franklin, who is middle-sized.

Nevertheless, this process of attaining to unison by conquering and subduing all impulses, this removing of all those individual traits which make for separateness and diversity, had to be achieved and accomplished. It is not until man has utterly seized power over himself, and gained complete knowledge of himself, down to the most minute and shameful of his desires and sensations, that he can really begin to be free. Then, when man knows *all,* both shameful and good, that is in man; and when he has control over every impulse, both good and bad; then, and only then, having utterly bound and fettered himself in his own will and his own self-conscious knowledge, will he learn to make the great choice, the choice between automatic self-determining, and mystic, spontaneous freedom.

When the great Greek-Christian will-to-knowledge is fulfilled; and when the great barbaric will-to-power is also satisfied; then, perhaps, man can recognise that neither power nor knowledge is the ultimate man's attainment, but only *being;* that the pure reality lies not in any infinitude, but in the mystery of the perfect *unique* self, incommutable; not in any eternity, but in the sheer Now.

The quick and issue of our being stands previous to any control, prior to all knowledge. The centre of creative mystery is primal and central in every man, but in each man it is unique and incommutable. When we know *all things* about ourselves we shall know this, know, and enter upon our being. But first we must know all things, both bad and good. For this, the great liberating truth, is the last to be realised, the very last.

When we know that the unique, incommutable creative mystery of the Self is within us and precedes us, then we shall be able to take our full being from this mystery. We shall at last learn the pure lesson of knowing not-to-know. We shall know so perfectly that in fulness of knowledge we shall yield to the mystery, and become spontaneous in full consciousness. Our will will be so strong that we can simply, through sheer strength, defer from willing, accepting the spontaneous mystery and saving it in its issue from the mechanical lusts of righteousness or power.

Benjamin Franklin [1923]

D. H. Lawrence*

The Perfectibility of Man! Ah heaven, what a dreary theme! The perfectibility of the Ford car! The perfectibility of which man? I am many men. Which of them are you going to perfect? I am not a mechanical contrivance.

Education! Which of the various me's do you propose to educate, and which do you propose to suppress?

*Reprinted from *Studies in Classic American Literature* (New York: Viking Press, 1961), 9–21.

Anyhow, I defy you. I defy you, oh society, to educate me or to suppress me, according to your dummy standards.

The ideal man! And which is he, if you please? Benjamin Franklin or Abraham Lincoln? The ideal man! Roosevelt or Porfirio Díaz?

There are other men in me, besides this patient ass who sits here in a tweed jacket. What am I doing, playing the patient ass in a tweed jacket? Who am I talking to? Who are you, at the other end of this patience?

Who are you? How many selves have you? And which of these selves do you want to be?

Is Yale College going to educate the self that is in the dark of you, or Harvard College?

The ideal self! Oh, but I have a strange and fugitive self shut out and howling like a wolf or a coyote under the ideal windows. See his red eyes in the dark? This is the self who is coming into his own.

The perfectibility of man, dear God! When every man as long as he remains alive is in himself a multitude of conflicting men. Which of these do you choose to perfect, at the expense of every other?

Old Daddy Franklin will tell you. He'll rig him up for you, the pattern American. Oh, Franklin was the first downright American. He knew what he was about, the sharp little man. He set up the first dummy American.

At the beginning of his career this cunning little Benjamin drew up for himself a creed that should "satisfy the professors of every religion, but shock none."

Now wasn't that a real American thing to do?

"That there is One God, who made all things."

(But Benjamin made Him.)

"That He governs the world by His Providence."

(Benjamin knowing all about Providence.)

"That He ought to be worshipped with adoration, prayer, and thanksgiving."

(Which cost nothing.)

"But———" But me no buts, Benjamin, saith the Lord.

"But that the most acceptable service of God is doing good to men."

(God having no choice in the matter.)

"That the soul is immortal."

(You'll see why, in the next clause.)

"And that God will certainly reward virtue and punish vice, either here or hereafter."

Now if Mr. Andrew Carnegie, or any other millionaire, had wished to invent a God to suit his ends, he could not have done better. Benjamin did it for him in the eighteenth century. God is the supreme servant of men who want to get on, to *produce*. Providence. The provider. The heavenly storekeeper. The everlasting Wanamaker.

And this is all the God the grandsons of the Pilgrim Fathers had left. Aloft on a pillar of dollars.

"That the soul is immortal."

The trite way Benjamin says it!

But man has a soul, though you can't locate it either in his purse or his pocket-book or his heart or his stomach or his head. The *wholeness* of a man is his soul. Not merely that nice little comfortable bit which Benjamin marks out.

It's a queer thing is a man's soul. It is the whole of him. Which means it is the unknown him, as well as the known. It seems to me just funny, professors and Benjamins fixing the functions of the soul. Why, the soul of man is a vast forest, and all Benjamin intended was a neat back garden. And we've all got to fit into his kitchen garden scheme of things. Hail Columbia!

The soul of man is a dark forest. The Hercynian Wood that scared the Romans so, and out of which came the white-skinned hordes of the next civilization.

Who knows what will come out of the soul of man? The soul of man is a dark vast forest, with wild life in it. Think of Benjamin fencing it off!

Oh, but Benjamin fenced a little tract that he called the soul of man, and proceeded to get it into cultivation. Providence, forsooth! And they think that bit of barbed wire is going to keep us in pound for ever? More fools they.

This is Benjamin's barbed wire fence. He made himself a list of virtues, which he trotted inside like a grey nag in a paddock.

1

TEMPERANCE

Eat not to fulness; drink not to elevation.

2

SILENCE

Speak not but what may benefit others or yourself; avoid trifling conversation.

3

ORDER

Let all your things have their places; let each part of your business have its time.

4

RESOLUTION

Resolve to perform what you ought; perform without fail what you resolve.

5

FRUGALITY

Make no expense but to do good to others or yourself—i.e., waste nothing.

6

INDUSTRY

Lose no time, be always employed in something useful; cut off all unnecessary action.

7

SINCERITY

Use no hurtful deceit; think innocently and justly, and, if you speak, speak accordingly.

8

JUSTICE

Wrong none by doing injuries, or omitting the benefits that are your duty.

9

MODERATION

Avoid extremes, forbear resenting injuries as much as you think they deserve.

10

CLEANLINESS

Tolerate no uncleanliness in body, clothes, or habitation.

11

TRANQUILLITY

Be not disturbed at trifles, or at accidents common or unavoidable.

12

CHASTITY

Rarely use venery but for health and offspring, never to dulness, weakness, or the injury of your own or another's peace or reputation.

13

HUMILITY

Imitate Jesus and Socrates.

A Quaker friend told Franklin that he, Benjamin, was generally considered proud, so Benjamin put in the Humility touch as an afterthought. The amusing part is the sort of humility it displays. "Imitate Jesus and Socrates," and mind you don't outshine either of these two. One can just imagine Socrates and Alcibiades roaring in their cups over Philadelphian Benjamin, and Jesus looking at him a little puzzled, and murmuring: "Aren't you wise in your own conceit, Ben?"

"Henceforth be masterless," retorts Ben. "Be ye each one his own master unto himself, and don't let even the Lord put His spoke in." "Each man his own master" is but a puffing up of masterlessness.

Well, the first of Americans practised this enticing list with assiduity, setting a national example. He had the virtues in columns, and gave himself good and bad marks according as he thought his behaviour deserved. Pity these conduct charts are lost to us. He only remarks that Order was his stumbling block. He could not learn to be neat and tidy.

Isn't it nice to have nothing worse to confess?

He was a little model, was Benjamin. Doctor Franklin. Snuff-coloured little man! Immortal soul and all!

The immortal soul part was a sort of cheap insurance policy.

Benjamin had no concern, really, with the immortal soul. He was too busy with social man.

1. He swept and lighted the streets of young Philadelphia.

2. He invented electrical appliances.

3. He was the centre of a moralizing club in Philadelphia, and he wrote the moral humorisms of Poor Richard.

4. He was a member of all the important councils of Philadelphia, and then of the American colonies.

5. He won the cause of American Independence at the French Court, and was the economic father of the United States.

Now what more can you want of a man? And yet he is *infra dig.*, even in Philadelphia.

I admire him. I admire his sturdy courage first of all, then his sagacity, then his glimpsing into the thunders of electricity, then his common-sense humour. All the qualities of a great man, and never more than a great citizen. Middle-sized, sturdy, snuff-coloured Doctor Franklin, one of the soundest citizens that ever trod or "used venery."

I do not like him.

And, by the way, I always thought books of Venery were about hunting deer.

There is a certain earnest naïveté about him. Like a child. And like a little old man. He has again become as a little child, always as wise as his grandfather, or wiser.

Perhaps, as I say, the most complete citizen that ever "used venery."

Printer, philosopher, scientist, author and patriot, impeccable husband and citizen, why isn't he an archetype?

Pioneer, Oh Pioneers! Benjamin was one of the greatest pioneers of the United States. Yet we just can't do with him.

What's wrong with him then? Or what's wrong with us?

I can remember, when I was a little boy, my father used to buy a scrubby yearly almanac with the sun and moon and stars on the cover. And it used to prophesy bloodshed and famine. But also crammed in corners it had little anecdotes and humorisms, with a moral tag. And I used to have my little priggish laugh at the woman who counted her chickens before they were hatched and so forth, and I was convinced that honesty was the best policy, also a little priggishly. The author of these bits was Poor Richard, and Poor Richard was Benjamin Franklin, writing in Philadelphia well over a hundred years before.

And probably I haven't got over those Poor Richard tags yet. I rankle still with them. They are thorns in young flesh.

Because, although I still believe that honesty is the best policy, I dislike policy altogether; though it is just as well not to count your chickens before they are hatched, its still more hateful to count them with gloating when they *are* hatched. It has taken me many years and countless smarts to get out of that barbed wire moral enclosure that Poor Richard rigged up. Here am I now in tatters and scratched to ribbons, sitting in the middle of Benjamin's America looking at the barbed wire, and the fat sheep crawling under the fence to get fat outside, and the watchdogs yelling at the gate lest by chance anyone should get out by the proper exit. Oh America! Oh Benjamin! And I just utter a long loud curse against Benjamin and the American corral.

Moral America! Most moral Benjamin. Sound, satisfied Ben!

He had to go to the frontiers of his State to settle some disturbance among the Indians. On this occasion he writes:

> We found that they had made a great bonfire in the middle of the square; they were all drunk, men and women quarrelling and fighting. Their dark-coloured bodies, half-naked, seen only by the gloomy light of the bonfire, running after and beating one another with fire-brands, accompanied by their horrid yellings, formed a scene the most resembling our ideas of hell that could well be imagined. There was no appeasing the tumult, and we retired to our lodging. At midnight a number of them came thundering at our door, demanding more rum, of which we took no notice.
>
> The next day, sensible they had misbehaved in giving us that disturbance, they sent three of their counsellors to make their apology. The orator acknowledged the fault, but laid it upon the rum, and then endeavoured to excuse the rum by saying: "The Great Spirit, who made all things, made everything for some use; and whatever he designed anything for, that use it should always be put to. Now, when he had made the rum, he said: "Let this be for the Indians to get drunk with." And it must be so."
>
> And, indeed, if it be the design of Providence to extirpate these savages in order to make room for the cultivators of the earth, it seems not improbable that rum may be the appointed means. It has already annihilated all the tribes who formerly inhabited all the seacoast. . . .

This, from the good doctor with such suave complacency, is a little disenchanting. Almost too good to be true.

But there you are! The barbed wire fence. "Extirpate these savages in order to make room for the cultivators of the earth." Oh, Benjamin Franklin! He even "used venery" as a cultivator of seed.

Cultivate the earth, ye gods! The Indians did that, as much as they needed. And they left off there. Who built Chicago? Who cultivated the earth until it spawned Pittsburgh, Pa?

The moral issue! Just look at it! Cultivation included. If it's a mere choice of Kultur or cultivation, I give it up.

Which brings us right back to our question, what's wrong with Benjamin, that we can't stand him? Or else, what's wrong with us, that we find fault with such a paragon?

Man is a moral animal. All right. I am a moral animal. And I'm going to remain such. I'm not going to be turned into a virtuous little automaton as Benjamin would have me. "This is good, that is bad. Turn the little handle and let the good tap flow," saith Benjamin, and all America with him. "But first of all extirpate those savages who are always turning on the bad tap."

I am a moral animal. But I am not a moral machine. I don't work with a little set of handles or levers. The Temperance-silence-order-resolution-frugality - industry - sincerity - justice - moderation - cleanliness - tranquillity - chastity-humility keyboard is not going to get me going. I'm really not just an automatic piano with moral Benjamin getting tunes out of me.

Here's my creed, against Benjamin's. This is what I believe:

"That I am I."

"That my soul is a dark forest."

"That my known self will never be more than a little clearing in the forest."

"That gods, strange gods, come forth from the forest into the clearing of my known self, and then go back."

"That I must have the courage to let them come and go."

"That I will never let mankind put anything over me, but that I will try always to recognize and submit to the gods in me and the gods in other men and women."

There is my creed. He who runs may read. He who prefers to crawl, or to go by gasoline, can call it rot.

Then for a "list." It is rather fun to play at Benjamin.

1

TEMPERANCE

Eat and carouse with Bacchus, or munch dry bread with Jesus, but don't sit down without one of the gods.

2

SILENCE

Be still when you have nothing to say; when genuine passion moves you, say what you've got to say, and say it hot.

3

ORDER

Know that you are responsible to the gods inside you and to the men in whom the gods are manifest. Recognize your superiors and your inferiors, according to the gods. This is the root of all order.

4

RESOLUTION

Resolve to abide by your own deepest promptings, and to sacrifice the smaller thing to the greater. Kill when you must, and be killed the same: the *must* coming from the gods inside you, or from the men in whom you recognize the Holy Ghost.

5

FRUGALITY

Demand nothing; accept what you see fit. Don't waste your pride or squander your emotion.

6

INDUSTRY

Lose no time with ideals; serve the Holy Ghost; never serve mankind.

7

SINCERITY

To be sincere is to remember that I am I, and that the other man is not me.

8

JUSTICE

The only justice is to follow the sincere intuition of the soul, angry or gentle. Anger is just, and pity is just, but judgment is never just.

9

MODERATION

Beware of absolutes. There are many gods.

10

CLEANLINESS

Don't be too clean. It impoverishes the blood.

11

TRANQUILLITY

The soul has many motions, many gods come and go. Try and find your deepest issue, in every confusion, and abide by that. Obey the man in whom you recognize the Holy Ghost; command when your honour comes to command.

12

CHASTITY

Never "use" venery at all. Follow your passional impulse, if it be answered in the other being; but never have any motive in mind, neither offspring nor health nor even pleasure, nor even service. Only know that "venery" is of the great gods. An offering-up of yourself to the very great gods, the dark ones, and nothing else.

13
HUMILITY

See all men and women according to the Holy Ghost that is within them. Never yield before the barren.

There's my list. I have been trying dimly to realize it for a long time, and only America and old Benjamin have at last goaded me into trying to formulate it.

And now I, at least, know why I can't stand Benjamin. He tries to take away my wholeness and my dark forest, my freedom. For how can any man be free, without an illimitable background? And Benjamin tries to shove me into a barbed wire paddock and make me grow potatoes or Chicagoes.

And how can I be free, without gods that come and go? But Benjamin won't let anything exist except my useful fellow men, and I'm sick of them; as for his Godhead, his Providence, He is Head of nothing except a vast heavenly store that keeps every imaginable line of goods, from victrolas to cat-o'-nine tails.

And how can any man be free without a soul of his own, that he believes in and won't sell at any price? But Benjamin doesn't let me have a soul of my own. He says I am nothing but a servant of mankind—galley-slave I call it—and if I don't get my wages here below—that is, if Mr. Pierpont Morgan or Mr. Nosey Hebrew or the grand United States Government, the great US, US or SOMEOFUS, manages to scoop in my bit, along with their lump—why, never mind, I shall get my wages HEREAFTER.

Oh Benjamin! Oh Binjum! You do NOT suck me in any longer.

And why, oh why should the snuff-coloured little trap have wanted to take us all in? Why did he do it?

Out of sheer human cussedness, in the first place. We do all like to get things inside a barbed wire corral. Especially our fellow men. We love to round them up inside the barbed wire enclosure of FREEDOM, and make 'em work. *"Work, you free jewel, WORK!"* shouts the liberator, cracking his whip. Benjamin, I will not work. I do not choose to be a free democrat. I am absolutely a servant of my own Holy Ghost.

Sheer cussedness! But there was as well the salt of a subtler purpose. Benjamin was just in his eyeholes—to use an English vulgarism, meaning he was just delighted—when he was at Paris judiciously milking money out of the French monarchy for the overthrow of all monarchy. If you want to ride your horse to somewhere you must put a bit in his mouth. And Benjamin wanted to ride his horse so that it would upset the whole apple-cart of the old masters. He wanted the whole European apple-cart upset. So he had to put a strong bit in the mouth of his ass.

"Henceforth be masterless."

That is, he had to break-in the human ass completely, so that much more might be broken, in the long run. For the moment it was the British Government that had to have a hole knocked in it. The first real hole it ever had: the breach of the American rebellion.

Benjamin, in his sagacity, knew that the breaking of the old world was a long process. In the depths of his own under-consciousness he hated England, he hated Europe, he hated the whole corpus of the European being. He wanted to be American. But you can't change your nature and mode of consciousness like changing your shoes. It is a gradual shedding. Years must go by, and centuries must elapse before you have finished. Like a son escaping from the domination of his parents. The escape is not just one rupture. It is a long and half-secret process.

So with the American. He was a European when he first went over the Atlantic. He is in the main a recreant European still. From Benjamin Franklin to Woodrow Wilson may be a long stride, but it is a stride along the same road. There is no new road. The same old road, become dreary and futile. Theoretic and materialistic.

Why then did Benjamin set up this dummy of a perfect citizen as a pattern to America? Of course, he did it in perfect good faith, as far as he knew. He thought it simply was the true ideal. But what we *think* we do is not very important. We never really know what we are doing. Either we are materialistic instruments, like Benjamin, or we move in the gesture of creation, from our deepest self, usually unconscious. We are only the actors, we are never wholly the authors of our own deeds or works. IT is the author, the unknown inside us or outside us. The best we can do is to try to hold ourselves in unison with the deeps which are inside us. And the worst we can do is to try to have things our own way, when we run counter to IT, and in the long run get our knuckles rapped for our presumption.

So Benjamin contriving money out of the Court of France. He was contriving the first steps of the overthrow of all Europe, France included. You can never have a new thing without breaking an old. Europe happens to be the old thing. America, unless the people in America assert themselves too much in opposition to the inner gods, should be the new thing. The new thing is the death of the old. But you can't cut the throat of an epoch. You've got to steal the life from it through several centuries.

And Benjamin worked for this both directly and indirectly. Directly, at the Court of France, making a small but very dangerous hole in the side of England, through which hole Europe has by now almost bled to death. And indirectly in Philadelphia, setting up this unlovely, snuff-coloured little ideal, or automaton, of a pattern American. The pattern American, this dry, moral, utilitarian little democrat, has done more to ruin the old Europe than any Russian nihilist. He has done it by slow attrition, like a son who has stayed at home and obeyed his parents, all the while silently hating their authority, and silently, in his soul, destroying not only their authority but their whole existence. For the American spiritually stayed at home in Europe. The spiritual home of America was, and still is, Europe.

This is the galling bondage, in spite of several billions of heaped-up gold. Your heaps of gold are only so many muck-heaps, America, and will remain so till you become a reality to yourselves.

All this Americanizing and mechanizing has been for the purpose of overthrowing the past. And now look at America, tangled in her own barbed wire, and mastered by her own machines. Absolutely got down by her own barbed wire of shalt-nots, and shut up fast in her own "productive" machines like millions of squirrels running in millions of cages. It is just a farce.

Now is your chance, Europe. Now let Hell loose and get your own back, and paddle your own canoe on a new sea, while clever America lies on her muck-heaps of gold, strangled in her own barbed wire of shalt-not ideals and shalt-not moralisms. While she goes out to work like millions of squirrels in millions of cages. Production!

Let Hell loose, and get your own back, Europe!

Benjamin Franklin and D. H. Lawrence as Conflicting Modes of Consciousness

Ormond Seavey*

I

D. H. Lawrence's essay on Benjamin Franklin in *Studies in Classic American Literature* has remained since 1923 the best-known treatment of Franklin. It is an angry attack, directed not only at Franklin's writings but at Franklin himself. Nor is Franklin the only target; a large number of contemporary phenomena, from the Ford car to Woodrow Wilson, are assailed in conjunction with Franklin. To Lawrence, Franklin stood for the most repellent qualities in American life—the fondness of Americans for the willful manipulation of their own behavior, their devotion to business and money-getting, their prurient desire to perfect the world. The essay makes no claim to present a dispassionate analysis; it is a work of denunciation, an attempt to exorcise a sort of demon from America.

What is there to learn about Franklin from this essay? Critics of Franklin commonly make reference to it, but it is often dismissed as a sort of literary curiosity. Certainly the essay makes no pretense of obeying the conventions of detachment and balance that are generally observed in serious critical discourse. Those who would discount the essay assert that in treating Franklin, Lawrence has found what he wished to find, rather than

*This essay was written especially for this collection and is published here for the first time.

what was truly there. According to this line of interpretation, we can learn something about Lawrence from the essay, but little about Franklin.

The essay does indeed say a good deal about Lawrence, but I think it is also right about Franklin in ways that much modern criticism has not been. According to Lawrence, Franklin sought to propagate a particular mode of consciousness, his own, as a norm for human behavior. The *Autobiography*, Lawrence insists, is not principally a delightful story about a young man's rise in the world, though this is its beguiling outward semblance. It is an ambitious attempt to stamp America in Franklin's image.

In certain ways Lawrence was specially equipped to understand Franklin. His novels and his criticism propagate his own version of how thought and feeling should coexist in a fulfilled human life; he had come to see Franklin as the most powerful advocate for the mode of consciousness he most strongly opposed. There was nothing freakish or casual about his choice of Franklin as an adversary. Unlike most novelists who write occasional essays on cultural questions, Lawrence did not treat criticism as an occasion for bright, disconnected observations. The essays in *Studies in Classic American Literature* received as much of his attention as his fiction. Before the book was published in August 1923, Lawrence had been working on the ideas in it for somewhere between eight and nine years.[1] He had published an earlier essay on Franklin in 1918, one quite different from the final version. In the five years between the first and second versions, Franklin grew in importance for Lawrence, becoming in his mind a far more formidable antagonist. The final version was written in America, where Lawrence was surrounded by reminders of the consciousness Franklin had fostered; he could see at close range the deleterious power Franklin had exercised.

Lawrence's insights into Franklin are worth taking further. It was not just the Franklin of the *Autobiography* who was preoccupied with propagating a mode of consciousness. The *Autobiography* was really the culmination of a lifetime of writing with a consistent aim. And Lawrence's denunciation reveals Franklin's achievements and their limitations in a particularly striking way.

Lawrence himself uses the term "mode of consciousness" (or simply "consciousness") in *Studies* as a central conceptual tool. By "mode of consciousness" he is referring to a pattern of attitudes and responses to the world that can be seen as internally coherent and unified. At several points he compares consciousness to the skin of a snake; it grows inside us and holds us together and can only be escaped through an awful writhing and straining.[2] A mode of consciousness is distinguishable from an ideology in that it is based on a consistency of character and personality, rather than of ideas. (One might, for example, not profess the ideas of the Puritans, and yet adopt a mode of consciousness characteristic of Puritanism.) Consciousness is also distinguishable from a world view; it consists not of opinions held or objects viewed, but rather more subtly of cultural reflexes and unstated assumptions. The characters of Lawrence's novels do not have ideas, in any developed way, nor do we recognize them by their opinions, convictions, or prejudices. Instead, they act consistently toward each other as if life is to be lived in a certain way—except for those peripheral figures (like Hermione in *Women in Love*) who fail to understand life at all. A person who thinks and feels within a certain mode of consciousness sees certain things as normal and right—as *what is*.

A mode of consciousness is not necessarily a consciously held pattern. Indeed, it may exercise its hold on people who resist it; Lawrence insists throughout *Studies in Classic American Literature* that the greatest American writers articulated something they denied recognizing. It is this sense of consciousness, as the great subject of American literature, that remains Lawrence's most resonant contribution to the study of that literature.

Lawrence begins with Franklin, after an opening chapter on what he calls the "spirit of place." It was Franklin who imposed, through a malign exercise of will, the prevailing consciousness on America.

> Old Daddy Franklin will tell you. He'll rig him up for you, the pattern American. Oh, Franklin was the first downright American. He knew what he was about, the sharp little man. He set up the first dummy American. (*Studies,* 9)

The essay concentrates on the two central features of Franklin's program for his projected United Party for Virtue, his creed and the plan for achieving moral perfection. Lawrence subordinates the narrative of Franklin's life to this program of self-improvement and its assumptions about life and belief. Franklin had deliberately set up "the first dummy American," a kind of self devoted to self-control, self-improvement, and the selfless advancement of the public good. As an outsider, Lawrence did not see in America a great diversity of human possibilities; instead he saw many duplicates of Franklin, people who labored within the constraints Franklin had established for the self.

Lawrence is responding in the essay to the Franklin of the *Autobiography,* to Franklin as a kind of self-created text. *Studies in Classic American Literature* treats American culture as a series of texts; Franklin does not occupy a different order of reality from Captain Ahab or Chingachgook. Of course, as a critic of Lawrence would insist, Franklin was really *not* a text; in an important sense he was not the figure who tells and acts in the *Autobiography*.[3] But he treats himself as a text, with episodes and errata in the *Autobiography;* that he should be read and interpreted follows inevitably from the metaphor of the self as book. Nor was this his first effort at projecting an image of character as a means of giving reality to an argued perspective. The Franklin who began writing his life story in 1771 had already been concerned about consciousness for a long time. The rhetoric of his earliest writing reveals an interest in altering not just the opinions of his audience but even their modes of perceiving.

II

Franklin's earliest writings appeared in Puritan Boston, and even the somewhat dilute Puritanism of the 1720s retained a concern for altering consciousness. But the Puritans did not provide him with a model he would use. Puritanism calls its believers away from any normal consciousness, since normality by the world's standards could only mean the ways of sin and death. The heightened consciousness inspired by divine grace must co-exist painfully with the attitudes and feelings of this world. Confrontation and denunciation are necessary elements of Puritan rhetoric. The normal way of the world must always be assailed, and the choice between God and Mammon must be continually drawn.

Franklin's own rhetoric—and his assumptions about consciousness—are different from this Puritan model from the very beginning. Franklin's earliest writings, his series of periodical essays under the name of Silence Dogood, pretend to be the productions of a Puritan matron, a minister's widow who has ideas about reforming the town. Most of the criticism of these elegant little squibs has seen them as basically but covertly satirical of individual Puritans or of Puritan customs.[4] But something beyond satire is also going on, which proves to be more basic to her characterization and more suggestive of the direction Franklin's writing would take later. Silence Dogood is not primarily a satirical object in herself; she is too knowing, too elusive. Her chatty letters do not assault Puritanism or undermine it; they simply leave it behind, as young Franklin himself indicates in the *Autobiography* he had done at around the same time.

Reality for Silence Dogood includes the old-time religion, but in a shriveled, vestigial role. Writing about pride of apparel, she says, in her pious way, that it "has begot and nourish'd in us a *Pride of Heart,* which portends the Ruin of Church and State."[5] The knowing Boston audience, though, would realize that this is no devout widow speaking but in fact another one of the smart-alecks who write for James Franklin's *Courant*. But as she proceeds with her thought, the sly ridicule of Puritan denunciations gives way to a more comprehensive view. "And I remember my late Reverend Husband would often say upon this Text, That a Fall was the *natural Consequence,* as well as the *Punishment* of Pride. Daily Experience is sufficient to evince the Truth of this Observation" (*Papers,* 1:22). Natural consequences, the sufficiency of daily experience—whatever happened to a realm of grace and revealed truth? Silence Dogood tends to treat religion as something mostly for menfolks to fret over, while she lives out her life by the dictates of womanly common sense. It is not accidental to Franklin's rhetoric that her husband the minister has passed on to his reward, while she keeps right on going. He is mentioned from time to time in the letters, most vividly in his bumbling efforts to court the young Silence. "The aukward [*sic*] Manner in which my Master first discover'd his Intentions, made me, in spite of my Reverence to his Person, burst out into an unmannerly

Laughter" (*Papers,* 1:12). Somehow nothing the late Reverend Dogood could say of an improving nature will escape being colored, in the reader's mind, by a recollection of this mortifying scene.

As Silence Dogood, Franklin is a kind of female impersonator, and the hint of naughtiness in the impersonation contributes to his rhetoric. Since she is a woman, Mistress Dogood does not have to worry about ideas or formal learning, because she occupies a reality where those considerations do not enter. Her world has no politics, no ideological constraints. In it, a simple good nature is sufficient to command the world. The impersonation is all a joke, of course, but somehow the mixture of her earnestness and the humor which she shares with her readers makes an insinuating suggestion. Perhaps her reality does comprehend as much as she confidently assumes it does.

Her world is rather like the world of Franklin's *Autobiography,* which he began almost fifty years later. In neither world are social classes acknowledged to fix one in a place. Silence Dogood begins her first letter by observing "that the Generality of People, now a days, are unwilling either to commend or dispraise what they read, until they are in some measure informed who or what the Author of it is, whether he be *poor* or *rich, old* or *young,* a *Schollar* or a *Leather Apron Man,* &c. and give their Opinion of the Performance, according to the Knowledge which they have of the Author's Circumstances . . ." (*Papers,* 1:9). (That people only "now a days" judge by such appearances suggests that social class awareness is some sort of recent development.) She proceeds, in apparent concurrence with those expectations, to provide an obviously spurious background, which forces her initial readers to discard considerations of authority. Silence Dogood is a model of self-sufficiency, and like the older Franklin she is full of suggestions for improving society. Lawrence would doubtless have found her just as repellent as her creator.

Young Franklin's rhetoric in these brief anonymous pieces of the 1720s is the more remarkable when considered in relation to the writings of his older brother and employer, James Franklin. James readily adapted the Puritan spirit of confrontation and denunciation in his newspaper, except that he turned his denunciations, so far as he dared, against Puritanism itself. The *Courant* at the time was involved in a campaign against smallpox inoculation, an innovation of the Mathers. James Franklin describes in his newspaper an altercation he had had with Increase Mather.[6] For both the old minister and the young printer the controversy was to be expressed in terms dictated by their common rhetoric. The elder Mather warned the impenitent James Franklin of an imminent death; the irascible Franklin responded in print that the misuse of anything so important as a moral denunciation was itself potentially wicked. James had no developed alternative to a Puritan consciousness in mind; when he confronted the Mathers, he used their weapons. Benjamin, meanwhile, had other possibilities in mind.

In some respects Franklin's capacity to bypass Puritanism derived from his reading of Addison, the great influence on his style as he describes in the *Autobiography*.[7] Addison offered a balanced elegance of style, a gracious aloofness that Franklin could use to escape the confrontational mode his brother was locked into. Addison's was a larger world than this little provincial seaport with its crabbed and dated habits of belief. Franklin tries, therefore, to invent a Boston for Silence Dogood in which the large-minded civility he found in Addison would govern. Silence Dogood portrays herself as an enemy to vice and a friend to virtue, a "hearty Lover of the Clergy and all good Men, and a mortal Enemy to arbitrary Government and unlimited Power" (*Papers,* 1:12–13). She feels it is her duty to serve her countrymen by her writing. Most of the letters discuss what are conceived of as public questions, such as the poverty of widows or the state of poetry and liberal education in Massachusetts. The reader of these letters is readily struck by the smoothness of their diction and the wit that is at play in them.

Yet somehow her Boston feels utterly unreal. In the evening she hears "many pensive Youths with down Looks and a slow Pace . . . now and then crying out on the Cruelty of their Mistresses; others with a more rapid Pace and chearful Air, would be swinging their Canes and clapping their Cheeks, and whispering at certain Intervals, *I'm certain I shall have her! This is more than I expected! How charmingly she talks!* &c" (*Papers*, 1:42). This street scene is a pastoral with an urban setting, but Boston was no city, nor could it pass for a scene of pastoral dalliance. If a reader had to choose between the letters of Silence Dogood and the sermons of Cotton Mather to find out what was really going on in the streets of Boston, the reader would do better with Mather. At least in Mather the reader would find a scene of belief in struggle with mercantile complacency, and that perception offers probably the best place to begin. Neither the realms of belief nor of trade enter into Franklin's youthful scene. Realistic social observation could only get in the way of young Franklin's more basic aim, which was to find in Boston a version of what he saw in Addison.

Silence Dogood is conscious of the problems of addressing an audience that is prone to confrontations. "I am very sensible," she writes, "that it is impossible for me, or indeed any *one* Writer to please *all* Readers at once. Various Persons have different Sentiments; and that which is pleasant and delightful to one, gives another a Disgust" (*Papers,* 1:13). But her real aim is to take everyone in as her audience, old and young, rich and poor, scholars and leather-apron men.

> He that would (in this Way of Writing) please all, is under a Necessity to make his Themes almost as numerous as his Letters. He must one while be merry and diverting, then more solid and serious; one while sharp and satyrical, then (to mollify that) be sober and religious; at one Time let the Subject be Politicks, then let the next Theme be Love: Thus

> will every one, one Time or other find some thing agreeable to his own Fancy, and in his Turn be delighted. (*Papers*, 1:13–14)

Young Franklin clearly welcomes this variety of roles, all of which would permit him to escape from his real role, as his brother's apprentice. But his *Autobiography* tells how little chance there was for him to make Mistress Dogood's possibilities his own. While she chattered about the varied possibilities in her writings, he was getting enmeshed in a complex of unresolvable confrontations with his brother and the colonial authorities. Boston was not interested in the mode of consciousness he was beginning to propagate.

In Philadelphia a little later, Franklin found a scene that was more amenable to his own kind of persuasion. Puritanism had provided a center in Boston what was lacking in Philadelphia: here there was no Harvard College, no unified body of clergy, little sense of a collective and defining history. The social and religious diversity of Philadelphia and its lack of a well-developed gentry class presented Franklin with opportunities he had lacked before. By the time he was 23 years old he had his own newspaper, a platform for advocacy of his own. By 1732 when he was 26 he had begun *Poor Richard's Almanack*, and in the following years he produced a series of proposals for public improvements in Philadelphia, anonymously or as the spokesman for some group. In Boston, Franklin had gotten his start through masquerading as a particular and unusual figure, a distinctive voice whose perspective necessarily looked unusual. In Philadelphia he was a printer, presenting himself as the impartial medium for communicating information to the public. Or he was the invisible spokesman for the public good.

If his major *persona* in Boston had been Silence Dogood, the major *persona* in Philadelphia was Richard Saunders, the supposed author of his almanac. The two figures represent stages in the development of his advocacy of the mode of consciousness he was advancing. Silence Dogood's observations on the world had been sometimes obtrusively disruptive to the prevailing orthodoxies; the new *persona* would be managed more subtly. Of the two, Silence is undoubtedly the sharper and more perceptive; Franklin endows her with verbal talents and a complexity of response that he carefully withholds from the Poor Richard who introduces himself in 1733.[8] She is capable of attacking Harvard College by use of an elaborate allegory. Poor Richard, by contrast, is utterly innocuous and innocent. Obliged by his own poverty and the scoldings of his wife to set aside his impractical researches into astrology, he begins the preface to his first almanac by admitting his own financial interest; he hopes to make a bit of money from the almanac, and he cannot help admitting it. "I might in this place attempt to gain thy Favour, by declaring that I write Almanacks with no other View than that of the publick Good; but in this I should not be sincere; and Men are now a-days too wise to be deceiv'd by Pretences how specious so ever" (*Papers,* 1:311). Silence Dogood had claimed to be concerned about the public good above all; the feckless astrologer is only trying to feed his family. No one could feel threatened by Poor Richard's superior intelligence; he is not likely to make anyone feel ridiculous. The maxims, as he modestly admits, are mostly not his own, but rather "the *Gleanings* I had made of the Sense of all Ages and Nations" (*Papers,* 7:350). Poor Richard provides another mode of insinuation for Franklin; his maxims speak with pungent force, but his own helpless simplicity invites the reader to attribute his maxims to the sense of all ages and nations.

Both Silence Dogood and Poor Richard are, in character and circumstance, greatly different from their creator. Silence is a woman with several children and a house of her own; Poor Richard is content with poverty and gullibly absorbed by a phoney science. Neither one is clearly connected to any traditional source of social influence—learning, religion, wealth, family connections—yet each is able to speak with authority. Both *personae* are naive, but with the complex naiveté of the knowing child who cuts through the accumulated obfuscations to the simpler truth beneath. Silence Dogood has no capacity for subtlety or indirection at all, as if concealment of motives were unimaginable for her. Their naiveté permits them to ignore certain significant considerations. Though they are both socially powerless by reason of poverty and sex, they seem to be unconscious of the limitations of their place in society. Neither has any sense of accumulated history, nor does either one sense the limitations of their own American setting. Silence Dogood betrays none of the anxiety about isolation and provinciality that weighed on the mind of her contemporary Cotton Mather. Poor Richard lives in some rural place, deliberately left ambiguous by Franklin, the sort of place that could be found anywhere in the colonies. Neither ever recognizes the limitations in size of the audiences addressed. Silence Dogood writes about her audience as if she wished to be addressing everyone; Poor Richard finds himself read everywhere and even quoted on public occasions.

Above all, they sound naive because they possess a mode of consciousness that sweeps these other considerations aside. They are both exemplars of self-possession, in full command of their own emotional situations and responses. Silence Dogood describes her courtship with the late Reverend Dogood as if he had carried a point in debate. "Whether it was Love, or Gratitude, or Pride, or all Three that made me consent, I know not; but it is certain, he found it no hard Matter, by the Help of his Rhetorick, to conquer my Heart, and perswade me to marry him" (*Papers,* 1:12). Now a widow, she fancies she could be persuaded to marry again, "provided I was sure of a good-humour'd, sober, agreeable Companion" (*Papers,* 1:12). Poor Richard's maxims about marriage say nothing about yielding to the dictates of the heart; instead they counsel prudence and restraint. The consciousness advocated in these maxims requires a measured distance from others who might entangle one; in fact, the most deeply involved relationship they contemplate is the relationship of creditor and debtor. In their apparent simplicity of heart, the two Franklin characters sidle up close to their readers, but the reader knows that they are in masquerade; their intimacy of tone is likely to inspire instead a careful detachment. When Silence Dogood argues that women have been maligned by men, the readers remember that this spirited defense of womankind was cooked up by some man. The humor of the Dogood essays and the *Poor Richard* maxims further encourages the detachment which is crucial to Franklin's mode of consciousness. "Nothing Humbler than Ambition, when it is about to climb," warns the 1753 almanac, and another apparent complexity of behavior is suddenly reduced to a starkly intelligible form.

The detachment of this mode of consciousness does not, however, lead to mere self-seeking. Out of the intensified awareness of one's own separateness comes a disposition to contribute to the general good. This is Silence Dogood's stated intention; it is also the intention of Franklin's first Philadelphia *persona*, the Busy-Body, who jocularly takes the public's general business into his own hands (*Papers*, 1:115). And it was around this same time that Franklin came up with the idea of a United Party for Virtue, consisting of young men who had undergone his program in moral perfection and subscribed to his all-purpose creed. The United Party for Virtue would be a secret society for the same reasons that caused Franklin to conceal his hand in Philadelpha—the large changes of consciousness needed would require subtle approaches untainted by the limitations of a particular advocate.

It may appear contradictory that the author of Poor Richard's maxims should also have advocated a disinterested advancement of the public good, but the audiences addressed are different. For most people, the advice of Poor Richard is sufficient: work hard, rely only on yourself, value your independence. But there is also the further detachment that may come to the enlightened and financially successful, out of which comes the capacity for benevolence. In Franklin's early plan for the United Party for Virtue, he says about the projected members that they would be "govern'd by suitable good and wise Rules, which good and wise Men may probably be more unanimous in their Obedience to, than common People are to common Laws.[9] The leading trait that sets them apart is a capacity for discipline.

The benevolence Franklin advocates is quite different from the Christian notion of charity. Charity requires the absence of deliberation; the left hand does not know what the right hand is doing. It is directed at individuals, who must be loved as they are assisted, if there is to be any merit at all in the giving. Franklin's benevolence, however, is a political, rather than a personal activity. The good works he advocates or performs always entail group action; groups are assembled to remedy the public need, and groups are the recipients of the instituted improvements. So instead of helping any one sick person, Franklin organizes the building and financing of the Pennsylvania Hospital. The very notion of assistance to some particular person is rather problematic in the terms Franklin creates, for it is assumed that everyone continually has the capacity to remedy his own difficulties and no one else can help him better than he himself can.

When Poor Richard talks in his maxims about the relations between particular people, he emphasizes the distance that should be maintained on both sides. "Fish and visitors stink in 3 days," says the almanac for 1736 (*Papers,* II, 137). Many maxims warn about the difficulties of coping with one's enemies; others caution against confiding in others, even in one's own friends. Poor Richard approves of marriage, but it is described as one of those satisfactions in life which one should be contented with and not ask too much of; as Poor Richard puts it for 1738, "Keep your eyes wide open before marriage, half shut afterwards" (*Papers,* 2:194). Numerous maxims describe the dangers of inappropriate marriages, to a woman much younger or higher in social rank. Industry and frugality, the specific emphases of *The Way to Wealth,* are only the economic corollaries to more basic message which pervades all of the maxims. Self-control and self-knowledge—these are what Poor Richard prescribes above all, and they are achieved alone.

There may not seem to be anything new in such an emphasis. The commandment to know thyself was inscribed on the oracle at Delphi, and the instructions for Franklin's self-control suggested to his contemporaries a linkage with Pythagoras. Indeed, part of the strategy of contriving such proverbs dictates the denial of their newness, so that they pass as the wisdom of all ages and nations. But in fact Poor Richard has a different view of self-knowledge from the ancient world. Self-knowledge and self-control are disconnected now from both religion and philosophy. For Sophocles, knowing oneself had meant the realization of one's limits in relation to unseen, malign forces at work in the universe; for Plato or Socrates, it had meant the life of philosophical discourse; for Augustine it led to the understanding of God and the contemplation of a divine system. Poor Richard has democratized and secularized self-knowledge; it now means the awareness of oneself as an economic being, with limited resources and wants which must be brought under control. "Who is strong? He that can conquer his bad Habits. Who is rich? He that rejoices in his Portion" (*Papers,* 2:395). The conquering of bad habits comes not from a reliance on God or from discussion and introspection; it comes from modifying one's own behavior according to plan. The proverb treats self-knowledge and self-control as behavioral rather than philosophical problems; they are possible for anyone to achieve, though Franklin recognizes that because of the weakness of human nature few will.

In the Franklin essay Lawrence describes himself as a child reading *Poor Richard* sayings in the almanacs his father used to buy. He admits that those sayings affected him strongly. "And probably I haven't got over those Poor Richard tags yet. I rankle still with them. They are thorns in young flesh" (*Studies,* p. 14). Lawrence recognizes that the kind of prudential maxims that Franklin codified delimit a world—"that barbed wire moral enclosure that Poor Richard rigged up." Each maxim offers what is supposed to be an unequivocal, invariable truth of experience; taken together, his maxims define a vision of the world. Lawrence knew the power of that vision, and his own vision was directly opposed to it. "Because, although I still believe that honesty is the best policy, I dislike policy altogether; though it is just as well not to count your chickens before they are hatched, its [*sic*] still more hateful to count them gloating when they *are* hatched" (*Studies,* p. 14). One can look in vain in the almanacs for sayings about how little we can know ourselves, or the benefits of taking it easy, or the supreme value of certain unexpected great experiences. Though the wisdom of all ages and nations has provided much material for maxims of that sort, they do not appear in Franklin's almanac.

Poor Richard does not offer anything to contradict the perceptions of experience which differ from his own. Contradiction would acknowledge the real existence of another view, and Franklin preferred to ignore adverse opinions if possible. In the *Autobiography* he reports that he chose to pay no attention to the criticisms of his electrical theories by his adversary Abbé Nollet. "I concluded to let my Papers shift for themselves; believing it was better to spend what time I could spare from public Business in making new Experiments, than in disputing about those already made" (*A.*, pp. 243–44). Abbé Nollet's arguments foundered because Franklin's theories explained the data better; the maxims of Poor Richard profess the same sort of unanswerable comprehensive sufficiency.

The rhetoric of *The Way to Wealth* is carefully arranged to exclude the possibility of diverse valid points of view. To that end, a new voice is invented, who represents Franklin at a second remove. Poor Richard himself is so bland and inoffensive, hardly capable of recognizing an orthodoxy, much less of propagating one. But Father Abraham, his undesignated spokesman, presents the maxims in a connected discourse as the inescapable basis for all decisions about the disposition of money and time. The question initially asked him by the people gathered at the vendue is political in nature: "*Pray, Father Abraham, what think you of the Times? Won't these heavy Taxes quite ruin the Country? How shall we ever be able to pay them? What would you advise us to?*" (*Papers,* 7:340) The accusations point toward the varied possibilities inherent in political life; they also hint at revolutionary action, since they are just the sort of questions the colonists would later ask during the Stamp Act crisis and afterwards. Father Abraham, however, quickly steers his response away from politics to ethics; the burdens we impose upon ourselves by our imprudence are far greater than any taxes imposed by government. "We are taxed twice as much by our *Idleness,* three times as much by our *Pride,* and four times as much by our *Folly,* and from these Taxes the Commissioners cannot ease or deliver us by allowing an Abatement" (*Papers,* 7:341). Economic decisions are therefore questions of personal morality, not of public policy, and even a divine sanction is enlisted in support of the right economic choices—"*God helps them that help themselves,*" as Poor Richard says, in his Almanack of 1733 (*Papers,* 7:341).

As revealed by Poor Richard's maxims, the realm of economic decisions is not truly a field of free choices, in the sense that one might select varied possibilities without penalty. "But, ah, think what you do when you run in Debt," warns Father Abraham; "*You give to another Power over your Liberty*" (*Papers,* 7:347–48). Misuse of leisure and even slight excess expenses can similarly deprive one of freedom. Only the fullest, most painstaking awareness can preserve one in a state that Poor Richard would call free. The choice, then, is not among options which afford differing kinds of satisfaction; the choice is between one's own best interest on the one hand and the variety of short-sighted, self-destructive possibilities on the other. Lawrence called this a barbed-wire enclosure; whatever bounds it, there is no question about the tightness of its confines.

III

The Way to Wealth, like the almanac in which it first appeared, is addressed to poor people, an amorphous group which would certainly have comprised the large majority of the American population in the 1750s. The *Autobiography* has a different audience and thus a different, more subtle rhetoric. The mode of consciousness advocated by the two works is substantially the same, except that the range of options for this intensely self-conscious being is far greater in the life Franklin describes.

D. H. Lawrence recognized what Franklin was aiming at in the *Autobiography*. "The Perfectibility of Man!" he exclaims at the beginning of his 1923 essay. "Ah heaven, what a dreary theme! The perfectibility of the Ford car! The perfectibility of which man? I am many men. Which of them are you going to perfect? I am not a mechanical contrivance" (*Studies,* p. 9). Here, then, are the choices as Lawrence sees them. The *Autobiography* presents the possibility of taking one's life under one's control and giving it a purpose and a direction. In fact, the *Autobiography* insists that a life thus organized is clearly superior to any other. Such an effort at perfecting one's life can only be accomplished by the imposition of a previously formulated standard and by the systematic elimination of divergent possibilities, other selves that might have been.

Seen in this light, the *Autobiography* is not just a narrative of events in Franklin's life, any more than *Women in Love* is just a story about two sisters and the men they marry. Lawrence sees Franklin as a rival in the shaping of the modern consciousness—the patterns of thinking and feeling which have succeeded those which claimed a religious sanction. Lawrence brushes past the events of Franklin's life, briefly acknowledging along the way that he finds certin things about Franklin admirable. He feels no obligation to offer a balanced appraisal, in part because he has no special regard for the conventions of critical fair-mindedness, in part because he honestly dislikes Franklin, and most of all because he finds Franklin's projected mode of consciousness repellent and dangerous. It is repellent to Lawrence because it is directly opposed to Lawrence's own consciousness, while implicitly denying that any viable alternative could ever exist. It is dangerous because its rhetoric is so seductive; Lawrence cannot escape acknowledging its appeal himself. "It has taken me many years and countless smarts to get out of that barbed wire moral enclosure that Poor Richard rigged up. Here am I now in tatters and scratched to ribbons, sitting in the middle of Benjamin's America looking at the barbed wire . . . And I just offer a long loud curse against Benjamin and the American corral" (*Studies,* p. 14).

Lawrence's rage about what he calls "perfectibility" points to the central postulate of Franklin's projected mode of consciousness. Quite simply, it is the assertion that one's life can be considerably changed by a concerted act of will. Change had not been concern in Father Abraham's speech, except when it is for the worse; in general the maxims of Poor Richard assume a static social and economic environment. But change is continual in the *Autobiography,* much of it brought about by Franklin himself. There is the basic movement from poverty and obscurity to affluence and reputation; there are also changes in the city of Philadelphia (increasing property values, varying amounts of paper currency in circulation, new institutions like the Library Company or the militia) and even the transformation of colony into nation that takes place in the course of the writing. Change was necessarily a subject in Puritan autobiography, from a fallen to a redeemed condition, but that was necessarily not of human origin; when Jonathan Edwards notes the shifts in his attitude toward predestination in his "Personal Narrative," he is noting an intellectual development that has been, fortunately for him, out of his own control. In asserting the powers he claims over his own basic nature, Franklin makes striking break from his Puritan antecedents.[10] In the appropriate places he nods respectfully to Providence for not interfering, but such gestures are peripheral to his central argument. The experiment in self-perfection is the instance Lawrence makes the most of, but the metaphor of the life as a book, which is carried through the first section systematically, shows just as much the degree to which Franklin believed a raw materials of experience could be given shape by the controlling will.

Not only is it possible to bring one's life into an unprecedented state of control; the controlled life is superior to any other. Franklin's own life, it should be noted, is not to be imitated throughout; it has its share of *errata* and local peculiarities. It is his personality, his patterns of response to the world, that is to be imitated. And the reader of the *Autobiography* sees enough of other personalities to recognize Franklin's superiority. There are numerous instances of failure in the *Autobiography:* John Collins, who leaves Boston for Philadlephia and becomes a nasty drunk; Samuel Keimer, a glutton with delusions about the extent of his own powers, "an odd Fish, ignorant of common Life, fond of rudely opposing receiv'd Opinions, slovenly to extream dirtiness, enthusiastic in some Points of Religion, and a little Knavish withal" (*A.*, 112–13); Governor Keith, who makes promises he cannot keep and appears last as a shamefaced private citizen on the street; David Harry, a potential printing rival who indulged in fine clothes and good living and neglected his business. Each instance illustrates how some form of indulgence led to personal failure. Even governor Keith, whose behavior might have seemed a case of casual malevolence, is described as someone who had succumbed to a personal weakness. "It was a Habit he had acquired. He wish'd to please every body; and having little to give, he gave Expectations" (*A.*, 95). The Art of Virtue, by contrast, describes how good habits can be formed; it appears in the narrative not where Franklin is in the greatest need of direction and organization in his life, but rather afterwards when he is getting established in his business in Philadelphia. It does not provide an emergency rescue for a soul helplessly beyond control, as a religious conversion does; instead it consolidates the disposition Franklin has gradually acquired. As Benjamin Vaughan writes, in the letter Franklin includes in the text, "For the furtherance of human happiness, I have always maintained that it is necessary to prove that man is not even at present a vicious and detestable animal; and still more to prove that good management may greatly amend him" (*A.*, 139). The *Autobiography* is designed to show the superiority of good management.

Franklin makes clear that he has adopted the self he presents at the expense of other selves that had to be discarded. His youthful longing for the sea, his ambitions to be a poet, his attempt at being a philosopher, and his prospects as a swimming teacher are all mentioned as fortunately rejected options. His friend James Ralph aimed at possibilities beyond him, and Samuel Keimer was always prone to impossible schemes. Franklin, who might have emphasized in his life story the range of his capabilities, insists rather on the limitations he accepted for himself and the small range of his talents. He was industrious and frugal; he was "a tolerable English writer." These traits are all he claims for credentials. The rhetoric of the *Autobiography* requires that his success can be duplicated by others, just as the rhetoric of Lawrence's novels invites the reader to a comparable trust in the deep passional self. Lawrence describes Franklin as a "snuff-coloured little man," while identifying himself in comparably drab terms, at his desk in a tweed jacket. But there are other versions of Lawrence, "other men in me, besides this patient ass who sits here in a tweed jacket" (*Studies*, 9). The creed Lawrence fashions for himself in imitation of Franklin asserts that in the dark forest of his soul "*gods, strange gods, come forth . . . into the clearing of my known self, and then go back*" (*Studies*, 16). Franklin insisted that the known self might be quite considerable in extent; the self would be understood and regulated best if the realm of unexplored life possibilities was left alone. Outside the territory that Franklin had brought under control lies only the domain of vanity, disorder, "Prattling,

Punning and Joking" (*A.*, 151)—tolerated weaknesses that are peripheral to the central self.

Poor Richard had offered a bleaker assessment of the self as it might be revealed to others. "Let all Men know thee, but no man know thee thoroughly: Men freely ford that see the shallows," warns the almanac for 1743 (*Papers*, 2:370). In keeping with this advice, the younger Franklin had sought for himself a range of concealments: Silence Dogood, whose first letter was submitted anonymously to the *Courant;* Poor Richard and a series of other *personae* in Franklin's early years; the committees of concerned citizens Franklin would assemble to advance the projects he had formed. But by the time the *Autobiography* was being written, concealment was becoming gradually impossible; he was too well-known. And, reversing the lesson of his earlier maxim, he had found ways of transforming limitations; the garrulousness, vanity, and disorderliness he admits in the *Autobiography* somehow do not appear as shallows in his character that can be freely forded. Franklin has no detectable fear in the *Autobiography* of all men knowing him thoroughly.

Lawrence's criticism makes clear why an autobiography should have been the culmination to Franklin's career of advancing his own mode of consciousness. Lawrence does not draw a distinction between the ideas in the *Autobiography* and the man himself, because he saw Franklin as an inextricable mixture of ideas, attitudes, and responses. The *Autobiography* demonstrates that the life Franklin advocates is actually possible. Poor Richard's precepts by themselves, with their exasperating sense of finality and certainty, stick like thorns in young flesh, but they become all the more dangerous when linked to a self presented with the subtlety and clarity of Franklin in the *Autobiography*. The characters Franklin had created earlier to carry his ideas had never fully understood the complexities of the societies they inhabited; their lack of sophistication was a necessary evidence of their trustworthiness. Moreover, they were primarily voices rather than actors, viewing and considering but removed from the scene. The earlier *personae* were distanced from the reader by the device of narration itself; now Franklin could establish a closer relation to his readers by speaking in his own voice and showing himself in action. The figure of Franklin links all the little lessons of experience—learning to write from the *Spectator*, setting up a matching grant arrangement for the Pennsylvania Hospital, rolling his wheelbarrow through town—into a complex whole of a sort that Lawrence could not dismiss.

Franklin came to recognize the superiority of his life story as a device for promoting his own mode of consciousness. In the 1760s he had begun talking about a treatise describing his program for achieving perfection, to be entitled the *Art of Virtue*. So far as can be gathered, he never began any separate writing on the project; the description he finally incorporates into the *Autobiography* suggests that he would have had difficulty in detaching the project from the developing course of his life. Benjamin

Vaughan's letter in the *Autobiography* points out the natural linkage between the *Art of Virtue* and the life (*A.*, 135). In a sense the *Autobiography* encompasses and supersedes the *Art of Virtue* just as it supersedes that other final statement, *The Way to Wealth*. Experience for Franklin was superior to precept, or to be more exact, legitimate precepts had to grow out of experience. Sailing from Boston to Philadelphia as a boy, Franklin gave up vegetarianism in favor of an especially savory meal of fresh cod; as he tells the story, a precept learned from his reading (that eating fish was a kind of unprovoked murder) was replaced by another, based on his experience: "So convenient a thing it is to be a *reasonable Creature*, since it enables one to find or make a Reason for every thing one has a mind to do" (*A.*, 87–88). Similarly, the *Art of Virtue* appears in the *Autobiography* embedded in details of Franklin's own life: the Quaker acquaintance who convinced him he was proud, the difficulties he had with Order, the story of the man with the speckled axe, the conclusions he has reached about the experiment now that he is 78 years old. He cites with approval his father's favorite Biblical verse: "Seest thou a Man diligent in his Calling, he shall stand before Kings, he shall not stand before mean Men" (*A.*, 144). But even the Bible is employed to fit Franklin's own model: he stood before no fewer than five kings, he says, and one of them sat down to dinner with him.

IV

Coming from a different society and carrying a different sense of what a healthy consciousness might be, Lawrence could recognize Franklin as a writer with designs on his readers, rather than as a genial old man artlessly telling his life to whoever would hear. Lawrence's Franklin is a more formidable, more ambitious figure than the good-natured grandfatherly person who tends to be featured in all the affectionate studies of Franklin. Lawrence felt he could see a large revolutionary strategy in the *Autobiography*, the overthrowing of the older, European mode of consciousness. "Benjamin, in his sagacity, knew that the breaking of the old world was a long process. In the depth of his own under-consciousness he hated England, he hated Europe, he hated the whole corpus of the European being. He wanted to be American" (*Studies*, 20). Writing at a time, right after World War I, when the cultural balance had shifted toward America, Lawrence felt he was seeing the culmination of Franklin's program. His Franklin is not bound by the eighteenth century; he exists in the present tense, as part of the cultural malaise Lawrence found about him in the twentieth century. Needless to say, there are limitations as well as opportunities in seeing Franklin as such a grandiose and menacing figure.

Franklin stood for a complex of rejected human activities which insistently confronted Lawrence in America. He stood for science and its products, from the lightning rod to the Ford car. He stood for social and political responsibility, lighting the streets of Philadelphia and engineering international revolution at the Court of Versailles. And he stood, above all, for economic life, the life of the market place of goods and services. It was this last association that set off Lawrence the most. What he found repellent about economic life was not senseless accumulation or the inequities of wealth, the traditional irritants for the moralist or the political reformer, but rather the discipline which the self must undergo to participate in that life. For Lawrence, one's final responsibility is never to society, always to the inner self. It is a moral duty to behave as the deep passional self dictates.[11]

For those who have embraced the consciousness that Lawrence has articulated, the disciplines of economic life represent a sort of death—or rather, the multiple deaths of all those other selves that would have to be sacrificed. But the case of Franklin suggests that such deaths can have their own considerable compensations. Franklin has stood for the prudent virtues of *Poor Richard's Almanack,* but for something else as well; as Lawrence recognized, Franklin was also a revolutionary with visions of national destiny and schemes for the renovation of the human character. As an advocate for this mode of consciousness, he has made those visions widely available; he has recast the once limited and straitened life of trade as an adventure. It would be foolish to attribute the hold of capitalism in America to Franklin; it is safe to say, however, that the rejection of economic life has been a problematic course for Americans, because the psychological rewards for economic life in America have been particularly substantial.

To participate in modern society, one must take on the role of economic man, willing to sell goods and services to potential buyers. In his first imagined form, in the eighteenth century, economic man was a particularly anonymous being. Adam Smith's *Wealth of Nations* includes no examples drawn from the lives of specific capitalists. To delineate the qualities of economic man might threaten his universality. It was Franklin's achievement to create for that role an appropriate personality. His *Autobiography* teaches how one can get ahead in the world, regardless of what activity one engages in, and yet be a distinctive personality and the embodiment of a national purpose.

Like Franklin and to some extent because of him, a significant number of Americans have looked upon economic activity as an end rather than as a means. To work, to earn money is a sufficing endeavor; it is a field on which one can project one's entire personality. The reader of the *Autobiography* continually notices that Franklin's shrewdest moves in economic self-advancement have the effect of bringing him to the notice of others. As he leaves poverty, he leaves obscurity and grows in his capacity to affect the world. The belief that economic life could afford such large satisfactions has distinguished the American capitalist from his European counterpart, at least during the nineteenth century. The English Industrial Revolution must seem to us the product of faceless beings, and it was in part the anonymity which capitalism fostered both in factory master and factory hand that horrified Carlyle, Dickens, and Ruskin. The great surge of economic activity in America, by contrast, manifested itself in the public mind as the accomplishment of a small group of particular and highly distinctive personalities—Vanderbilt, Carnegie, Rockefeller, Ford, and others. American fiction has supplied its own depictions of the appeal of buying and selling. Adam Verver, the capitalist of James's *The Golden Bowl*, is not a repellent money-grubber. He has a large, even imperial sense of the possibilities of life, and he is creating in "American City" a place of cultural splendor. Jay Gatsby's wealth is at times repugnant, but somehow also grand and beautiful. In a scene full of comic ambiguities, he piles on his bed a heap of expensive shirts, and Daisy Buchanan sobs at the loveliness of accumulation. The political reaction against these self-aggrandizing modes of capitalist activity has taken the form of a criticism of a style of personality. "Rugged Individualism," a mode of behavior, has been blamed for American economic problems—as if a less personally assertive mode of capitalist accumulation would have avoided those problems.[12]

It is quite understandable, then, that Lawrence should have seen America as a society constituted of calculating, ultimately disconnected individuals, bound to each other only for the sake of certain mutual advantages. He considered such a society revolting. For him the basic ties between people must be instinctual and unconscious, and nothing was more important than preserving intact those deep connections. As he puts it elsewhere in *Studies in Classic American Literature*, "Men are free when they are in a living homeland, not when they are straying and breaking away. . . . Men are free when they belong to a living, organic, *believing* community, active in fulfilling some unfulfilled, perhaps unrealized purpose. Not when they are escaping to some wild west" (*Studies*, 6). Lawrence wanted the world to consist of networks of excited relationships among attracted opposites. In *Women in Love*, for example, Gudrun, Ursula, Birkin, and Crich form such a pattern of strong continuing ties with particular others. Americans had run away from Europe to escape from that sort of connectedness.

In America Lawrence found something at variance with his ideal, yet with intriguing possibilities. Americans, he noted, retreated from human community into states of isolation. It is easy to think of instances of this phenomenon in American literature: Ishmael takes off on the *Pequod;* Hester Prynne withdraws to the neglected edge of the settlement; Thoreau sets up at Walden; Ike McCaslin repudiates his property rights. Yet Lawrence did not consider this phenomenon a denial of his desired world of excited relationships; it offered rather an intriguing variant. "The essential American soul," he writes in the chapter on Cooper's Leatherstocking Tales, "is hard, isolate, stoic, and a killer" (*Studies*, 62). These harsh words actually serve as a celebration of that essential American male soul for its capacity to find the company of other males sufficient.[13] Franklin, however, represented for Lawrence a different, impalatable form of aloofness, which had nothing to do with any pattern of human relationship that Lawrence could value.

Lawrence ultimately accuses Franklin of *not* withdrawing from community. Franklin was a schemer and a manipulator, with secret designs of mastery over his fellow-beings. He sought control not just over other people but, worst of all, over himself. He despised his origins and preyed upon them because in his heart he had never really left behind his cultural parentage. In its secret desire to destroy Europe and the European consciousness, the Franklin consciousness has been "like a son who has stayed at home and obeyed his parents, all the whole silently hating their authority, and silently, in his soul, destroying not only their authority but their whole existence" (*Studies,* 21). But all this conscious resistance to an inherited identity can only be futile, Lawrence asserts. Lawrence's simile is curiously chosen. It denies the central event of Franklin's *Autobiography,* his journey from Boston to Philadelphia as a sixteen-year-old runaway apprentice. Lawrence's Franklin is a figure for whom that journey at some deeper level never took place; his Franklin is implicated in a conspiracy against his own culture.

There is something quite wrong about Lawrence's perception of Franklin at this point, something which marks the limits of Lawrence's direct usefulness in understanding Franklin's mode of consciousness. The simile of the child who stays at home betrays a lapse in perception. The real Franklin did not remain at home despising and manipulating his human or cultural parents. It is clear from the *Autobiography* that he was a loyal son to his father. He clung to his cultural parentage in Great Britain until he was repudiated and publicly slandered in the last years before the outbreak of the Revolution. Franklin cannot be thus readily dismissed. The author of the *Autobiography* was not a sullen, hateful child, but an old man untroubled by such conflicts. And he was securely and comfortably an American, accustomed to playing the role in the best house of Europe; the attempt to make him seem a recreant European, a regressive stage in the evolution of a genuinely American identity, will not work.

Lawrence's talk about sullen children hating their parents is really an attempt to talk about politics, an area where he could not offer valuable insight. Despite a deep interest in history, Lawrence was ill-equipped to understand political life, whether in his own time or in the past, in part because politics offers certain kinds of intimacy and passion that have no sexual basis or component. This blindness prevents Lawrence from understanding the connections between consciousness and politics in the *Autobiography*. In *The Way to Wealth* Father Abraham had steered his audience away from poltical questions, but in the *Autobiography* such questions are intimately linked to daily life. Politics offers the ultimate field of display for the mode of consciousness Franklin advocates in the *Autobiography;* his establishment in business provides him the opportunity to engage in a growing range of projects, from the establishment of the Library Company to the provisioning of General Braddock's army. History as Lawrence saw it consists of large unseen forces operating on people who are unconscious of them. Such a perception can make little sense of much of Franklin's life. Franklin did not hate "the whole corpus of the European being," though he came at the end of his life to wish that Americans would be different from Europeans. Precisely because of his political sense and his sense of the connection between politics and consciousness, he turned the record of his life into the life of a model American.

Despite this serious inadequacy, Lawrence's essay deserves its large following. It will continue to be read as long as Franklin himself is read. Lawrence took Franklin seriously, as a continuing presence in the twentieth century, not just a figure frozen in a lost historical moment. In his insistence on the loathesome relevance of Franklin to the present, Lawrence was particularly true to his subject; much of the rhetoric of the *Autobiography* is designed to insure Franklin's freedom from the limitations of historical contingency. It is addressed for the imitation of his posterity, who are invited to learn from it regardless of their place or time.

The problem Lawrence has with Franklin is really the most important one. It is the question of how we should live our lives. As Lawrence puts it, "Either we are materialistic instruments, like Benjamin, or we move in the gesture of creation, from our deepest self, usually unconscious" (*Studies*, 20). To such a question no definitive answers can be found of the sort that delight scholars. But I think the confrontation between Lawrence and Benjamin constitutes a classic occasion. Everyone continually faces the choice between a life directed by the conscious will and a life spent following the deep promptings of one's inner gods. Franklin and Lawrence exemplify the advantages and pitfalls of either choice better than anyone else.

Notes

1. In a 1919 letter to B. W. Huebsch, Lawrence describes the essays as the result of five years of persistent work. "They contain a whole *Weltanschauung*—new, if old—even a new science of psychology—pure science." (D. H. Lawrence, *Collected Letters*, ed. Harry T. Moore [New York: Viking, 1962], 1:595–96).

2. D. H. Lawrence, *Studies in Classic American Literature* (1923; rpt. New York: Viking, 1961), 20, 52–53, 65. Further page references to this text are given in parentheses.

3. David Levin discusses the way Franklin creates himself as a character in "*The Autobiography of Benjamin Franklin:* The Puritan Experimenter in Life and Art," *Benjamin Franklin: A Collection of Critical Essays*, ed. Brian M. Barbour (Englewood Cliffs, N. J.: Prentice-Hall, 1979), 76–78.

4. Cf. Perry Miller, *The New England Mind: From Colony to Province* (Cambridge: Harvard University Press, 1953), 340–44; Leo Lemay, "Benjamin Franklin," *Major Writers of Early American Literature*, ed. Everett Emerson (Madison: University of Wisconsin Press, 1972), 205–9; Melvin H. Buxbaum, *Benjamin Franklin and the Zealous Presbyterians* (University Park: Pennsylvania State University Press, 1975), 47–75.

5. *The Papers of Benjamin Franklin*, ed. Leonard W. Labaree et al. (New Haven: Yale University Press, 1959-), 1:22. Further references to this edition are given in parentheses as *Papers*.

6. *New-England Courant*, 27 November 1721, 15 January 1722, 29 January 1722.

7. In contrast to Franklin's own tribute to Addison, Leo Lemay argues that Mathew Gardner, one of the other local writers for the *Courant*, was the major influence on Franklin's earliest writing. (Lemay, "Benjamin Franklin," 205–6).

8. James A. Sappenfield discusses the kinships that develop between Poor Richard and Franklin over the long period during which Franklin was writing the almanac (*A Sweet Instruction: Franklin's Journalism as a Literary Apprenticeship* [Carbondale: Southern Illinois University Press, 1973], 121–77). I would maintain that despite those interesting similarities between the life experiences of Franklin and his character, he always restricted Poor Richard to a naive and innocent formulation of perceptions which he himself entertained in a more complex and ambiguous way.

9. *The Autobiography of Benjamin Franklin*, ed. Leonard W. Labaree et al. (New Haven: Yale University Press, 1964), 161–62. Further references to the *Autobiography* are given in the text as *A*.

10. For a somewhat different view of Franklin's connection to his Puritan forebears, see Levin, "Puritan Experimenter," 79–83 or A. Whitney Griswold, "Three Puritans on Prosperity," *New England Quarterly* 7 (1934):475–93.

11. Cf. D. H. Lawrence, *Women in Love* (1920; rpt. New York: Viking, 1960), vii–viii.

12. On the connection between American individualism and economic life, see, for example, Richard Hofstadter, *Social Darwinism in American Thought*, rev. ed. (Boston: Beacon, 1955), 102–22, 201–3; Matthew Josephson, *The Robber Barons* (New York: Harcourt Brace, 1934); E. C. Kirkland, *Dream and Thought in the Business Community, 1860–1900* (Ithaca: Cornell University Press, 1956), 1–10, 29–50; Peter d'A. Jones, ed., *The Robber Barons Revisited* (Boston: Heath, 1968); Robert Bannister, *Social Darwinism: Science and Myth in Anglo-American Social Thought* (Philadelphia: Temple University Press, 1979), 10–11, 114–36, 201–25.

13. See Marguerite Beede Howe, *The Art of the Self in D. H. Lawrence* (Athens, Ohio: Ohio University Press, 1977), 87–92.

Political Concerns

Benjamin Franklin and the Nature of American Diplomacy

Jonathan R. Dull*

The period of the American Revolution appears to be an anomaly in the history of American diplomacy. It is one of the few occasions on which consensus reigned, at least on essentials—if, of course, one excepts the loyalists. The revolutionaries agreed that America must be fully independent (the doubters were given time to accede to this); that America needed to accept foreign help, but only to the extent that it was indispensable; and that Canada should be added if possible to the union. There were debates on the right ministers for foreign posts and on the relative desirability of Newfoundland fishing rights versus western lands, but on fundamental principles there seems to have been little conflict.

This interpretation is based on the work of diplomatic historians like James Hutson and political historians like Jack Rakove.[1] Their emphasis on consensus reflects a recent shift in the historiography of revolutionary diplomacy. Until a short while ago, the most influential diplomatic history of the revolution probably was Felix Gilbert's *To the Farewell Address: Ideas of Early American Foreign Policy*.[2] Gilbert portrayed the revolutionaries as torn between Enlightenment idealism and considerations of power politics. Hutson, however, demonstrated an almost total absence of Enlightenment influence on the diplomacy of the revolution. For him realism reigned supreme in a generation united in the goals of security and survival.[3]

This new interpretation is very persuasive, yet an important question remains not fully answered. Much of American diplomatic history, if not most, has been marked by fierce conflicts about ends as well as means. Does conflict about diplomatic goals date only from the 1790s, as Hutson claims, or do fundamental conflicts exist, at least in embryo, in the generation of the Founders?

If Benjamin Franklin is representative of that earlier generation such conflict did exist.[4] Within Franklin's diplomacy were fundamental fissures. I shall examine those fissures and suggest how in practice they were bridged. Gilbert held that "the basic issue of the American attitude towards

*Reprinted by permission from the *International History Review* 5, no. 3 (August 1983): 346–63.

foreign policy" has been "the tension between Idealism and Realism.[5] However oversimplified this formulation, I believe it nonetheless remains a useful analytic tool for studying the contradictions in the diplomacy of Benjamin Franklin and a suggestive way of looking at Franklin's America.[6]

I

The popular conceptions of Franklin's mission are very contradictory. Often he has been portrayed as charming the French into an alliance with America; this triumph of public relations supposedly was a product not only of his benevolence, but even of his pursuit of pleasure (or dissipation, as the dour John Adams put it).[7] It is argued that Franklin's frivolity, his relaxed attitude towards religion, and his cosmopolitanism, unique among his Puritan countrymen, accorded perfectly with the worldview of the dissolute French aristocracy. Another popular view of this American in Paris stresses opposing qualities. In this view, Franklin, the canny Yankee, beat French diplomats at their own game. His naïveté was a mask, his indolence a cover, and his American mannerisms a device to win publicity. It was not his lovable qualities, but his craftiness which enabled him to best the French. From one perspective, though, the contradictions between these perceptions are more apparent than real. While some of Franklin's contemporaries viewed him as too trusting, the Franklin of myth hardly was an innocent abroad; whether his cunning was that of angels or that of serpents, he was no one's fool.

Historians, too, have seen his success as the result of a calculated policy. One of the most sophisticated treatments of Franklin's mission to France is in Gerald Stourzh's *Benjamin Franklin and American Foreign Policy*.[8] Stourzh sees him as an exemplar of enlightened self-interest. In Stourzh's view, Franklin's demonstrating trust of France and gratitude for the alliance represented a reasonable policy, given that America and France had the same basic interest, the independence of the United States. By using France and Britain as diplomatic counterweights, moreover, he showed his mastery of practical politics. In particular, he was not inhibited by the French alliance from rigorously pursuing US territorial aims and reconciliation with Great Britain.

Stourzh presents strong evidence to support his treatment of Franklin as a model of rationality. By concentrating on Franklin's thought, however, Stourzh may have a skewed vision of his motivation. Furthermore, this model statesman shows little sign of strain in reconciling the "realistic" and the "idealistic" sides of his diplomacy. The popular image of Franklin often downplays his seriousness; Stourzh's image, in contrast, makes him appear rather bloodless.

Neither treatment of Franklin gives adequate attention to the enormity of the physical, mental, and emotional challenge represented by the mission to France. First of all, Franklin, almost 70, was of an extremely advanced age for an eighteenth-century envoy.[9] His health was frail, moreover, and his strength limited. Nonetheless, he risked the dangers of an autumn voyage and British capture and then endured a year of rejection and frustration until the alliance was signed. During the next five years, he accepted the responsibilities of making the alliance work and of negotiating a settlement with Britain. For a total of eight and a half years, he represented America at its most vital diplomatic post, working with a limited staff, uncertain finances, and little guidance from Congress. To succeed at such tasks would have been a major accomplishment for a person half his age. How did he do it?

I believe Franklin drew the strength for his mission from the depth of his passions: his love for his compatriots and his rage at the government of Britain, which had shunned his counsels, murdered his fellow-citizens, and alienated from him his beloved son William, whose loyalism the father never forgave.[10] Beneath Franklin's cosmopolitanism and charm lay the heart of a zealous patriot as uncompromising as Samuel Adams. This produced behaviour we do not always associate with him. On the one hand, he often acted with exceptional selflessness: for example, he donated his salary as postmaster general to disabled American war veterans.[11] By the standards of the time, he was unusually scrupulous in not mixing public and private business, as did, for example, Silas Deane and Robert Morris. In the interests of the revolution, he willingly left family and friends to go to France, endured more homesickness than he publicly admitted, and postponed a retirement for which, at least partially, he longed. On the other hand, he at times revealed his rage at the British. He was prepared to burn Glasgow or Liverpool in retaliation for the burning of American cities.[12] He and his colleagues also threatened retaliation in kind for British mistreatment of American prisoners.[13] Lord North's administration provoked in him a fierce hatred; in one of his many embittered letters to English friends he described his feelings: "I . . . never think of your present Ministers and their Abettors, but with the Image, strongly painted in my View, of their Hands, red, wet, and dropping with the Blood of my Countrymen, Friends, and Relations."[14]

For the most part, however, Franklin used the weapons of calculation and manipulation developed in a lifetime as a successful businessman and politician. Even his public image, that of a simple Quaker in a fur cap, served his purposes (although, as we shall see, he was cautious in making use of his popularity). Before leaving for France he drafted a dummy peace proposal, which he felt might be useful, among other things, for frightening the French into an alliance with America.[15] Once in France, though, Franklin was very cautious about using the threat of Anglo-American reconciliation, fearing the French would perceive the bluff as weakness.[16] When news of the victory at Saratoga arrived, however, he was glad to foster the illusion America was dealing with both sides. He discussed with three different Englishmen what concessions Britain needed to make to America;

although these negotiations were totally without promise, they served to pressure the French. The American commissioners even blandly informed the French foreign ministry about Silas Deane's meeting with Paul Wentworth, a major operative of the British intelligence service. The comte de Vergennes, the French foreign minister, meanwhile was trying to win his idealistic king's consent to war and to lure the Spaniards into a joint alliance with America. Vergennes thus was enthusiastic in playing up the magnitude of the supposed threat.[17]

Once agreement had been reached with France, Franklin assumed the role of dutiful ally. His main function in Paris was that of wheedling money out of the French government. In this he was notably successful, in large part because of his care in not overplaying his trump card, the threat of American bankruptcy and military collapse. The French cited his influence when they granted America money, although on one occasion they caught him trying to collect the same loan twice.[18] Franklin also was cautious about pressing for a French expeditionary force in America. In February 1779, perhaps succumbing to Lafayette's enthusiasm, he exceeded his Congressional instructions by asking the French for help not only in capturing Canada, but also in recapturing Newport, Rhode Island. He appears to have regained quickly his normal prudence, though; he withheld from Congress information about what he had done and refused to promise the French a welcome for any expeditionary force sent to America. It was George Washington, apparently alarmed about the British expansion of the war to the American south, who informed Lafayette that such an expeditionary force would be welcome. Within a few weeks of receiving this news, the French government approved the sending to America of the army eventually entrusted to Rochambeau.[19]

The masterpiece of Franklin's talent for calculated ambiguity, however, was the peace negotiations of 1782. There his task was to foster contradictory impressions. To induce the British to make concessions he led them to think America might desert France in order to make a separate peace; at the same time, he was able to preserve the French alliance by reassuring them that America would not make peace separately. He accomplished both tasks with such skill that not even the clumsiness of John Jay could undo his work. The provisional Anglo-American agreement of 30 November 1782 is a marvel of Jesuitical evasion. As it was conditional on a general agreement, it did not technically violate the terms of either the French alliance or the American peace commissioners' instructions from Congress. Franklin even had the nerve to apologize to the French for neglecting a point of etiquette and then to ask for an additional loan—which he received! In actuality, the provisional agreement effectively took America out of the war and forced her allies to make whatever peace they could. Franklin, however, was not to blame for the French surprise at learning of the American *fait accompli;* he repeatedly urged his fellow peace commissioners, Jay and John Adams, to inform Vergennes of the progress of their negotiations, safe in the knowledge his two colleagues would vote to overrule his advice.[20]

II

Thus far this account of Franklin's diplomacy is largely a record of duplicity. There was another side, however, to this complex and elusive man. In a number of ways, Franklin was the most traditionalist of the diplomats of the American Revolution: in his tendency to approach diplomacy as a search for compromise; in his use of diplomacy as a tool for peace; in his scrupulosity about working in proper channels; and in his care to adhere to the norms of good manners and civility.

His search for compromise reflects his general approach to social and political issues. As a younger man, he made a reputation as an advocate of voluntary association, which he urged for a variety of purposes, such as self-improvement, fire-fighting, insurance, and civil defence. As a politician, he was noted as a builder of coalitions and as a seeker of consensus.[21] Although in 1776 he was among the most radical members of Congress on the issue of American independence, one of his closest associates in that body was Robert Morris, among its most cautious and conservative members. Because Franklin had avoided unduly associating himself with any faction in Congress, he subsequently was protected from the danger of being recalled from his post in Europe; critics he had, but few enemies. This job security came not because he had avoided taking political stands, but because he had avoided alienating those with whom he disagreed. It should also be noted, though, that he had an intense dislike of face-to-face confrontations, probably as a result of childhood experience.[22] His avoiding the provocation of colleagues was not always of service to his country; for example, with victory apparently near at hand in the 1782 peace negotiations, he acceded to a time-consuming dispute with the British over the credentials of their negotiator rather than disagree with his colleague John Jay. On balance, however, Franklin's willingness to compromise was a great asset, particularly in dealing with France, whose diplomatic and military needs sometimes differed greatly from America's.

Related to Franklin's proclivity to compromise was his hatred of bloodshed. In 1764 he opposed the Paxton Boys, who hoped to repeat in Philadelphia their frontier Indian lynchings. Franklin defended the Indians who had found refuge there; a dozen years later, he promised to help protect the rights of conscience of those who wished to support the revolution without bearing arms.[23] His lifelong love of peace placed him within a diplomatic tradition which predates the Renaissance,[24] the tradition that the greatest duty of the diplomat is the service of peace. Franklin hated war, fought to avert it, and when this proved impossible, worked to minimize its extent, to restrict it to the battlefield, and to reduce its suffering. At every stage of the revolution, he was at the forefront of such efforts. In the winter of 1774–5, he engaged in negotiations with members of the North government to avert war.[25] He helped negotiate the French alliance in order to speed the end of a war whose successful outcome he seems never to have doubted. He devoted enormous efforts to alleviating the conditions of American prisoners of war and securing their exchange.[26] During the 1782 peace negotiations, he sought not only the end of hostilities, but also genuine reconciliation with Great Britain.[27] Finally, he tried unsuccessfully to incorporate in the definitive peace treaty protection for non-combatants in case of future war.

Franklin was a traditionalist about the means of conducting diplomacy as well as about its ends. While in France he played by an established set of rules, among the most important of which is that of working within proper channels. This care to remain within proper channels is not in accord with the usual picture of him. According to the stereotype, he secured the French government's acquiescence in the alliance by winning the hearts of the French people. This is a misinterpretation of both French diplomacy and his own. Franklin's popularity in France certainly did reinforce the popularity of the American cause, but unlike John Adams in the Netherlands, he did not try to use public opinion to win over the French government. For example, he made few contributions to the press; indeed, during his first year in France he probably wrote only one original article.[28] He did provide older pieces as well as copies of some of his correspondence, but these were sent to the French government's own covertly run periodical, the *Affaires de l'Angleterre et de l'Amérique*. His contacts with the public were largely restricted to the rich, the nobility, fellow scientists, and intellectuals, and, above all, his neighbours in the Parisian suburb of Passy. He used these contacts to reassure the French privileged classes that the American Revolution posed no threat to them.

He played his role masterfully. His wearing of a fur cap instead of a wig, his fractured use of the French language, even his witticisms made him appear picturesque and unfrightening. His public appearances and utterances, moreover, served the French government's campaign of preparing the public for war with Britain. In 1777, French high society used the word "stormonter" for "to tell a falsehood"; this came as the result of a witticism of Franklin's about Lord Stormont, the British ambassador.[29] Franklin used public opinion to smooth the path for the French government, not to lobby it—a drastic change from his former practice as a colonial agent in London.

There are other ways in which Franklin took care not to operate outside proper channels. At least in theory, France was an absolutist state, but this does not mean it lacked politics. Vergennes, its foreign minister, had political rivals both inside and outside the government. Much to Stormont's disappointment, Franklin took great care to avoid Vergennes's rivals, such as the duc de Choiseul, a former foreign minister. He also took care not to alienate Vergennes's allies. Silas Deane, while serving as the first American diplomatic representative, was foolish enough to criticize the comte de Maurepas, the de facto first minister in the French government, upon whose support Vergennes depended.[30] Franklin avoided such mistakes. Congress grumbled at the lack of court news in Franklin's letters, but, given the possibility of interception and publication by the British, his silence was wise. He was equally reticent about Congress's internal squabbling when he communicated with the French or with his friends in England.

Franklin also avoided the common failing among inexperienced diplomats of trying to influence a ruler or foreign minister through his subordinates. He had had years of experience as a colonial agent at the British court to learn the futility of such efforts. His successor in France, Thomas Jefferson, was more naïve about the power of Vergennes's undersecretaries. He complained, for example, of the anti-American bias of Rayneval, the undersecretary Vergennes sent when bad news had to be given the American.[31] Even experienced ambassadors could make the same mistake. Sir James Harris, the British representative in St. Petersburg during the American Revolution, snubbed the Russian foreign minister and wasted his time and money bribing Empress Catherine's favourites.[32] In contrast to ambassadors like Harris, Franklin dealt only with the foreign minister to whom he was accredited (or with the foreign minister's delegated representatives) and kept relations on a business level.

More fundamentally, Franklin believed in an envoy's going only where he would be received. His mission to France was not approved in Philadelphia until a letter from one of his French friends led Congress to believe official American representatives would be welcome.[33] When he arrived in France, he did not appear in public in an official capacity until he was certain neither the French government nor his own would suffer embarrassment.[34] He viewed with distaste the unsolicited journeys of Arthur Lee to Spain and Arthur and William Lee to Germany, telling the former that he had not changed his opinion that America should not go suitoring for alliances, but should wait with decent dignity for the application of others.[35]

This care to work within channels was only a part of his concern for observing the dictates of established diplomatic practice. The rules of diplomacy were more than hollow formality; they were a code of ethics by which diplomats earned the respect of their profession. According to this code, the true diplomat tries to understand those with whom he is negotiating. He works by establishing trust and avoids as best he can the telling of falsehoods or issuing of threats. Franklin tried to live by these standards and succeeded well enough to be treated by his European counterparts as a professional. This distinguishes him from a John Adams or an Arthur Lee, who often acted as if good manners were a sign of weakness.

With Adams, abrasiveness was a matter of policy; he did feel that his older colleague's deference and tact created an impression of subservience.[36] With people like Arthur Lee, the use of bluster seems to have been less a question of calculation than a reflection of underlying arrogance, although on the face of things, Americans seem hardly to have had grounds for feeling superior. The United States was an underdeveloped country, increasingly dependent on foreign assistance as the war continued, Washington's army shrank, and Congress lost its ability to finance the war. American statesmen continued to act, however, as if America's moral superiority made her unconquerable by Britain and superior to older states like France and Spain. This belief was reinforced by an inflated view of the importance of American trade, which Americans believed gave them a central position in the balance of power.

Franklin's optimism was surpassed by few and his self-righteousness about America by perhaps even fewer. On the other hand, his years in London had taught him something of how to approach a court. Moreover, his eighteen months in Congress, including service on dozens of Congressional committees, made him exceedingly well-informed about American shortages of money, material, and manpower. Ironically enough, for all their arrogance, lesser statesmen like Lee and Deane proved all too willing to offer sweeping trade concessions in exchange for French help.[37] Franklin took a different approach: America needed foreign assistance to hasten her inevitable victory, but prudence dictated that she ask for help politely and not too often. Congress flooded him with loan office certificates to pay and requests for further French financial aid. Repeatedly, it ignored his warnings that the French government was not made of money. Franklin's role in negotiating the alliance and in eliciting loans and grants from the French government was dependent on his winning a degree of trust. By not crying wolf when it wasn't necessary, he was able to obtain help when it was vital (as in 1781, when French financial help kept Congress from bankruptcy). In one way, though, the Lees and Deane and Adams were a help to Franklin. The French government was all the more willing to deal with Franklin so it would not have to deal with his insufferable colleagues.

III

Franklin's contradictions are hardly unique among diplomats. He is not the only statesman ever to use duplicity and manipulation in the pursuit of peace or compromise; such contradictions, however, can exert a price in human stress.

While evidence is not conclusive, there are many clues that Franklin suffered from psychological stress during the period of his French mission (although it is sometimes difficult to differentiate this stress from homesickness, exhaustion, or anxiety about the mission's success, each itself perhaps symptomatic). Even if one considers his numerous physical ailments (including psoriasis, gout, and kidney stones) to be merely the results of age and of primitive medical treatment, there is both direct and indirect evidence of the mental burdens he bore. Numerous indications of psychological discomfort, even agony, can be found in his correspondence. His letters to his British friends often contain eloquent statements of his hatred of war and disillusionment with man's inhumanity to his fellow man. To Bishop Shipley, for example, he wrote: "After much Occasion to consider the Folly and Mischiefs of a state of Warfare, and the little or no Advantage obtain'd even by those Nations, who have conducted it with the most Success, I have been apt to think, that there never has been, nor ever will be, any such thing as a *good* War, or a *bad* Peace."[38]

He also wrote frequently to America about his eagerness for peace and his desire to retire from public life. He even submitted his resignation when Congress sent him an unwanted helper, John Laurens (although in this case his motives probably were mixed).[39] Nonetheless, his reiterated desire to return to America suggests the posibility of burdens he wished to shed.

Franklin's dissatisfaction with the dictates of his official life is suggested even more strongly by the contrasting tenor of his personal relationships in France. It is hardly unusual that he should have found relief in social activities; the life of dissipation that Adams criticized was in fact a life of dinner parties. Franklin not only shared the tables of others, but hosted weekly dinners for fellow Americans in Paris. One suspects that the check to his gregariousness caused by the peace negotiations not only prompted many letters to his friends, but may also have helped to undermine his health.[40] More symptomatic of his discomfort with his official life is the pattern of relationships he established with the American mission. Here he encouraged an atmosphere of informality, trust, openness, and disregard for any precautions to maintain security. By treating the members of the American mission as a family, Franklin may have provided relief for himself. He certainly provided opportunities for British spies.

Three friends in particular violated Franklin's unquestioning trust: his fellow commissioner Silas Deane, the commissioners' unofficial secretary Edward Bancroft, and Deane's secretary William Carmichael. Deane helped to cement a friendship begun in joint congressional service by sharing in Franklin's disputes with their irascible colleague Arthur Lee. Unknown to Franklin, however, Deane formed a partnership with Bancroft and Samuel Wharton, an American associate in England, to speculate on the London stock market. Bancroft and Deane used for this purpose their inside knowledge of the negotiations which led to the Franco-American alliance.[41] There is no evidence, however, that Deane provided information to the British government, or that Franklin had any suspicion of Deane's speculations.[42] In 1781 when Deane did sell his services to the British, Franklin broke relations with him.[43]

More serious were the activities of Edward Bancroft, a long-standing friend who, like Franklin, was a fellow of the Royal Society. Bancroft had become an agent of the British intelligence service long before Franklin joined Deane in Paris. Bancroft's importance to the British can easily be overestimated, however; his motives were pecuniary and his spying was strictly a sideline to his stock speculations. King George III at any rate viewed his services as disappointing.[44] Bancroft did succeed in fooling Franklin, who maintained their friendship for the remainder of his life.

Most dangerous, though, were the actions of William Carmichael, a wealthy young Marylander who was a good friend of Franklin's grandson and personal secretary, William Temple Franklin. The evidence is inconclusive about whether Carmichael provided information to the British. There is the likelihood, however, that in the summer of 1777 Carmichael attempted to provoke a war between France and Britain in the hope it would lead to a reconciliation between Britain and the American colonies. In pursuit of this goal Carmichael (perhaps with the connivance of Deane) apparently gave secret instructions to the privateer captain Gustavus Conyngham to disregard the commissioners' prohibition of cruising against British shipping. Conyngham's subsequent provocation of the British created the impression of French complicity and caused a major diplomatic crisis. It even briefly appeared that France would be forced into a war with Britain for which she was not yet prepared. Although war was averted by France's expelling other American warships from her ports, the American commissioners were badly discredited with the French government. Franklin does not seem to have realized what Carmichael had done, and remained friends with the young man even after Deane and Lee had become estranged from him.[45]

The security of the American mission was also endangered by its hospitality to visiting countrymen, such as James Van Zandt, a New Yorker who went through Deane's papers and sent numerous intelligence reports to London.[46] When Franklin was warned that his own papers were exposed, his reaction was to deny that there was any need for security precautions.[47] Such a denial seems in fact the denial of the realities of his position as a foreign envoy of a power at war, and as such suggests that Franklin may have been under considerable strain.

It would have been surprising had Franklin been immune from such stress. The Revolution imposed severe strains on ways of thought and action shared by most Americans. A provocative recent book, Charles Royster's *A Revolutionary People at War*,[48] describes the tension between the military ideals of the revolutionaries and the realities of the war. A similar set of tensions was produced by the conduct of revolutionary diplomacy.

Part of this tension came from the conflict between the dictates of diplomacy and American religious beliefs. Distrust of Catholicism was still ingrained in American thought; even Franklin took care to send his younger grandson to be educated in Geneva as a Protestant and a republican.[49] Although religious leaders like Samuel Cooper took pains to defuse this tension, an alliance with Catholic France was repudiation of the traditional view of America as part of an embattled Protestant world alliance.[50]

Similarly, the alliance with France forced a rethinking of a widely held distrust of French character, government, and diplomacy. Among the revolutionary diplomats, Franklin alone seems to have been immune from at least incipient francophobia, perhaps because he had made French friends before the war from his scientific writings and his visits to Paris. More common was the view of John Adams that in the long run France potentially posed an even greater danger to America than did Britain.[51]

On a larger scale, the war forced Americans into the very participation in European diplomacy that Thomas Paine and Franklin hitherto had claimed was the result of America's ties to England.[52] The war for independence thus was paradoxical: for Americans to maintain their identity as free-born Protestants working out their own destiny they had to ally with a Catholic absolutist state and participate in the European balance of power. What could justify such a departure from tradition?

The obvious answer is survival, an issue which possessed a significance that transcended the fate of the revolutionaries themselves. As Royster points out, many of them derived their zeal from a sense that upon them depended not only the survival of freedom in the world, but also the inauguration of the Christian millenium. Franklin at least shared the first half of this view. To his friend Samuel Cooper he wrote from France, " 'tis a Common Observation here, that our Cause is *the Cause of all Mankind,* and that we are fighting for their Liberty in defending our own. 'Tis a glorious task assign'd us by Providence; which has, I trust, given us Spirit and Virtue equal to it, and will at last crown it with success."[53]

This messianic vision, moreover, was dynamic in nature. The war had hardly begun when the revolution sought to expand geographically. From the army beseiging Boston a small detachment left to liberate Canada from the British yoke. Before war's end similar tiny armies would contest with the British for control of the area west of the Appalachians, envisaged by Franklin and others as the future home of an ever growing American population.[54] The revolution thus was of an international, if not metaphysical importance, expansive in both space and time. Were not compromises justified in such a cause?

IV

Finally, let us return to the two questions posed by Gilbert, the narrower one of conflict versus consensus in the revolution and the wider one of idealism versus realism, pervading not only the revolution but all of American diplomatic history. Does Franklin's mission help to prove or to disprove the arguments set forth by Gilbert?

First, it seems clear Franklin's differences with his colleagues related to diplomatic tactics rather than to fundamental disagreements over the aims of revolutionary diplomacy. American diplomats abroad thus shared in a broad national consensus about the justice and purposes of the war. This high degree of consensus stemmed from more than the nature of the cause.

It was also fed by outrage against the way the British conducted the war. The burning of cities, the hiring of foreign mercenaries, the supposed inciting of Indians to attack the frontier—these atrocities acted as a force for unity much as did the 1941 bombing of Pearl Harbor. Franklin not only shared but helped to shape the American response to them. The war itself thus reinforced the desire for unconditional independence. By 1777 at the latest, the only real British chance of victory lay in American economic collapse and general exhaustion;[55] any hopes of winning American hearts and minds were illusory. Apart from a sizable but badly outnumbered and disorganized group of loyalists, the only meaningful division in America was between the strong and weak of heart, (perhaps more accurately, between the resilient and the exhausted). With the possible exception of Silas Deane, the faint-hearted were not to be found at the American mission in France.

If the unity of the revolutionaries is striking, so too are the deep divisions among them, divisions cemented by the need for survival and victory. These divisions manifested themselves in issues which on the surface appear secondary: the choice of envoys for diplomatic posts in Europe or the precise formulation of US peace terms. Such issues, however, served to bring to the surface deeply divided feelings. As Edmund Morgan has shown, the Congressional debate over Silas Deane's conduct as commissioner really was a debate over the very meaning of the revolution.[56] The question of whether Newfoundland fishing rights should be presented to Britain as an ultimatum for peace was also a question for the distribution of political power among the disparate sections of a country not yet unified.[57] The consensus on foreign policy thus was a fragile one and the issues that would divide Americans in the 1790s would draw on many of the same unresolved underlying tensions.

The striking unity among revolutionary diplomats abroad derived much of its strength from never having been tested. In particular, the chief reason serious conflicts did not arise during the peace negotiations of 1782 is that they were never given the chance. By buying the Americans out of the war with massive concessions, the British spared them the necessity of choosing between possibly competing goals. The consensus between Franklin and his colleagues, although real, was somewhat artificial.

Finally, how can we judge Gilbert's claim that the central foreign policy issue dividing Americans was the choice between realism and idealism; indeed, that this issue is central to all of American diplomatic history?[58] To judge it, we must first understand clearly what Gilbert means by "idealism" and "realism." The idealism he describes is really a form of enlightened self-interest. Because one nation's welfare is served by that of others, peace, the rule of law, and friendly trade are practical as well as moral aims for statecraft. By realism, Gilbert means the amoral struggle of states for power, advantage, and security, a struggle in which ethical considerations are irrelevant, if not foolish.

Hutson has argued that the diplomcy of the revolution was based on the latter of these world-views. It certainly is difficult to contradict his assertion that the statesmen of the revolution universally accepted the practice of *realpolitik,* involving great power diplomacy, the use of trade as a political weapon, and reliance upon military preparedness and strength.[59] US diplomatic history in general is filled with a similar "realism." An important part of US historical dealings with other peoples has been a pattern of expansionism, racism, economic imperialism, and readiness for war. Such a pattern stems from the very beginnings of the English settlement of America and seems almost to be ingrained in the US character. Yet so bleak a picture obscures the complexity of US diplomatic history. In this history there has been a real debate between those finding "realism" in naked self-interest and those who have defined it more broadly. There are genuine differences between the savagery and amorality of a Henry Kissinger and the decency and restraint of a Cyrus Vance, whatever continuities exist between their policies. Can such differences be traced to the generation of the Founding Fathers?

Over the conduct of the war, they certainly can be found. John Shy has shown a clear difference in the way Charles Lee and George Washington proposed fighting the British.[60] It is largely to the latter's credit that the war, savage as it was, did not degenerate into the sort of blood feud recently seen in Lebanon. Such differences are less easily visible in foreign policy, but they did exist, particularly during the peace negotiations. Jay's willingness to abandon the French alliance and his encouragement of a British attack on America's de facto ally, Spain, contrast sharply with Franklin's approach, even though such differences related partly to diplomatic tactics.[61] Franklin's greater idealism also was manifested in his insistence on national dignity. His hatred of begging and his insistence that America not sell herself to obtain an alliance or financial support, contrast with the shortsightedness of Deane and Lee, who were willing to mortgage American trade or threaten peace with Britain if French help were not forthcoming. Above all, Franklin's belief in the reciprocity of national interests and his desire for peace and reconciliation with Britain (shown so clearly by Stourzh) speaks for a deeper moral purpose underlying his diplomacy.

Notes

1. James H. Hutson, "Intellectual Foundations of Early American Diplomcy," *Diplomatic History I* (1977), 1–19; James H. Hutson, *John Adams and the Diplomacy of the American Revolution* (Lexington, Ky, 1980); Jack N. Rakove, *The Beginnings of National Politics: An Interpretive History of the Continental Congress* (New York, 1979). Rakove does feel the divisiveness of the 1779 debate over war aims did lasting damage to congressional consensus: see pp. 243–74. Another recent example of a consensus approach to the origins of American politics and foreign policy is Robert W. Tucker and David C. Hendrickson, *The Fall of the*

First British Empire: Origins of the War of Independence (Baltimore and London, 1982), especially pp. 333–41, which argue that this consensus suddenly emerged in 1774.

2. Felix Gilbert, *To the Farewell Address: Ideas of Early American Foreign Policy* (Princeton, N.J., 1961).

3. This is discussed in Reginald C. Stuart, *War and American Thought: From the Revolution to the Monroe Doctrine* (Kent, Ohio, 1982), pp. 35–36.

4. My concern in this paper will be with Franklin's mission to France (1776–85). He served as one of three commissioners (along with Arthur Lee, Silas Deane, and Deane's replacement John Adams) until in February 1779 he became minister plenipotentiary. As a collateral duty he served as peace commissioner (1781–3); during the peace negotiations he was joined by his fellow commissioners John Jay, John Adams, and Henry Laurens.

5. Gilbert, p. 136.

6. In doing so I will elaborate on some of the arguments I presented in *Franklin the Diplomat: The French Mission* (Philadelphia, 1982). Published in: American Philosophical Society, *Transactions*, vol. LXXII, pt. 1. (Hereafter Dull, *Franklin*.) An earlier version of the present paper was presented to the Society for Historians of American Foreign Relations.

7. Lyman, H. Butterfield, ed., *Diary and Autobiography of John Adams*, 4 vols. (Cambridge, Mass., 1961), II, 346.

8. Gerald Stourzh, *Benjamin Franklin and American Foreign Policy*, 2nd ed. (Chicago and London, 1969).

9. Dull, *Franklin*, p. 68n gives examples.

10. Dull, *Franklin*, pp. 70–71.

11. Leonard W. Labaree, William B. Willcox, et al., eds., *The Papers of Benjamin Franklin*, 23 vols. to date (New Haven and London, 1959–), XXII, 218–19 (hereafter *Papers*).

12. See Francis Wharton, ed., *The Revolutionary Diplomatic Correspondence of the United States*, 6 vols. (Washington, 1889), II, 326. Albert Henry Smith, ed., *The Writings of Benjamin Franklin*, 10 vols. (New York and London, 1907), VII, 299, 401–2 (hereafter Smyth).

13. *Papers*, XXIII, 548–49.

14. Smyth, VII, 101.

15. There is no indication, however, that Franklin ever used it: *Papers*, XXII, 630–33.

16. See particularly Silas Deane's testimony, published in Charles Isham, ed., *The Deane Papers*, 5 vols. (New York, 1887–91), V, 438.

17. Dull, 29–32; Jonathan R. Dull, *The French Navy and American Independence: A Study of Arms and Diplomacy, 1774–1787* (Princeton, N.J., 1975), pp. 89–101. (Hereafter Dull, *French Navy*.)

18. Dull, *Franklin* pp. 50n, 65.

19. Dull, *Franklin*, pp. 50–51; Stanley J. Idzerda, ed., *Lafayette in the Age of the American Revolution: Selected Letters and Papers, 1776–1790*, 4 vols. to date (Ithaca, N.Y. and London, 1977), II, 313–19; Jonathan R. Dull, "Lafayette, Franklin, and the Coming of Rochambeau's Army," *Proceedings of the Annual Meeting of the Washington Association of New Jersey* (1980), pp. 15–24.

20. Dull, *Franklin*, pp. 53–64.

21. For Franklin's system of values see Paul W. Conner, *Poor Richard's Politicks: Benjamin Franklin and His New American Order* (New York, 1965), for his political career, James H. Hutson, *Pennsylvania Politics, 1746–1770: The Movement for Royal Government and Its Consequences* (Princeton, N.J., 1972) and Benjamin H. Newcomb, *Franklin and Galloway: A Political Partnership* (New Haven and London, 1972). More critical of Franklin's politics is William S. Hanna, *Benjamin Franklin and Pennsylvania Politics* (Stanford, Calif., 1964).

22. Franklin's childhood is discussed in Arthur Bernon Tourtellot, *Benjamin Franklin: The Shaping of Genius. The Boston Years* (Garden City, N.Y., 1977), 108–43 and Claude-Anne Lopez and Eugenia W. Herbert, *The Private Franklin: The Man and His Family* (New York, 1975), pp. 5–10.

23. Hutson, *Pennsylvania Politics*, 84–121; Melvin H. Buxbaum, *Benjamin Franklin and the Zealous Presbyterians* (University Park, Pa. and London, 1975), pp. 185–219; *Papers*, XXII, 57–58.

24. See Garrett Mattingly, *Renaissance Diplomacy* (Boston, 1955).

25. *Papers*, XXI, *passim* provides documentation, but there has yet been no adequate monographic study of the negotiation.

26. Catherine M. Prelinger, "Benjamin Franklin and the American Prisoners of War in England during the American Revolution," *William and Mary Quarterly*, 3rd ser., XXXII (1975), 261–94.

27. Stourzh, pp. 186–213.

28. This article compared Great Britain and America as credit risks: Smyth, VII, 1–8. In Dull, *Franklin*, p. 17n, I mistakenly attributed to Franklin a set of memoirs more likely written by Edward Bancroft, for which see Butterfield, *Diary and Autobiography of John Adams*, IV, 73. For Franklin's only known contribution to the British press in 1777 see *Papers*, XII, 112–14.

29. Alfred Owen Aldridge, *Franklin and His French Contemporaries* (New York, 1957), p. 196. According to the head of the Paris police Franklin said in response to Ambassador Stormont's report of an American defeat, "La verité et le Stormont sont deux." Benjamin Franklin Stevens, ed., *Facsimiles of Manuscripts in European Archives Relating to America, 1773–1783*, 25 vols. (London, 1889–98), XVIII, no. 1648.

30. Isham, I, 212; Dull, *French Navy*, pp. 6, 48.

31. Julian P. Boyd, ed., *The Papers of Thomas Jefferson*, 20 vols. to date (Princeton, N.J., 1950–), II:96.

32. Isabel de Madariaga, *Britain, Russia, and the Armed Neutrality of 1780: Sir James Harris's Mission to St. Petersburg during the American Revolution* (New Haven: Yale University Press, 1962).

33. *Papers*, XII, 453–55.

34. *Papers*, XXIII, 29.

35. *Papers*, XXIII, 511.

36. Stourzh, pp. 154–64.

37. Isham, I:184–95, 361–64; Brian N. Morton and Donald C. Spinelli, eds., *Beaumarchais Correspondance*, 4 vols. to date (Paris, 1969–), II, 171–76.

38. Smyth, VIII, 454.

39. Dull, *Franklin*, 48–9 gives details.

40. For Franklin's health see Lopez and Herbert, p. 236 and Dull, *Franklin*, pp. 58, 66.

41. Although there as yet is no scholarly biography of Deane there is an excellent study of his early life: Kalman Goldstein, "Silas Deane: Preparation for Rascality," *Historian*, XLIII (1980–1), 75–97. The manuscript of Deane and Bancroft's financial accounts is at the Connecticut Historical Society.

42. Dull, *Franklin*, pp. 33–37. A contrary view of Deane is presented by Julian Boyd in "Silas Deane: Death by a Kindly Teacher of Treason?" *William and Mary Quarterly*, 3rd ser., XVI (1959):165–87, 319–42, 515–50.

43. See Isham, V, 70–71.

44. Sir John Fortescue, *The Correspondence of King George the Third from 1760 to December 1783*, 6 vols. (London, 1927–8), III, 481–82, 532.

45. For details see Dull, *Franklin*, pp. 37–40. For Franklin's continued esteem for Carmichael see Franklin to Carmichael, 8 February 1778 (National Archives).

46. For Van Zandt's activities see Stevens, *Facsimiles of Manuscripts, passim* and Dull, *Franklin*, pp. 33–34, 38–39. The identification of his first name is tentative.

47. Juliana Ritchie to Franklin, 12 January 1777 and William Alexander to Franklin, 1 March 1777, *Papers*, XXIII, 162–63, 414–15. For Franklin's response see *Papers*, XXIII, 211.

48. Charles Royster, *A Revolutionary People at War: The Continental Army and American Character, 1775–1783* (Chapel Hill, N.C., 1979).

49. Franklin to John Quincy Adams, 21 April 1779, Smyth, VII, 288–89. In a letter to Samuel Cooper of 9 December 1780 (Library of Congress; American Philosophical Society) he spoke of educating his grandson at Geneva as a Presbyterian and a Republican. William C. Stinchcombe, *The American Revolution and the French Alliance* (Syracuse, N.Y., 1969), pp. 1–13, discusses the change of American attitudes which resulted from the need for an alliance with Catholic France.

50. Stinchcombe, pp. 91–103. See also Charles W. Akers, *The Divine Politician: Samuel Cooper and the American Revolution in Boston* (Boston, 1982).

51. For this distrust of France consult Hutson, "Intellectual Foundations of Early American Diplomacy," pp. 14–15.

52. *Papers*, XXI, 509, 603–4; Philip S. Foner, ed., *The Complete Writings of Thomas Paine*, 2 vols. (New York, 1945) I, 18–19 ("Common Sense").

53. Franklin to Samuel Cooper, 1 May 1777, Smyth, vii, 56; for above, Royster, pp. 155–61.

54. Conner, pp. 69–107; Stourzh, pp. 98–100.

55. For a case study of the economic effects of the war see Richard Buel, Jr., *Dear Liberty: Connecticut's Mobilization for the Revolutinary War* (Middletown, Conn., 1980).

56. Edmund S. Morgan, "The Puritan Ethic and the American Revolution," *William and Mary Quarterly*, 3rd ser., XXIV (1967), 3–43.

57. Rakove, pp. 262–74; H. James Henderson, *Party Politics in the Continental Congress* (New York, 1974), pp. 196–213.

58. Gilbert, p. 136. For Gilbert's discussion of the contrasting aims of realism and idealism see pp. 56–66.

59. Hutson, "Intellectual Foundations of Early American Diplomacy," pp. 9–19.

60. John W. Shy, "Charles Lee: The Soldier as Radical," in George Athan Billias, ed., *George Washington's Generals* (New York, 1964), pp. 22–53.

61. Compare Dull, *Franklin*, pp. 58–64 and Richard B. Morris, *The Peacemakers: The Great Powers and American Independence* (New York, 1965).

Franklin's Last Years in England: The Making of a Rebel

William B. Willcox*

No man, the old adage has it, can be a hero to his valet. He can be and often is to his biographer, and most of the lives of Franklin are tinged to some degree with hero-worship; the authors are selective, as historians have to be, and consciously or unconsciously sift out the evidence unfavor-

*This essay was written especially for this collection and published here for the first time.

able to their subject. This an editor cannot do, at least when he is committed as we are to including everything of the least significance that the editee, if there is such a word, has written or that has been written to him. Because such an editor has no selectivity, he sees his man in the round as the valet see his, *e pede Herculem,* and recognizes that even Hercules has traces of clay around the toes. At least that has been my experience. Franklin is incomparably the most interesting historical figure with whom I have been in close contact, and greatness he unquestionably had. But unflawed through-and-through greatness at all times, secular sainthood, he did not have. To impute it to him outrages truth as much as it would have outraged him.

He grew by stages from provincial politician to statesman and diplomat. Some of the stages were slow, but one that was not was the closing years of his British mission. During that period he broke with what had been deep loyalties.

He had two English missions, separated by an interval so short that they constituted virtually a single sojourn of eighteen years. He arrived in 1757, sent by the Pennsylvania assembly to lobby for its claim to tax the Penns' vast landholdings in the province. Although he got nowhere with the claim, he had a wonderful time. He had been briefly in London as a young man, and now he took to the city like a duck to water. (He was urban by temperament, and never put down country roots; his dream for retirement was not a Braintree or Mount Vernon or Monticello, but a more spacious town house.) He found London more exciting than Philadelphia, and was soon at home in it. His landlady, Mrs. Stevenson, and her daughter Polly replaced his own family. He cultivated British friends whom he had already made by correspondence, and quickly acquired new ones. He had a small entree to government by way of the post office, because since 1753 he had been one of the two deputy postmasters general in North America, and he soon familiarized himself with the corridors of power; before he left in 1762 he secured for his son William, who was both young and illegitimate, the governorship of New Jersey.

Franklin had only two years in Philadelphia before he returned to England, again as agent for the assembly and again on a fruitless errand, which was to have the province transformed from proprietary to royal government. But this objective soon became secondary as other business absorbed him. His reputation had spread through the colonies, and in the next few years he became agent for New Jersey, for the commons house of Georgia, and for the Massachusetts House of Representatives. He was thus closely connected with four of the thirteen colonies, and was nearer than anyone else to being the spokesman for them all.

Pennsylvania, once the hope of changing its government faded, gave him little more than routine business. New Jersey under the skillful management of his son presented few problems to be guided through the maze of Whitehall. In Georgia the governor was at perpetual loggerheads with the commons house, and prorogued and dissolved it so regularly that no business could be done; Franklin's appointment lapsed and his salary remained unpaid. Massachusetts was quite another matter. When its house appointed him agent in 1770, the year of the Boston Massacre, the tumultuous province was already assuming the leadership in the movement toward rebellion. He played a part, probably a greater one than he ever intended, in accelerating the pace; and the Bostonians' brand of radicalism came to affect his thinking almost as much as their actions dominated his political life. He continued to speak for America only because the other colonies made common cause with Massachusetts.

During those years he had little official standing with the government; none of the agents had as agent. Each colony employed at least one, and most of his business was routine—to keep an eye on lawsuits in which his constituents had a stake, to defend their legislation as it made its slow way through the board of trade to the privy council for allowance or rejection, to expedite a petition to the king or parliament. The agents themselves were a scratch lot, English and American; they ranged from men little known even in their day to such public figures as Franklin and Edmund Burke. They went their own ways, with little or no sense of having a common constituency, and even a great crisis rarely brought them together to try to concert common action. The government might have used them, if it had had the imagination, as informal representatives through whom to feel the pulse of colonial opinion. But imagination was in short supply among ministers, most of whom were content to preserve inviolate their ignorance of what Americans were thinking.

The outstanding exception was in 1766. The Stamp Act had touched off the first great explosion of colonial anger, and the Rockingham administration was considering repeal. Even the House of Commons showed a glimmer of curiosity about why Americans behaved as they did, and in an effort to find out summoned Franklin and others for questioning. His examination was long. From all sides of the House questions came at him, some friendly and some hostile. The friendly ones gave him openings to explain the colonial position. The hostile ones he deftly parried; trying to trap him was like trying to grab a drop of quicksilver. His answers were calm and deliberate, and he did not mince words. Taxing the Americans, he said, threatened to bring into question the sovereignty of Parliament; arguments had been made "that if you have no right to tax them internally, you have none to . . . make any other law to bind them. At present they do not reason so, but in time they may possibly be convinced by these arguments." Coercing the colonies would be as dangerous as taxing them. "Suppose a military force sent into America; they will find nobody in arms. . . . They will not find a rebellion; they may indeed make one." Nine years before Lexington he saw the shadow of coming events.

Although this scene in the House of Commons undoubtedly enhanced his reputation as a colonial spokesman, and may have contributed to repeal, the effect of that measure was transient. Parliament combined it with proclaiming, in the Declaratory Act, its right to legislate for the colonies in all cases whatsoever. Such a proclamation may have been necessary at the time, as a sop to the opposition; but in the long run it proved a disaster, because enunciating a principle in absolute terms precludes future compromise. Junius, the pseudonymous writer of philippics against the government, made the point succinctly: Parliament, he said, had relinquished the revenue and judiciously taken care to preserve the contention.

As that contention grew, it put greater and greater strain upon Franklin's loyalties. His ties to England were close, and the last thing he wanted was division between his two homes. He had been so long away from Philadelphia that he was becoming a Londoner by adoption, and he had friends all over the British Isles. He loved the country and its people. He held office under the crown, and had a royal governor for son. Last but not least, he was working on the government for a land grant from which he hoped to make a fortune. He and many associates organized what came to be known as the Walpole Company, which petitioned in 1770 for a grant of twenty million acres west of the Alleghenies and south of the Ohio River. This vast tract, if the crown agreed to grant it, offered riches untold to every one in the company—to Franklin and his son, to friends in Philadelphia, to prominent London politicians, to seedy backwoodsmen on the Mononghahela. But the grant would also be disastrous to outsiders who had claims of their own, such as George Washington; and they put every obstacle they could in the way of the application. The result was a long and devious struggle, which came to the surface in hearings before the Board of Trade and the Privy Council and opinions from the law officers of the crown. Under the surface the pulling and hauling went on for years, and at one point precipitated a cabinet crisis and the resignation of the secretary of state for the American colonies.

To study land speculation in this period, I may say parenthetically, is to risk madness; and the Walpole grant is a case in point. The speculators' first step was to cajole the Indians into ceding territory out of which claims could be carved. Even if the land had belonged to the grantors (Indians liked to bargain away the hunting grounds of other tribes) the boundaries were vague. They were surveyed and resurveyed, and each time the size of the tract seemed to grow; the maps sent to London, even when not intentionally falsified, were highly unreliable. Harassed bureaucrats in Whitehall had little idea of what was going on, and protected themselves by endless delay. The harassed modern scholar has even less idea, with so much of the evidence gone, and has no refuge in delay; he must deal as best he can with details, about which no two historians apparently agree, of a project that was as unproductive as it was murky. For after all the promoters' efforts, the Walpole grant never materialized.

Franklin did not share for long his associates' high hopes for the Company. He was realistic enough, and versed enough in the ways of Whitehall, to expect the negotiations to move as they did, at the pace of a sluggish glacier; and his interest in them seemed to wane. A possible explanation is that the prospect of riches did not deeply concern him. He liked money, and was intent on having enough to support his style of life; he kept accounts to the penny (or rather he tried to) and could be waspish about whatever smacked of extravagance in his family. But years earlier he had amassed a comfortable nest egg, and did not have the impetus to add to it that someone like Washington had. He did not live expensively and had no plantation to support; he seems to have been content with what he had, and indifferent to anything more that was due him. When Pennsylvania for some reason cut his salary as agent, he made no protest; for years Massachusetts and Georgia paid him nothing, and he continued to act for them on the chance, which proved to be a good one, of eventual reimbursement. This attitude was perhaps calculated: insistence on being paid may not have fitted his image of himself as a philosopher. But that was not all. The author of "The Way to Wealth" did not at bottom, I am convinced, care a tinker's dam for riches.

He certainly cared much more for other things that cannot be bought, and high among them were friends and acquaintances. He was the most gregarious of men, and his catholic taste meant a range of contacts. He was constantly meeting people, writing to people, visiting people, working with people. He moved easily into the circle of his landlady and her daughter. Through them he knew a flibbertigibbet spinster of good county family, another woman who was a power in the East India Company, two brothers who were carriage-makers (he helped one of them perfect a new method of making wheels), and numerous odd characters of varying degrees of respectability. He looked after his and his wife's English relatives, many of whom were indigent and almost illiterate. He hobnobbed with politicians, encouraged scientists in their experiments, visited bankers and noblemen at their country estates. He had a remarkable gift for getting on with children, who apparently sensed that he took them seriously. His deism was no barrier to friendship with an Anglican bishop and with the great revivalist, George Whitefield. He loved to travel; new scenes were a tonic to him, and everywhere he went—Ireland, Scotland, Germany, France—he met interesting people, and kept in touch with many of them by correspondence. In the same way he maintained his American ties. If he had done nothing but write the letters that have survived, his time would have been filled.

His life in England differed essentially from his subsequent mission to France. The Franklin of Paris and Passy was building, consciously or unconsciously, myths about himself; he was at one and the same time the elder statesman of science, the apostle of liberty, the flirtatious man of the world, and that embodiment of homespun republican virtues, Bonhomme Richard. In London he did not have so many hats to wear. Without an assignment on which his country depended, he was much less in the public eye, and could be himself and enjoy himself. He needed no embroidery of myth.

His British years were busy ones. He gave full rein to his curiosity, not only about people and places but also about the workings of nature. His great period as an electrical scientist was over, but that was only the best known example of his itch to investigate. Anything in the world around him could spark his interest, and almost everything did. The post office told him that some pocket ships had a longer voyage to America than others that sailed a greater distance, and he was immediately baying after the reason; he soon learned it from a Nantucket whaling captain, an old friend, who informed him that masters of some packets did not know about Atlantic currents and others did, and this kindled what proved to be his lifelong interest in the Gulf Stream. Another sea captain gave him data proving, it seemed, that the aurora borealis was a sure portent of a southerly gale; Franklin conjectured why, but neither he nor any one since, as far as I know, has fully explained the connection. He was interested in the fall of rain, in the nature of sunspots, and the way windmills were built in Poland, in the common cold and what causes it (here he mixed the medical mythology of his day with more common sense than most of his contemporaries had), in recipes for cheese, Parmesan in particular, in the best way to teach a person how to swim (he was an avid swimmer from boyhood), in the shocks delivered by a creature called the torpedo fish. During his last winters in England he warmed himself with an improved stove of his devising, which consumed its own smoke, and took the model home with him to Philadelphia. He was fascinated by the effect of oil on calming waves, and conducted experiments in the Lake country, on London ponds, and in the English Channel with cooperation from the Royal Navy. In his spare time he turned from the physical world to design a phonetic alphabet, rewrite the Lord's Prayer, and contribute to a drastic shortening, on deistic lines, of the Book of Common Prayer.

The list could be prolonged, but why bother? Here was a man in his middle to late sixties, busy with public affairs, who somehow found leisure and energy to pursue these other interests. He lived in an age, it is true, that was probing its world and churning with the excitement of discovery; but which of his contemporaries among the philosophers ranged from sunspots to the common cold? Not that his ranging contributed much to the sum of knowledge; it did not. He seldom went deeply enough into a subject, electricity and stoves excepted, to leave his mark on its history; in general his mind met a problem, struck sparks from it, and then moved on. But his curiosity, at a time of life when most men's is becoming sated, remained incredibly active.

During these years his reputation was still growing in England and on the continent. Foreigners visiting London, he told his son with pleasure, went out of their way to call on him. In 1752, while still in America, he had been elected a fellow of the Royal Society; but that was only the beginning of his honors. The climax came in 1772, when he received the accolade of membership in the Académie royale des sciences. In the following year a Parisian friend and disciple published a sumptuous two-volume French edition of his works, and it spread his fame far and wide among the French-speaking intelligentsia of Europe. In their eyes he was not the best known of his countrymen; he was the only one known. "The modern Prometheus," as Immanuel Kant had called him years before, as the single American who was a recognized figure in the Enlightenment, and this recognition soon afterward stood him and his country in good stead.

Although much of his renown rested upon his achievements as scientist, the other cardinal interest of his life had always been politics; and, as the Anglo-American quarrel moved inexorably toward war, politics more and more absorbed him. His ongoing dialogue with his constituents in Massachusetts kept him abreast of developments there, and he took on himself to present the American case in London through an outpouring of communications to the press. They were sometimes serious, sometimes anecdotal, sometimes satiric. Through them and his private correspondence he revealed the development of Franklin the politician, who was a quite different person from Franklin the scientist; the difference is the measure of the man's complexity.

His scientific thinking had certain characteristics. First, the range of his curiosity was extremely broad; he found a challenge in almost any phenomenon that came his way. Second, he handled the challenge objectively, by gathering experimental data, drawing tentative conclusions, testing them by further experimentation, to arrive eventually at a theory about what was going on; he regarded facts with disciplined aloofness, in other words, to let them speak for themselves and lead him to an explanation. Third and last, he was detached about his findings, which he left to stand or fall on their merits; when others assailed them, as they often did with more heat than politeness, he made no defense. "I have an extreme Aversion to Public Altercation on philosophic Points," he said, "and have never yet disputed with any one who thought fit to attack my Opinions."

These characteristics of his scientific thinking are all absent from his political thinking. There his range was narrow, and its focus was America. Developments around him that appeared to be unrelated to that focus did not greatly concern him. War and threats of war in Europe were for him no more than the roll of distant thunder unless Britain was likely to be involved, and then only because involvement might teach her to value her colonies as a source of strength. Her domestic politics left him equally unmoved. Grenville gave place to Rockingham, Rockingham to Chatham, Chatham to Grafton, Grafton to North; Franklin scarcely noticed. Neither was he much interested, surprisingly enough, in the upsurge of popular discontent that was so skillfully manipulated by John Wilkes. Wilkes's brother Israel was an old acquaintance, but John and his doing barely impinged on Franklin's consciousness. He occasionally pointed out that the establishment was oppressing Englishmen as much as Americans, yet all that really concerned him was colonial grievances. In 1768 a new cabinet post was created, that of secretary of state for the American colonies; and for the next seven years the policies of the two incumbents, Lord Hillsborough until 1772 and Lord Dartmouth thereafter, mattered more to Franklin than all the rest of British politics put together.

As a politician, secondly, he was not in the least objective. Far from letting the facts speak for themselves, he seized instinctively on those that suited his turn and ignored the rest. His political writings give the impression that conclusions were the starting point, not the end point, and that the supporting facts were ammunition. Consider for instance one of his most famous satires, written in the summer of 1773, "Rules by which a Great Empire May Be Reduced to a Small One." It catalogs, as its title implies, the kinds of measure that the British government had taken to antagonize the colonists, with never a hint that the colonists had done anything to antagonize the British government. After the Bostonians' recent provocation, this was selectivity with a vengeance. Satire always is. The purpose is not to show both sides of a question, or even argue a case, but to demolish an opponent's position by making it ludicrous. Nothing could be further from the scientific method.

As a politician, lastly, Franklin was to a degree contentious. He is traditionally portrayed as standing above the controversies raging around him, and in science to a large extent he did. But not in politics. Here he was the polemicist through and through; the last thing he could have professed was "an extreme Aversion to public Altercation." Whatever he construed as an attack on colonial rights, particularly in the London press, set his pen working. He was usually good-natured, and rarely indulged in the heavy-handed bludgeoning so common at the time; his weapon was sometimes the rapier, sometimes the dart, sometimes the reasoned argument. Under this equable surface, nevertheless, was the dedicated partisan, who did not stand above controversy but waded into it with zest. The word that his old friend David Hume applied to him was factious.

Controversy advanced his thinking. He was not a political philosopher in the sense that Jefferson was; he was too much of a pragmatist to be in love with first principles. If he had written the Declaration of Independence instead of making a few verbal changes in Jefferson's draft, the document would doubtless have contained as powerful a denunciation of King George, but would not have contained the thundering universals that echoed around the world. Franklin did not think in those terms. Contention jogged him into developing his position, a little here, little there, and he rarely defined it at any particular moment. His letters to Massachusetts, for example, contained almost no constitutional doctrine. All he had to offer was simple if ambiguous advice; stand firm in asserting your rights, but do not be provocative.

The Bostonians had no need of his help in concocting new doctrine, and ignored his advice to be unprovocative. At the beginning of 1773 Governor Hutchinson, alarmed at the rising tide of radicalism, delivered to the two houses of the General Court a closely reasoned statement, in the traditional vein, of the relationship between a colony and the mother country. The House and Council replied at length in writing; the replies elicited a second speech and second pair of answers. In this interchange the governor's opponents hammered out, on the anvil of his own logic, a concept of the constitution that was completely incompatible with his or with Whitehall's. They interpreted the colony's charter as the source of inalienable rights of self-government; neither Parliament nor the crown, by this line of reasoning, could claim any effective control over Massachusetts. Franklin accepted the reasoning without comment. He does not seem to have been much interested, and probably was not; political abstractions left him unmoved.

A factor that may perhaps have moulded his way of thinking was a negative one: he had had, unlike most of the Founding Fathers, no legal training. Does this help to explain a certain fluidity, at times even ambiguity, in his ideas? The lawyer is practiced in analyzing specific situations to fit them into a structure of rules, in marshaling precedents, in developing a case that is armored against an opponent's logic. Franklin did not work that way. He could develop a case, and an extremely effective one; but the bar at which he practiced was that of public opinion, which demands less rigor than the legal bar.

Although he was not by nature a rigorous political thinker, he did develop during these years several political theories. The best known had to do with the crown, which he considered for a time to be the institution that held the empire together. As the issue of Parliament's taxing power raised the larger issue of Parliamentary sovereignty, he was one of many Americans who came to deny that sovereignty; and he replaced it with the king. When colonists emigrated, he was insisting privately as early as 1769, they left the realm and were no longer subject to its legislature; the king governed them through the legislatures that he empowered them to establish, and each of these was on a constitutional par with that at Westminster. This idea had an enormous future but no present. In the nineteenth century it burgeoned into the dominion concept, and in the twentieth into the Commonwealth of Nations; in the 1770s it was impossible, because it ran counter to the whole course of British constitutional development since Stuart times. That development had resolved the struggle between crown and Parliament by fusing the two: the crown in Parliament—the constitutional trinity of the king, lords, and Commons—was the ultimate sovereign, and the crown outside Parliament, in other words the prerogative alone, operated in a jealously circumscribed sphere. The notion that George III might govern a colony in any way except through Parliament would have been as unthinkable to him as it was to the Lords and Commons. The trinity was indivisible, and Franklin was indulging in a dream.

The indulgence was brief. His experience with Massachusetts soon drove home the truth that the crown offered no more hope than Parliament of solving the imperial dilemma: when the House of Representatives sent him petitions to the throne for redress, and one after another they were brusquely rejected, he was forced to realize that the crown and its ministers, the ministry and Parliament, were parts of one whole; and that this monolithic government had no intention of retreating. Once the realization sank in, the role of mediator that he had tried to play lost all meaning. He had pled for restraint, had searched long and hard for common ground on which the questions at issue might be compromised. There was no such ground, but instead a chasm that he could not straddle.

At the end of 1772, while still trying to mediate, he began to play a quite different part. He injected himself as a participant in events by an action that he expected, or so he said, would help to bridge the chasm, but that widened it instead. The result within the next fourteen months was to destroy such political usefulness as he still had in London, and to expose him to the one great political humiliation of his life.

His personal involvement in late 1772 grew out of events years before. The story began in Massachusetts in the aftermath of the Townsend Acts. Those ill advised statutes revived the issue of taxation, dormant since repeal of the Stamp Act, and stung the Bostonians to fury. Royal officials went in fear of the mob; the newly created customs commissioners fled for their lives to a fort in the harbor; troops were called in. The violence in the air appalled conservatives, whose world seemed to be coming to an end. Among them were Thomas Hutchinson, then chief justice and lieutenant governor of the province, and Andrew Oliver, its secretary. Both men were in correspondence with an Englishman, Thomas Whately, who was a member of Parliament and the chief lieutenant of George Grenville, the former first minister and, as Franklin put it, "the Centre to which flow'd all the Correspondence inimical to America." In writing Whately, Hutchinson and Oliver bemoaned the times, viewed with alarm, and called for a strong line. What it should be they did not say. But they harped on the theme that something must be done, and soon.

The next scene was in August 1772. Grenville was dead; Whately was dead; Hutchinson was governor of Massachusetts and Oliver lieutenant governor. Franklin was talking with someone—we do not to this day know his identity—who told him that the government's American policy did not originate in London but was instigated by Americans. Franklin was incredulous. His informant, whom we have to call X, promised to prove his point, and returned a few days later with a packet of letters. They were originals in Hutchinson's and Oliver's hands, apparently random sample of their correspondence with Whately some years before. Franklin was convinced. He concluded, or so he said, that the letters provided the means of resolving the quarrel between Massachusetts and the mother country: they would convince his constituents that their grievances began at home, and so redirect their fury from Whitehall to their own officials; Whitehall would then have the opportunity to dissociate itself from those officials and try real conciliation. Franklin persuaded X to allow him to send the originals to Boston, on condition that they would not be published but shown only to a small group, and that X's role would remain an inviolable secret.

The next scene opened in the spring of 1773, when Franklin's letter and the enclosed packet of correspondence arrived in Boston. He was pledged to say nothing about how he had obtained the packet, he said, and to forbid its publication. But it arrived in a period of tension that he had not foreseen, and fell like a grenade into an open keg of powder; he might as well have forbidden the powder to explode. Hutchinson's popularity that spring was at the vanishing point. He had just terminated his constitutional debate with the House and Council by dissolving the General Court. No one had won the debate, but everyone had a heightened awareness of the gulf between the conservative and radical positions; and the governor, to his opponents, stood out as the king's henchman and the enemy of the province. They seized upon his letters, old as they were by now, as priceless ammunition; by late June the correspondence in pamphlet form was being disseminated through the colonies, while the House was petitioning the king to have Hutchinson and Oliver removed from office. Franklin's intention of resolving the quarrel with Britain had instead brought it to a new crisis.

The final act opened in London in August, when he received the petition and started it on its way to the throne. The town was by then buzzing with rumors about how the letters had been obtained, and above all by whom. The man most strongly suspected, at the time and since, was John Temple, a relative of the Grenvilles, the son-in-law of a prominent Boston merchant, Franklin's acquaintance of long standing, and a customs commissioner in Massachusetts—the only popular one—at the time the letters had been written. Hutchinson and Oliver had had nothing good to say of him, and he had subsequently lost his position. He returned to England soon after the death of Thomas Whately, whose brother William gave him access to the dead man's papers. Did access mean the chance to help himself? Temple insisted in a letter to the press that it did not, and that William Whately would bear him out. William, also in public, declined to do so, and implied that Temple could have taken any letters he chose. This altercation brought on a duel, and Whately received some slight wounds; as soon as he recovered, rumor had it, the two would fight again.

At that point, Christmas Day 1773, Franklin intervened. he published a brief announcement that he had been responsible for obtaining the letters, that they had never been in William Whately's possession, and hence that Temple could not have taken them from him. This revelation opened Franklin to his enemies, and they were soon in full cry. He had never believed that his part in the affair would long remain secret, or made much effort to keep it so. Now that it was public, however, he stood to lose almost everything that he cherished in his London world: friends, reputation, such little official favor as he still enjoyed, and with it his political usefulness. he must have realized, although he never said so, that his decision twelve months before to send the letters had backfired disastrously. That act had produced the petition, which left no room for compromise. The government could not reject it without making the quarrel worse, or grant it without abject surrender.

Was this outcome not predictable when he sent the letters? How could he have expected the hotheads in Boston, once he provided them with such ammunition against the governor, to become more charitable toward the mother country, or the mother country more charitable toward them? He said and went on saying that these were his expectations, but his words are hard to believe. He had been amply exposed to the paranoia endemic in Massachusetts, and to the legalistic inflexibility in Whitehall. If he thought that revealing the letters would bridge the gap between the two, instead of widening it, he was a political simpleton. And that is an epithet that no one has ever applied to him.

The motives he gave are not the only questionable aspect of what he did. His critics attacked him on ethical grounds, and with some reason. Hutchinson and Oliver, they argued, had been corresponding with Whately as private individuals; Franklin had accepted a stolen segment of this correspondence and sent it to Boston in full knowledge that it would destroy the writers' reputations. How could he use pilfered private letters in this way and still call himself a gentleman? (The word may have lost much of its force today, but had a great deal then.) He could not hide behind the old excuse of *salus populi suprema lex*, because to the unbiased eye nothing in the letters threatened the people's safety; he was a scoundrel and a thief. This was the line of attack. The fact that many of the attackers were scoundrels themselves has nothing to do with the question, which goes on nagging, of whether their charges were valid.

By the beginning of 1774 troubles were crowding in on Franklin. On 7 January William Whately instituted a suit against him in chancery, one of the purposes of which was to force him to break his promise by divulging under oath the identity of X. On the 24th the Walpole Company asked for and received his resignation, and thereby recognized the fact that he had become anathema to officialdom. For good reason. The previous September he had published his famous satires ridiculing British policy, and they were a goad to Whitehall. The ministry believed that he was tarred with the radicalism of his constituents in Massachusetts, which to some extent he was, and that he had provided them with their constitutional ideas, which he had not. But he had, by his own recent admission, incited them to attack the king's representatives. Probably nothing more was needed to provoke the ministerial bull, but further provocation came: on 20 January arrived the news of the Boston Tea Party. Franklin had no direct responsibility for that explosion, and had not foreseen the excitement that produced it; tea, nevertheless, played its part in ending his political career in London. He was the spokesman for the Bostonians, who by now were intolerable to Whitehall. First they had taken a stand, in the debate with Hutchinson, that was close to a declaration of independence. Next they had demanded the Governor's and Oliver's removal. Finally they had destroyed the property of the East India Company, and thereby in one stroke defied the law, the administration, and the mercantile giant in India House. This was insurrection.

The final scene was on 29 January when the Privy Council held a hearing in the Cockpit, in Whitehall Palace, on the petition from the Massachusetts House of Representatives. Franklin was summoned to attend as its agent. Hutchinson also had his agent, who engaged as counsel to look after his interests no less a person than Alexander Wedderburn, the king's solicitor general. Franklin insisted that no legal issue was involved, but perforce engaged counsel of his own. London was agog with anticipation of the coming performance, and the Cockpit was filled to capacity. Almost all the privy councilors were there, including Lord North and Lord Dartmouth. Among the spectators were Lord Shelburne's young protégé, Jeremy Bentham, and the famous dissenting minister and chemist Joseph Priestley, Franklin's friend of many years, who had been admitted to the gathering, to his surprise, under the wing of Edmund Burke.

Franklin's counsel opened the proceedings. The petitioners, he pointed out, were not asking that Hutchinson and Oliver be punished, but only that they be removed from office because they had lost the confidence of the people; the sole question was whether the king's interests would be better served by removing or retaining them, and that was a matter of policy, not law. Wedderburn then took the floor, and held it for more than an hour. He was one of the most formidable, as well as disagreeable, lawyer-orators in Britain; and scruples he had none. He quickly brushed aside the substance of the petition as the work of a few trouble-makers, of whom the foremost was the man standing there, the agent of the House. The rest of the speech was a personal indictment of Franklin, and in particular of his sending the Hutchinson letters. Wedderburn employed, according to one observer (probably Arthur Lee), "all the licensed scurillity of the bar, decked with the finest flowers of Billingsgate." The scurillity in fact went so far beyond what the bar licensed that the speech was laundered before it was later printed; some of the choicest bits, such as the charge that Franklin was a thief, were preserved only in listeners' notes. Most of the audience was delighted with Wedderburn, and laughed merrily at his quips; only Lord North, among the privy councilors, preserved a sense of decorum. But neither he nor anyone else attempted to recall the speaker from his victim to the business before the council, which was the petition and not the agent. Franklin stood silent through the diatribe. He had no chance to reply, and presumably would not have taken it if given. What had he to say to that gathering?

The next day he was curtly dismissed from his office as deputy postmaster general for North America. The government gave all possible publicity to his downfall in order to punish him and, through him, his constituents; the king's subsequent dismissal of the petition as "scandalous and seditious" was anticlimax. The question of whether Franklin deserved punishment is beside the point; so is the question of why the ministry chose such an egregious, almost childish, way to vent its pique. The point is the effect on Franklin. He was in his way a proud man, and the only safe way to bring down the proud is to squash them; if not squashed they become dangerous. Virgilian Rome could perform the Roman mission, *debellare superbos;* Whitehall could not. Franklin rarely cherished a grievance, but this one he neither forgot nor forgave. Four years later at Versailles, he had his revenge in another public scene, the French court's acceptance of the alliance with the United States. He wore, according to tradition, the same suit in which he had appeared at the Cockpit.

After his debacle he stayed in London for more than a year. In the final months before he went home he was involved in unofficial negotiations to try to stop the drift toward war, but they were abortive. Once Massachusetts had defied Whitehall, and Whitehall had responded with the Intolerable Acts, and the colonists had made the revolutionary answer of summoning the first Continental Congress, what was left to negotiate? Franklin's political usefulness ended in the Cockpit, and that scene is as good a point as any to close this survey of his British years.

If the American Revolution occurred first in men's minds, as John Adams said, when did it occur in Franklin's? On 29 January 1774 is much too simple an answer. He had no single moment of realization; that was not in his nature. He was a pragmatist, and it may be argued that no pragmatist turns easily to revolution. His bent is for working with the political structure as he finds it. He may patch it here and there, even refashion it in places; but he is loath to destroy it in the hope of building a better in its place. Only when long experience convinces him that the structure is too decrepit to be patched, too rigid to be in any way refashioned, does he despair of working within it. So with Franklin. His years in England were littered with hopes betrayed, and each betrayal had its effect. He welcomed the appointment of Hillsborough as the first colonial secretary in 1768, but soon detested the man. He greeted Dartmouth's succession to the office in 1772 as the dawn of a better era, but concluded within a year that the new minister was, in effect, a jellyfish. So it went. Slowly but surely he became disillusioned with first one part of the system and then another. The way in which Parliament legislated for the colonies persuaded him, sooner than many Americans, that its authority was illegitimate; but he did not reject royal sovereignty until further experience taught him that the king was deaf to American grievances. Through one disappointment after another he became convinced that the structure of British government and British thinking could not be changed.

He was brought to that point by a process in the heart as well as the head. As late as 1773 he said that he was considered in England too much of an American, and in America too much of an Englishman; and this duality was what made him valuable on both sides of the Atlantic as long as he had some hope of mediating the quarrel. Just after the scene at the Cockpit he wrote that he appeared to be too much of an American. When the government pillored him for being just that, and fanning sedition in Boston, it superimposed on all his past disillusionment a sense of personal outrage; and when it went on to punish his constituents he rapidly ceased to be an Englishman. His long delay in sailing for home shows that he continued to love the world of London; on his last day before departure he was in tears. Whether they were for losing that world, or for the war that he knew was impending, they were a sign of his pain in choosing between his two countries. In fact, however, he had no choice; his whole past life had made it for him.

Economic Concerns

Benjamin Franklin's Economic Thought: A Twentieth Century Appraisal

Tracy Mott and George W. Zinke*

Benjamin Franklin has been lionized in the popular mind and examined and appreciated by scholars for his many contributions to politics, letters, political history, and science.[1] His historical role as an economist has generally found him credited as such but placed in a ranking below the significant developers of the discipline. Those who know his work know of his contributions to the history of economic thought mainly through his influence on and mutual interaction with the physiocratic school and with Adam Smith. They also rightly acknowledge the wisdom and worth of Franklin's pamphlets and letters on economic matters. And, indeed, this is the reason generally given by those who know him for Franklin's status as a contributor to the historical development of economics but not as a giant of that history: his attention to economics focused itself mostly on economic theory as a guide to practical policy matters.

This is not to say, however, that Franklin did not contribute to the development of economic theory as theory. In fact, Karl Marx praised Franklin's genius in the area of pure theory. Franklin, though, did not write a systematic treatise on "the cause of the wealth of nations" or on "the principles of political economy." His economic ideas and theoretical insights are rather to be found in tracts on specific issues with an eye to guiding practical policy. As Marx noted, "Franklin's analysis of exchange-value had no direct influence on the general couse of the science, because he dealt only with special problems of political economy for definite practical purposes."[2]

According to this view then, the key to Franklin's economic thought is to be found in Carl L. Becker's biographical sketch, as he writes that:

> Science was after all the one mistress to whom he gave himself without reserve and served neither from duty nor for any practical purpose. Nature alone met him on equal terms, with a disinterestedness matching his, . . . in dealing with nature he could be, . . . entirely sincere, pacific, objective, rational. . . .[3]

*This essay was written especially for this collection and published here for the first time.

Political economy he took to be the stately art of giving reasoned support to arguments for public policy making. This is the domain in which persons interact in a process that most nearly resembles a game—one not to be taken lightly and to be played with finesse. Becker can imagine Franklin saying,

> This is an interesting, alas even a necessary, game; and we are playing it well, according to all the rules; but men being what they are it is perhaps best not to inquire too curiously what its ultimate significance may be?[4]

Yet despite, or perhaps even because of, this practical orientation, we believe that Franklin's work is extremely relevant to the history of economic theory and practice both in his own day and in ours. Franklin's vision of and contributions to the political economy of his day belongs to a category within which we also place his contemporaries and, indeed, colleagues and friends Adam Smith and David Hume. We feel that this attitude toward our discipline was largely lost to economics until the advent of the work of John Maynard Keynes in our own century. We do not mean that Franklin and the others were simply anticipating "Keynesian economics" or "the economics of Keynes,"[5] or that this particular spirit represents all that is good and worthwhile in economics. We do mean, however, that there was a similar attitude among these men toward how one is to approach economics and to apply its ideas, and we call this attitude "pragmatic classicalism." Let us begin by examining the salient characteristics of Franklin's economic thought to set the stage for our particular appraisal.[6]

FRANKLIN'S RELATION TO HIS CONTEMPORARIES

In an unfortunately typical way, historian Massimo Salvadori wrote in 1963: "Concerning economics on the theoretical level, he [Franklin] can be describe as a moderate physiocrat."[7] Well, what's in name, provided that it is not taken to mean that he borrowed his idea of the primacy of agriculture (over manufacturing as a source of riches) from the French physiocrats. He was indeed personally well acquainted with them. Yet in his tract on population published in 1751—sixteen years before he met with leading physiocrats—he expressed a conviction that economic development must proceed from agriculture as its foundation.[8] Then, in the very opening of his 1766 essay "On the Price of Corn," a not-so-imaginatively created character declares, "I Am one of that class of people that feeds you all and at present is abus'd by you all; in short I am a *Farmer*."[9]

This essay came to the attention of the Physiocrat Pierre Dupont (then still dreaming of founding a pastoral estate in North America), and he had the essay translated and published in *Ephêmérides du Citoyen*, of which he was the editor. Franklin, then, had his thought firmly on the ground quite before his contracts with the French philosophers, who seemed to see value growing out of the soil analytically, if not actually. In a 1747 tract, Franklin pointedly placed himself in the ranks of "we . . . the middling People, the Farmers, Shopkeepers and Tradesmen. . . ."[10] Some writers have indeed called him "not an authentic agrarian," or an "urban agrarian,"[11] or something like that.

The physiocratic vision of the economy was that agriculture is the only source of a "net product." Manufacturing consisted merely of an alteration but not a creation of value, which only nature could accomplish. Franklin's attraction to the physiocratic school lay mainly in his agreement with their notion that the removal of restraints on agricultural production in the form of mercantilistic imposts and tariffs was the way to increase the wealth of nations in conformity with the laws of nature:

> [T]here seem to be but three Ways for a nation to acquire Wealth. The first if by *War* as the Romans did in plundering their conquered Neighbours. This is *Robbery*. The second by *Commerce* which is generally *Cheating*. The third by *Agriculture* the only *honest Way;* wherein Man receives a real Increase of the Seed thrown into the Ground, in a kind of continual Miracle wrought by the Hand of God in his Favour, as a Reward for his innocent Life, and virtuous Industry.[12]

Franklin also was in harmony with the physiocrats in advocating laissez-faire as the proper economic policy conforming to the natural order. Commerce as a way to acquire wealth is "generally *Cheating*" because if exchanges involve honest trades of value for equal value, one is not increasing one's wealth through exchange but merely altering its form. Agriculture again is the only way to obtain an honest increase from the hand of God in the miracle of nature. Free trade, then, without government mercantile restrictions designed to secure an advantage for one party, is the only way to let nature's riches unfold themselves for humankind.

On numerous occasions in his writings Franklin was happy to repeat the classical antimercantilist arguments, as for example:

> Suppose a country, X, with three manufacturers, as *cloth, silk*, and *iron*, supplying three other countries, A, B, and C, but is desirous of increasing the Vent, and raising the price of cloth in favor of her own clothiers.
>
> In order to do this, she forbids the importation of foreign cloth from A.
>
> A in return, forbids silk from X. Then the silk-workers complain of a decay of trade.
>
> And X, to content them, forbids silks from B.
>
> Then the iron workers complain of decay. And X forbids the importation of iron from C.
>
> C, in return, forbids cloth from X.
>
> What is got by all these prohibitions?
>
> *Answer:* All four find their common stock of the enjoyments and convenience of life diminished.[13]

Franklin's thoughts along these lines were not limited to his own writings. Jacob Viner noted in his classic *Studies in the Theory of International Trade* Franklin's influence on another free-trader, George Whatley. Concerning Whatley's book, *Principles of Trade,* Viner pointed out, "Benjamin Franklin helped in the preparation of this book, and the notes, which are generally superior to the text, have especially been attributed to him."[14]

Franklin's influence on perhaps the most famous free-trader—Adam Smith—is well known. Franklin was in London in 1773 when Smith arrived with a manuscript of the *Wealth of Nations,* which would be published three years later. In 1775 Franklin left in grief with Parliament's and the King's thick-headedness. In the meantime, between 1773 and 1775 the two men met and conversed. Smith is known always to have been open to suggestions and in their light occasionally making alterations and additions in the manuscript. He valued Franklin's views in general but in particular those on the state of affairs of the "North American Colonies." In fact, it is chapter 7 of book 4, "Of Colonies," that contains the greatest number of revisions made between 1773 and 1776. Here there is a section referring to high wages in America which some writers think was written by Benjamin Franklin. In any event, one cannot fail to recognize the spirit of Franklin in numerous passages.[15]

But having noted Franklin's vigorous support of free trade, we then find him writing in a private letter to a friend in Connecticut who had solicited his opinion of a five percent import duty newly imposed by that colony on its neighbor colonies that he generally disparages this sort of thing. "Yet, if you can make some of the Goods, heretofore imported, among yourselves, the advanc'd price of five per cent may encourage your own Manufacture, and in time make the Importation of such Articles unnecessary, which will be an Advantage."[16]

Today we would categorize this as "import substitution," often advocated for less-developed economies in our world. In Franklin's world, British North America was a less-developed economy, albeit developing at an astonishing rate. If we excuse Franklin on these grounds, we may drop any charges of onsetting protectionism, even though a number of analogous remarks should be found in his works. After all, he did introduce free trade resolutions in the Continental Congress and sign with Friedrich the Great of Prussia a treaty which contained a free trade clause.

We must note that Franklin was consistent in his advocacy of laissez-faire policy to the poor as well as to the rich. He argued vehemently against the continuation and extension of the Elizabethan Poor Laws in both England and North America. Some have identified him as anticipating Malthus's population principle by which aid for the poor was considered useless due to the tendency for population to equal the subsistence in wages made available. The evidence, however, more clearly warrants acknowledging Franklin's belief that poor relief encouraged idleness and made the poor dependent and weak rather than able and self-supporting.[17]

FRANKLIN ON VALUE, MONEY, AND LAND

Marx's appraisal of Franklin's economic writings begins as follows:

> It is a man of the New World—where bourgeois relations of production imported together with their representatives sprouted rapidly in a soil in which the superabundance of humus made up for the lack of historical tradition—who for the first time deliberately and clearly (so clearly to be almost trite) reduces exchange-value to labour-time. This man was *Benjamin Franklin* . . . [italics in original].[18]

Marx sees Franklin as having made a significant advance upon William Petty, the father of the "classical" economists, in his understanding of the labor theory of value:

> The celebrated Franklin, one of the first economists, . . . who saw through the nature of value, says: "Trade in general being nothing else but the exchange of labour for labour, the value of all things is . . . most justly measured by labour." . . . Franklin is unconscious that by estimating the value of everything in labour, he makes abstraction from any differences in the sorts of labour exchanged, and thus reduces them all to equal human labour. But . . . he says it (and always acts on this *Einfühlung*). He speaks first of "*the one* labour," then of "*the other* labour," and finally of "*labour*" without further qualification as the substance of the value of everything.[19]

The reference is to Franklin's 1729 tract, "A Modest Enquiry into the Nature and Necessity of a Paper Currency." Franklin began his statement of the labor theory by simply paraphrasing Petty as follows:

> . . . Suppose one Man employed to raise Corn, while another is digging and refining Silver; at the Year's End, or at any other Period of Time, the compleat produce of Corn, and that of Silver are, the natural Price of each other; and if one be twenty Bushels, and the other twenty Ounces, then an Ounce of that Silver is worth *the Labour* of raising a Bushel of that Corn.[20]

Franklin then continued to follow Petty by stating that if by reason of improved mining technology 40 ounces of silver are extracted and refined are extracted and refined "and the same labour is still required to raise Twenty Bushels of Corn, then Two Ounces of Silver will be worth no more than the same Labour of raising One Bushel of Corn, and that Bushel of Corn will be as cheap at Two Ounces, as it was before at one; *caeteris paribus*."[21]

Franklin's penchant for practicality may have indeed detracted from his direct influence on the historical development of economic doctrine and perhaps explains his "unconsciousness" that he had stumbled upon the concept of *abstract universal labor* as the proper measure of value in the passage Marx cited. Yet this emphasis on the practical may also have enabled Franklin to achieve valuable insights into economic questions which other classical economists, such as David Ricardo, missed due to an overzealous concern for pure principles of economic theory.

Franklin's political economy was motivated throughout by a vision of the good society to which sound economic policy should lead. This vision was called "Happy Mediocrity," which did not mean in the eighteenth century what it would be taken to mean today.[22] Rather, it signified the strengthening of the middle class and of a society without extremes of conduct and of wealth or poverty.

As early as the tract on "Paper Currency," Franklin included himself among those suffering at the time from low wages and depressed farm prices and severely burdened by high levels of debt, aggravated by a shortage of cash money.[23] He pressed forward a colonial demand for the issuance of paper currency to grease the wheels of trade. John Kenneth Galbraith has remarked that the printer's advocacy of paper money had "an immensely practical touch. He printed money for the colonial governments on his own printing press."[24]

Franklin's argument, however, stands on theoretical grounds that today we would recognize as "Keynesian":

> . . . if Money grows scarce in a Country it becomes more difficult for People to make punctual Payments of what they borrow, Money being hard to be raised; likewise Trade being discouraged and Business impeded for want of a Currency, abundance of People must be in declining Circumstances, and by these Means Security is more precarious than where Money is plenty. On such Accounts it is no wonder if People ask for a greater interest for their Money. . . . Thus, we always see, that where money is scarce, Interest is high, and low where it is plenty.[25]

Keynes claimed this to be the chief insight of the mercantilist school of economic thought, though he credits John Locke as the first to state the principle in theoretical terms that the quantity of money would affect the rate of interest.[26] Franklin reached this position from his observations of the economic distress caused by the chronic net outflow of specie from the colonies to Britain.

Franklin's second significant tract on money, "Remarks and Facts Concerning American Paper Money," (1767)[27] is a scathing refutation of Parliament's "Report of Trade" (1764). This was an attempt to rationalize Parliament's outright forbidding the colonies to issue more paper money. This tract on "American Paper Money" expresses many insights into the nature and necessity of adequate purchasing power as a means ultimately to reach the good society of Happy Mediocrity. Franklin wrote,

> . . . when [in Pennsylvania] in 1723, Paper Money was first made there, [it] gave new Life to Business, [and] promoted greatly the Settlement of new Lands, by lending small Sums to Beginners on easy Interest, to be repaid by Installments. . . . Pay is now become so indifferent [low] in

> New England, at least in some of its Provinces, through the Want of Currency, that the Trade thither is at present under great Discouragement. . . .Bills were in a short time gather'd up and hoarded, it being a very tempting Advantage to have Money bearing Interest, and the Principal . . . ready for Bargains that may offer, which Money out on Mortgage is not.[28]

The problems of the inadequacy and maldistribution of credit that might be remedied by the introduction of colonial paper money were well known at the time to be important factors in the periods of commercial distress in pre-Revolutionary America. In particular, chronic indebtedness of Tidewater planters to Scottish factors and the chronic net outflow of specie to Britain from the colonies, aggravated by various policies favoring British over colonial merchants (and offset at times by colonial reactions such as dumping East India Co. tea into Boston harbor), have been noted as the common thread uniting the rebellion against Great Britain. Both North and South and rich and poor could agree on the desirability of establishing the colonies' own right to decide what was legal tender and what commercial policies, especially regarding the importation of goods and the enforcement of credit agreements, ought to be followed.[29]

The death-blow to the mercantilist argument had supposedly been dealt in 1752 by Franklin's friend Hume in his development of the specie-flow mechanism coupled with the quantity theory of money: "It is of no manner of consequence, with regard to the domestic happiness of a state, whether money be in a greater or less quantity."[30] This follows from the argument that the quantity of money determines sooner or later only the overall level of prices and none of the "real" economic magnitudes, such as output, employment, or relative exchange-rations among goods or labor.

Keynes pointed out, however, that Hume "was still enough of a mercantilist" to realize that even according to quantity-theory reasoning an inflow or increase of money would cause prices to be rising and that rising prices are a stimulus to production and trade.[31] Franklin realized this as well. Though he embraced the classical position of free trade against mercantilist protectionism, he anticipated Keynes in realizing that plentiful money caused low interest and increased borrowing, and thus high levels of production and demand for goods and services.

Franklin's argument was very much along the lines of Hume's, though of course with a different end in mind—to argue in favor of *paying attention* to the quantity of money rather than ignoring it, as Hume had urged. For Franklin actually presented a kind of quantity-theory argument in order to fend off criticism of wanting to cheapen the value of currency, making the point which Hume had conceded, that rising prices are good for trade. This in fact is the place where Franklin is led to making his insights about value which Marx praised. Franklin wanted to show that the real value of commodities is determined by the labor it took to make them, so that a rise of commodities in money-value cannot affect their real value but will serve to stimulate more production of them, resulting in more commerce and employment for masters and workers.[32]

Franklin also pointed out those who he felt were likely to oppose paper currency. They would be men who already "are Possessors of large Sums of Money, and are disposed to purchase Land. . . ," for such will favor the high rates of interest they are presently earning on lending out their money and the low price of land which they can thus purchase more easily.[33] One can almost hear Keynes calling for "the euthanasia of the rentier."

Franklin then agreed with Hume that the value of money was determined by the quantity of money relative to the work it had to do. Nevertheless, he saw in this not a reason to be indifferent toward the availability of money but rather a reason not to be afraid of having an excess of money. In other words, Franklin took the quantity theory of money as an argument for ignoring the *quantitative* aspect of the value of money in favor of its *qualitative aspect*.

Thus, his concern with money did not represent a regression to mercantilist ideas but rather an awareness that merchants, manufacturers, farmers, and laborers had to have the means of carrying on the business of the economy[7]. This type of thinking belongs properly to the classical school of political economy with its concern for freeing the progressive classes of society to bring about economic growth.

The classical economists, and most forcefully Adam Smith, sought to replace the mercantilist doctrines of state policies designed to favor the nation's merchants against foreign, even colonial competition, by the policy of laissez-faire. Smith argued that it was the widening of the market (as opposed to the mercantilist restriction of the market) that would increase the division of labor and so the productivity of labor and the wealth of the nation. Competition among merchants and manufacturers rather than governmental protection would make economic growth and welfare follow as if guided by an "Invisible Hand" and would prevent the business classes, "who have generally an interest to deceive and even to oppress the public. . . ," from being able to do so.[34]

After the 1729 "Paper Currency" tract we see an increasingly sophisticated criticism of British export-policy in Franklin's writing and correspondence. In the drive for export surpluses, England is represented as having gone in for industrialization at forced draught, with the inevitable results of overcrowded new towns and bad working condition. Franklin wrote, "Manufactures are founded in poverty. It is the multitude of poor without land in a country, and who must work for others at low wages or starve, that enables undertakers to carry on a manufacture, and afford it cheap enough to prevent the importation of the same kind from abroad, and to bear the expence of its own exportation. But,"he continued in a significant sentence, "no man who can have a piece of land of his own, sufficient by his labour to subsist his family in plenty, is poor enough to be a manufacturer and work for a master."[35]

Franklin himself became involved in a petition for a grant to settle a very extensive land area containing a part of Virginia to the south of the Ohio River and extending several degrees of longitude westward from the western ridge of the Appalachian Mountains. The plan, although cast in the language of traditional British land grants to such persons as William Penn, was unique in that it contemplated giving access to ordinary small-scale farmers. Even more significant than opening such access was that this was to be facilitated by what Franklin had mentioned favorably before: "lending small Sums to Beginners on easy Interest, to be repaid by Installments. . . ."[36]

The petition was denied by the Lords' Commissioners for Trade and Plantations on the grounds that, among other things, these lands included "immense tracts of unpeopled desart." The petitioners' response contained the following passage:

> . . . we answer, we shall, we are persuaded, satisfactorily prove, that in the middle colonies, *viz*, New Jersey, Pennsylvania, Maryland, and Virginia, there is hardly any *vacant land*, except such as is monopolized by great landholders, for the purpose of selling at *high prices;* that the poor people of these colonies, with large families cannot pay these prices; that some have *already* settled upon the Ohio; that we do not wish for, and shall not encourage one single family of his Majesty's *European subjects* to *settle* there, (and this we have no objection to be prevented from doing,) but shall *wholly* rely on the voluntary superflux of the inhabitants of the middle colonies for settling and cultivating the lands in question.[37]

Here, it is perhaps worthwhile to tie Franklin's practical concerns once more to the progress and problems of classical economic theory. Classical political economy in its understanding of the accumulation of wealth attendant upon the freeing-up of capital to seek profits driven by competition, thus continually dividing labor and increasing its productivity, ran into the following logical conundrum: The growth of the wealth of nations was seen essentially by the classicals to be an unfolding of the bounty which nature held waiting for us and which heretofore had been left dormant by the feudal and mercantile barriers to the releasing of nature's bounty. Yet it was recognized that what "nature giveth, nature eventually taketh away," that is to say, there are *natural* limits to nature's riches. Specifically, the classical school generally held in one form or another that the process of capital accumulation would lead to the "Stationary State"—a time when no further economic growth could take place.

The argument basically was that the growth in population following upon the growth in social wealth would lead to decreasing fertility per unit of land as the scale of cultivation was increased to feed the new numbers. Eventually the addition to product of cultivating one more acre of land would be just sufficient to feed the newly grown workers hired to tend it.

Thus there would remain no promise of profits to spur more growth, and the logical development of this position by the classical school was what caused economics to be called "the dismal science."[38]

Franklin again observed that no one who had sufficient land would work as an industrial laborer. Without more land brought into cultivation, however, the progress of society would become checked eventually by the high cost of food to feed the workers as the fertility of land diminished rapidly with the increased intensive cultivation of what land lay available. We can therefore appreciate the hope of the British classical economists that American would be the source of fertile tracts to delay the approach of the stationary state by many generations.

The hope of America to men like Smith and Franklin lay in its potential as a place where the growth of freedom and material riches following from the spread of laissez-faire need not lead to "dark, Satanic mills." Instead, there would develop in America a society of independent farmers and craftsmen, owning their own land and their own tools, trading with each other as free men at exchange-ratios determined by the labor embodied in their products, and increasing the peace and prosperity of the bountiful land.[39]

The importance of the availability of land in determining the cost of food (and thus the labor-value or cost of labor's wages) also explains the point of another of Franklin's often-cited and frequently misunderstood passages from a letter to Lord Kames:

> Food is *always* necessary to *all*, and much the greatest Part of the Labour of Mankind is employed in raising Provisions for the Mouth. Is not this kind of Labour therefore the fittest to be the Standard by which to measure the Values of all other Labour, and consequently of all other Things whose Value depends on the Labour of making or procuring them? May not even Gold and Silver be thus valued.[40]

The idea that agricultural labor represents the standard measure of labor-value was suggested as well by Smith, who was criticized consequently by Ricardo. The controversy can be summarized as follows: According to the labor theory of value, the value of the contribution of labor itself is determined by the labor-value of the commodities making up the bundle purchased by labor's wage. If these commodities are the basket of food considered sufficient for a laborer's subsistence under current historical and cultural standards, as according to classical economic doctrine, then the productivity of agricultural labor will determine the value in labor-time of these commodities. Franklin's point that agricultural labor is the standard by which we should measure the value of all commodities, even gold and silver, means, then, that since the purchasing power of a commodity is measured by how much labor this commodity can buy, the value of a commodity should be determined by the labor-value of the (agricultural) commodities making up the basket purchaseable by labor's wages.

eynes pointed out the problem with such "long-run equilibrium" ar-
its in the following oft-quoted passage:

'he] *long-run* is a misleading guide to current affairs. *In the long run* e are all dead. Economists set themselves too easy, too useless a task if tempestuous seasons they can only tell us that when the storm is long ast the ocean is flat again.[43]

ranklin's policies favoring cheap money and cheap land, then, might own to be irrelevant in long-run equilibrium. If, however, one re- ers that by the time such an equilibrium might be reached, other ions will surely have changed, one will see with Keynes that "it is transition [towards equilibrium] that we actually have our being."[44] ermore, Franklin, like Smith, was primarily concerned with eco- development, which by definition means continual transition. The ense that equilibrium can be given in this context is that of an equi- m path of growth, which could involve such "Keynesian," "demand- concerns, rather than an equilibrium state of rest.

Ve believe that classic example of such a position in Franklin's work following: In arguing against the Poor Laws, he held, along with , that the solution to poverty lay in having a prosperous economy to le high levels of employment and rising wages. Franklin then went on that in fact all the revenue expended in the economy over a period of went to wages.[45] This cannot be accurate reasoning because in any pe- hat part of society's spending that represents expenditures on capital and on consumption goods for the non-wage earning members of so- will accrue to profits and rent rather than to wages.

Nevertheless, there is a way in which these capital and luxury con- tion expenditures are helpful to labor in that they furnish higher lev- employment the higher they are. This follows from their contribution gregate demand for employment to produce the capital and luxury .[46]

Franklin's argument that luxury consumption benefits the poor does tell an important truth. Its significance in the history of economic doc- is that only a few economists, such as Bernard de Mandeville and ius, saw this point, while the dominant view of the classical school, as for example in Ricardo, was that luxury consumption was an unpro- ve expenditure that represented a drag on the capital accumulation ss. And, as Keynes wrote, "Ricardo conquered England as completely e Holy Inquisition conquered Spain."[47] Expenditure on luxuries was as taking spending away from economic growth. If, indeed, there no problem of aggregate demand to increase trade and employment, vould be true. The technically brilliant Ricardo failed to see the prob- however, the insightful and practical Franklin did not miss this point.

Ricardo disliked this idea of "labor-commanded" bor-value and so attacked Smith, insisting on "labor-e labor-time necessary to produce a commodity, as th value.[41] Labor-embodied will equal labor-commanded value going to profits and rent as a deduction from tl bodied in a commodity and thus included in the lab purchasing a commodity. If we identify labor-comma the wage paid to labor, which is less than the full val as Smith agreed, we fall into Smith's and Franklin's e

This was to argue that a change in agricultural through its effect on wage, cause all prices to move i by the amount of the change in wages. Ricardo succe that in this case prices overall would not change bec labor-embodied in commodities had only changed i Still, a change in the labor-value of agricultural prod *share* of subsistence-goods in the national product an growth rate of the economy and its ability to produce cessities. Though Smith and Franklin were technica mains a worthwhile point about the importance of agr to the wealth of the economy in their analysis.

FRANKLIN'S APPRECIATION OF "DEMAND-S

The spirit of Franklin's economic thinking on the within the attitude towards economic matters that with the classical school of political economy. This att dogma as advocacy of laissez-faire in policy, oppositio adherence to the labor theory of value, all of which w

We see Franklin deviating from at least one d thought, however, in his apparent appreciation of the gate demand in determining the level of output and classicals, except for Thomas Malthus, accepted uncri the notion that "supply creates its own demand." We awareness of the need to consider demand conditio supply to his view of political economy as a guide to ec or betterment, rather than as a means to establish the the equilibrium of the economy as a balance of forces.

Franklin's previously discussed arguments concer of cheap money, cheap land, well-distributed purch substitution, and the like all exhibit these sorts of "K Adherents to classical economics, old and new, claim t in these policies. Economists overly concerned with ar ciples to the conclusions to be found in the equilibr against cheap money and import-substitution policies demonstrate the errors in Franklin's position.

CONCLUSIONS: FRANKLIN AS A "PRAGMATIC CLASSICAL"

Since Franklin's day the economist has become much more of a technician and economics much more unwilling to deal with the moral question of what society should be in favor of the technical question of how society might achieve whatever ends it decides to desire. Franklin's vision of "Happy Mediocrity" and his concern for the practical effects of economic policy would therefore be something that a modern economist might not disagree with but might feel awkward or "unprofessional" about advocating. To be sure, modern economists are glad to talk about the practical consequences of various policies, but rarely with open consciousness of what type of society or of what type of individual their policies are designed to create.

Franklin and his contemporaries, though, were less shy about presenting their vision of the good society. They were generally advocates of laissez-faire, of course, but more out of a positive belief in the freedom and dignity and productivenes of the individual rather than from not knowing what else to advocate, as we fear is often the case today. This is why we believe that in matters of economic policy the legitimate heirs today of Franklin's ideas and goals are to be found in the populist, interventionist, Keynesian tradition rather than with the free-marketers who have become conservative and anti-egalitarian in their latest incarnations.

Franklin's vision of the good society to be brought forth in colonial America might be considered utopian. However, the strong concern with practical matters in Franklin's economics, as indeed in Franklin's scientific and diplomatic work, gives us rather practical policies to fulfill the vision of a good society growing naturally from the opportunities presented.

Franklin saw economic theory as a tool to show us how to make life better. Recall, for instance, Marx's comments on Franklin's unconsciousness regarding his insights into the determination of value because of limiting his concern to practical matters. Inexcusable perhaps in a German Hegelian like Marx, but appropriate for a North American of British descent.

And what were Franklin's practical economic policies to make things better? For one thing, he helped alleviate the chronic shortage of money in the colonies and thus relieved their debt and encouraged economic growth. Moreover, opening up the West relieved the crowding on the eastern seaboard and forced down the high cost of living that had prevented economic development. Together these policies constituted a vision of an economy in which there is access on easy terms to capital and land so that the conditions of the distribution of income might furnish no barrier to a high rate of growth.

The advocates of policies and aims such as these on down to our own time have not been either the conservative proponents of the status quo or of policies favoring inequality in the distribution of income on the grounds that the saving of the rich is good for the economy, nor have they been the revolutionaries crying that there is no hope to be had from any of these reforms within capitalism. Rather, these have been traditionally the kind of policies favored by liberal or populist reformers—those who have advocated such measures as cheap money and cheap land, progressive taxation, and agricultural cooperatives.

It is true that during the era of the New Deal Franklin's name was invoked by some opposing Roosevelt's program and that many conservative economists today sport Adam Smith neckties, drawing upon the letter, though not the spirit of Smith's economics. The common ground between their views and Franklin's and Smith's comes in that both are opposed to governmental policies creating a *rent,* that is, an income accruing merely due to a scarcity caused by a monopolization of some commodity. A difference arises where there is rent created due to natural or social conditions apart from direct governmental action. The modern conservatives see this always and everywhere either following in some circuitous manner from government intervention or else a necessary spur to growth by attracting further investment and competition or by allocating inevitably scarce resources to their most efficient uses.

The "pragmatic classicalism" of Franklin, however, realized, as Keynes was to realize in our own century, that the monopoly on land and on money-capital *given by mere ownership* was something that governmental policy must always and everywhere keep from supporting by its own actions and if necessary, overcome. This meant in Franklin's day removing the British monopoly on the provision of legal tender at the expense of the colonies and removing restrictions on Western settlement. It has meant in our day progressive taxation, government credit programs for farmers and homeowners, and the use of monetary and fiscal policy to stimulate economic growth: the modern private enterprise cum positive-state intervention economy which we know today in the North Atlantic Community.

Would Benjamin Franklin have approved of the New Deal? Professor Dudley Dillard in his *Economcic Development of the North Atlantic Community* offers potent circumstantial evidence:

> Whatever may have been the motives, ideas, and interests of the makers of the Constitution, their essential contribution to the economic development of the United States was a document which increased the power in the hands of the federal government.[48]

Dillard then reminds us that the economy of the United States could not have evolved in the manner it did without the elimination of interstate hinderances to trade, without the consequent emergence of the world's largest domestic market, without a uniform national currency, or without authorization for the federal government to levy and collect taxes as well as to adopt fiscal policies of public debt management. Dillard concludes that "the Constitution created the type of strong national State required for the economic development of the American economy,"[49]

The classical concern for political economy as mainly a theory of economic development called for whatever policies freed the progressive elements in society to bring about the growth of "the wealth of nations." The principle of laissez-faire was embraced because it was seen to conform to natural liberty and to channel the energies of the budding capitalists by enforcing competition to spur them on. A positive role for the state was associated in the minds of the classical school with the oppressive and unwise mercantilist doctrines. To the extent that laissez-faire represented a means to an end, rather than the end itself, a "pragmatic classical" like Franklin, or like Keynes, could advocate positive government policy, *if it actually supported liberty and a system of liberty*.

Notes

1. Professor Mott claims to be a direct descendant of Benjamin Franklin's brother John but feels that this has given him no privileged insight.

2. Karl Marx, *A Contribution to the Critique of Political Economy* (New York: International Publishers, 1970), 57.

3. Carl L. Becker, *Benjamin Franklin* (Ithaca, N.Y.: Cornell University Press, 1946), 36.

4. Becker, *Franklin*, 36.

5. For the difference between these see Axel Leijonhufvud, *On Keynesian Economics and the Economics of Keynes* (New York, 1968).

6. The best-known previous studies of Franklin's economic theories are Paul W. Conner, *Poor Richards' Politicks* (New York: Oxford University Press, 1965); W. A. Wetzel, *Benjamin Franklin as an Economist* (Baltimore: Johns Hopkins Press, 1985); and Lewis J. Carey, *Franklin's Economic Views* (Garden City, N.Y.: Doubleday, 1928). We wish to acknowledge the assistance of these works.

7. Massimo Salvadori, in *The American Economic System*, ed. Salvadori (Indianapolis: Bobbs-Merrill, 1963), 4.

8. Benjamin Franklin, "Observations Concerning the Increase of Mankind" (1751), in *The Papers of Benjamin Franklin*, vol. 4, ed. Leonard W. Labaree et al. (New Haven: Yale University Press, 1959–) 225–34 (hereafter, *Papers*).

9. Franklin, "On the Price of Corn" (1766), *Papers* 13:512.

10. Franklin, "Plain Truth" (1747), *Papers* 3:201.

11. See, for example, Virgil Glenn Wilhite, "Benjamin Franklin: Urban Agrarian," in *Founders of American Economic Thought and Policy* (New York, Bookman Associates, 1958), 283–319.

12. Franklin, "Positions to be Examined"(1769), *Papers*, 16:109.

13. Franklin, "Wail of a Protected Manufacturer," in *The Writings of Benjamin Franklin*, vol. 1, ed. Albert Henry Smyth (New York: Macmillan, 1906), 149–50.

14. Jacob Viner, *Studies in the Theory of International Trade* (New York, Harper & Bros., 1937), 85–86, n. 35.

15. See, for example, Wetzel, *Franklin as Economist*, 51–53.

16. Franklin, "To Jared Eliot" (1747), *Papers*, 3:151.

17. See Howell V. Williams, "Early American Political Economists and the Poor Law," Ph.D. dissertation, University of Chicago, 1942, 21–83.

18. Marx, *Critique of Political Economy*, 55

19. Marx, *Capital*, vol. 1 (New York: International Publishers, 1967), 51, n. 1.

20. Franklin, "A Modest Enquiry into the Nature and Necessity of a Paper Currency" (1729), Papers 1:149.

21. *Papers* 1:49.

22. Conner, *Poor Richard's Politicks*, p 36, discusses this point, mentioning that the term "happy mediocrity" as used by Franklin is best understood as meaning "quite comfortable."

23. Franklin, "Paper Currency," *Papers* 1:139–57.

24. John Kenneth Galbraith, *The Age of Uncertainty* (Boston: Houghton Mifflin, 1977), 180.

25. Franklin, "Paper Currency," *Papers* 1:154.

26. John Maynard Keynes, *The General Theory of Employment, Interest, and Money* (New York: Harcourt, Brace, Jovanovich, 1964), 333–53.

27. Franklin, "Remarks and Facts Concerning American Paper Money" (1767), *Papers* 14:76–87.

28. *Papers* 12:79–86.

29. See Marc Egnal and Joseph A. Ernest, "An Economic Interpretation of the American Revolution," *William and Mary Quarterly* 29 (January 1972) 3–32.

30. David Hume, "On Money" in *Political Discourses* (Edinburgh, 1752); quoted in Keynes, *General Theory*, 343, n. 3

31. Keynes, *General Theory*, 343, n. 3.

32. Franklin, "Paper Currency," *Papers* 1:148–50.

33. *Papers*, 1:146.

34. Adam Smith, *The Wealth of Nations* (New York: Modern Library, 1937), 250.

35. Franklin, "The Interest of Great Britain Considered with Regard to Her Colonies" (1760), *Papers* 9:73.

36. Franklin, "American Paper Money," *Papers* 14:79.

37. The Lords' remarks and the petitioners' response, influenced but not written by Franklin, can be found in Smyth, *Writings of Franklin*, vol. 5, 465–527.

38. See David Levine, *Economic Studies* (London: Routledge and Kegan Paul, 1977), 115–52.

39. See Drew McCoy, "Benjamin Franklin's Vision of a Republican Political Economy for America," *William and Mary Quarterly* 35 (October 1978): 605–28.

40. Franklin, "To Lord Kames" (1769), *Papers* 16:47.

41. See David Ricardo, *The Principles of Political Economy and Taxation* (Cambridge, Eng.: Cambridge University Press, 1966), 11–51.

42. See Maurice Dobb, *Theories of Value and Distribution since Adam Smith* (Cambridge, Eng.: Cambridge University Press, 1973), 73–84.

43. Keynes, *A Tract of Monetary Reform* in *The Collected Works of John Maynard Keynes* (London: Macmillan, 1973), vol. 4, 65.

44. Keynes, *General Theory*, 343, n. 3.

45. Franklin, "On the Labouring Poor" (1768), *Papers* 15:105–6.

46. To see this, consider the following model:

wages = workers' consumption.

profits = capitalists' consumption plus investment.

national output = wages plus profits.

If capitalists' (luxury) consumption rises, profits will rise by the amount of the rise in luxury consumption. Workers will benefit as there are idle hands and resources which the now-higher level of luxury spending draw into production of more national output. (See Michal Kalecki, "Determinants of Profits," in *Selected Essays on the Dynamics of the Capitalist Economy* (Cambridge, Eng: Cambridge University Press, 1971), 78–92. See also George W. Zinke, *The Problem of Malthus: Must Progress End in Overpopulation?* (Boulder: University of Colorado Press, 1967), 65–77.

47. Keynes, *General Theory*, 32.

48. Dudley Dillard, *Economic Development of the North Atlantic Community* (Englewood Cliffs, N.J.: Prentice-Hall, 1967), 212–13.

49. Ibid, 212–13.

Scientific Concerns

The Science of Benjamin Franklin

I. Bernard Cohen*

Many Americans tend to think of Benjamin Franklin as a tinkerer or gadgeteer, an inventor or practical man who "allegedly" made one experiment: the lightning kite. American historians generally have not understood that Franklin was, in fact, a true scientist of a "serious" scientist. They would be at a loss to explain how Joseph Priestly and other contemporaries could have referred to Franklin as a "Newton," in fact as the "Newton," of electricity. But the evidence as to the importance of Franklin in basic or fundamental science is not hard to find. His book on electricity, *Experiments and Observations on Electricity, Made at Philadelphia in America* (first published in London in 1751) was one of the most often reprinted books of the age. In the eighteenth century it appeared in five editions in English, three in French (in two separate translations), one in German and one in Italian—all prior to his rise to international political fame during the Revolution. Containing Franklin's unitary theory of electrical action and the many experiments that illustrated the theory, this book established the basic language that we still use in discussing electrical phenomena; such terms as negative or minus, positive or plus, battery—introduced into electrical discourse for the first time by Benjamin Franklin.

Franklin, furthermore, was honored by the scientific community to a degree that was unmatched in his day. He was awarded the Copley Medal of the Royal Society of London and was then elected a Fellow of that society and a member of its Council. He was elected in 1773 (two years before the Declaration of Independence) a "foreign associate" of the French Academy of Sciences in Paris, a very great honor indeed, since by the statutes of the Academy there could be only eight such foreign scientists as associates at any one time. No other American would be distinguished enough in his research to be so honored for another hundred years, when Louis Agassiz became a "foreign associate." Yet, despite such visible signs of eminence in the domain of pure or basic or fundamental science, Franklin's place in the history of science remains obscure and most Americans (even

*Reprinted by permission from *Meet Dr. Franklin*, ed. Roy N. Lokken (Philadelphia: Franklin Institute, 1981), 265–86.

historians) do not recognize his stature and eminence in science as such and have not even tended to confuse his scientific research and thought with his inventions.

For many years I have pondered as to why most Americans have not appreciated Franklin's stature as a scientist. A probable reason is to be found in the fact that, well into the twentieth century, the United States was a "developing nation," or an "underdeveloped nation," with regard to the sciences. Before that time the country produced very few first-rate scientists on a world scale. The physicist J. Williard Gibbs stands out as a great nineteenth-century exception, and he was recognized abroad long before his own countrymen knew of him. Until the present century, there was no adequate provision in America for advanced scientific education and very little opportunity for a lifetime of research. Americans specialized in applied science and invention, rather than pure science. Science, for all too many, was equated with practical needs rather than advances in knowledge. Accordingly, being a scientist was not traditionally included among the careers that led to greatness. The nation's rise to true scientific eminence came during the 1930's, following the immigration of so many scientific refugees from Europe, and national support of science on the present large scale dates only from the 1950's. Now that the United States has at last assumed a leading role among the scientific nations of the world, it is time that our history books set Benjamin Franklin in the proper perspective of the greatness of his scientific achievement, as a leading theoretical and experimental physical scientist of the Age of Reason.[1]

Franklin first became aquainted with the subject of electrical science sometime around 1744.[2] Between 1747 and 1751 he made his major discoveries and began to win scientific acclaim. Contrary to the supposed general rule that the great discoveries in physics are made by men in their twenties and thirties, Franklin began his scientific work at about the age of 40; he had previously been too busy earning a living to devote much time to scientific pursuits. Having been successful in the world of affairs and now finding the pursuit of truth congenial to his tastes and gifts, he decided, as he tells us in his autobiography, to give up his business and to spend his time conducting experiments. No sooner had he retired from business, however, than a great national crisis arose and he put aside his scientific research in order to participate in the defense of Philadelphia. From then on until he died, he pursued his research only in his spare time. His city, colony and nation never ceased to require his services. At 81 years of age, American independence had been won, and when his work in Paris was finished and he was ready to come home to America, Franklin wrote to his most initimate scientific correspondent, the Dutch physician and physicist Jan Ingenhousz, that he was once more a free man "after fifty years in public affairs." He hoped that his friend would come with him to America, where "in the little remainder of my life . . . we will make plenty of experiments together."[3] Alas, even this was to be denied him, for ahead there lay not days of joyful interrogation of nature but the trying and tedious work of the Constitutional Convention. Long before, Franklin had been forced to choose between the role of a quiet philosopher and a "public man." He had decided the issue without hesitation, saying: "Had Newton been pilot of but a single common ship, the finest of his discoveries would scarce have excused, or atoned for his abandoning the helm one hour in time of danger; how much less if she carried the fate of the Commonwealth."[4]

As we read these lines today, we cannot help thinking of our own scientists who, during World War II, gave up their own individual research to serve their nation. But there is a fundamental difference between their problem and Franklin's. In Franklin's day, the one outstanding American scientist, the only one with a world-wide reputation, found that he could serve his country best by going abroad to plead its cause, rather than by applying his scientific skills to devising new instruments of destruction. Yet such was Franklin's stature in science—and he *was* the Newton of his age—that some suspected the man who dared to tame the lightning bolts of Jove had turned his talents to the perfection of a new and terrible weapon. "The natural philosophers in power," wrote Horace Walpole in 1777, "believe that Dr. Franklin has invented a machine of the size of a toothpick case, and materials that would reduce St. Paul's to a handful of ashes."

Benjamin Franklin made scientific contributions in many fields, including pioneer studies of heat conduction, the origins of storms, and so on, but his most significant work was done in electricity. He worked in electrostatics—the science of electricity at rest or in sudden swift surges. Before Franklin, the known facts of this subject were meager and their explanation was inadequate. When he left the field, a whole new set of observed data had been entered in the record and the Franklinian theory of electrical action had unified all the known facts, preparing the way for the progress of the future.[5]

Franklin's theory of electrical action is simple and straightforward. It is based on the fundamental idea that there is a "common matter," of which the bulk of bodies is composed, and an "electrical matter," or, to use other 18th-century terms, "electrical fluid" or "electrical fire."[6] In its normal state, every body contains a fixed amount of the electrical fluid. But a body may, under certain conditions, gain an excess of the electrical fluid or lose some of its normal complement of it. In such a state a body is "electrified" or "charged"; in the first case, when there is an excess of the fluid, said Franklin, the charge is to be denoted as "positive" or "plus," indicating that something has been added to it; in the second case, "minus" or "negative," indicating that something has been lost. When a piece of glass has been rubbed with a silk rag, the glass acquires an excess of the electrical fluid and becomes charged plus. Franklin insisted that electric charges are not "created" by friction, as some of his contemporaries believed, but rather are the redistribution of the electrical fluid that results from the act of rubbing. If the glass gains an excess of fluid, Franklin held, the silk must have lost the very same amount, thereby gaining a negative charge of the same magnitude. Today we call this principle the law of conservation of charge. This principle declares that whenever charges appear or disappear, they do so in exactly equal quantities of positive and negative charge. Although this principle had been implicit in the thought of other scientists, it was Franklin who made it central to his theory and illustrated it by a number of different experimental examples.[7]

Franklin applied his theory to a number of experiments, including the following. He placed two experimenters on insulated glass stools, one charged plus and the other minus. When the two experimenters touched hands, both lost their charges because the excess of one supplied the deficiency of the other. If a third uncharged experimenter touched either of the charged ones, he drew a spark or got a shock, because he had relatively more electric fluid than the man charged minus, and less than the man charged plus.[8]

This was a simple, dramatic demonstration of Franklin's contention that electrical phenomena are caused by the action of a single "fluid."[9] The chief rival theory held that electrical phenomena derive from two "currents" of an electric matter "which differ only in direction, not in kind," and which "nearly or exactly balance, so that a body can never be emptied of its electrical matter." These jets of matter ("effluences" and "affluences") produce electrical attraction and repulsions from "the direct impact of the electrical matter in motion."[10] A French contemporary pointed out that the beauty of Franklin's theory over its rival was that "Franklin says: do that and this is what must happen; change that circumstance and this will be the result. In this way you can take advantage of a certain thing; in that you will suffer an inconvenience."[11] The late J.J. Thomson, discoverer of the fundamental properties of moving electrons, wrote only a few years ago: "The service which Franklin's one-fluid theory has rendered to the science of electricity by suggesting and coordinating researches can hardly be overestimated."[12]

To understand the application of Franklin's theory, let us follow him through two series of significant experiments.[13] The first begins with one of the many facts first discovered by Franklin and now part of the basic data of the science—what he called the "wonderful effect of pointed bodies, both *drawing off* and *throwing off* the electrical fire." Franklin found that if a pointed conductor such as a needle is brought into the neighborhood of a charged insulated body, the needle will draw off the charge, but it will do so only if it is grounded, that is, in contact with the experimenter's hand or a grounded wire. If the needle is inserted in wax, a non-conductor or insulator, it will not draw off the charge.[14] He also found that if you try to charge a metal object with a jagged edge or point, the object will "throw off the charge" as fast as you put it on. He discovered further that a charged object could be discharged by sifting fine sand on it, by breathing on it, by burning candle near it, or by surrounding it with smoke.

For at least 50 years before Franklin's research, there had been speculation that lightning is probably electrical in nature. But what distinguished Franklin from his predecessors was the fact that he was able to design an experiment to test his hypothesis.[15] He made a small model showing how a discharge might take place between two electrified clouds and between a cloud and the earth. He then predicted that since a small pointed conductor would draw off the charge from an insulated charged body in his laboratory, a large pointed conductor erected in the ground ought to draw the electricity from passing clouds. This suggested to his active mind that "the knowledge of this power of points might be of use to mankind, in preserving houses, churches, ships, &c., from the stroke of lightning, by directing us to fix on the highest parts of those edifices, upright rods of iron made sharp as a needle, and gilt to prevent rusting, and from the foot of those rods a wire down the outside of the building into the ground, or down round one of the shrouds of a ship, and down her side till it reaches the water."[16]

The experiment which proposed to test his hypothesis was described by him in these words: "On the top of some high tower or steeple, place a kind of sentry-box . . . big enough to contain a man and an electrical stand. From the middle of the stand let an iron rod rise and pass bending out of the door, and then upright 20 or 30 feet, pointed very sharp at the end. If the electrical stand be kept clean and dry, a man standing on it when such clouds are passing low, might be electrified and afford sparks, the rod drawing [electrical] fire to him from the cloud. If any danger to the man should be apprehended (though I think there should be none) let him stand on the floor of his box, and now and then bring to the rod the loop of a wire that has one end fastened to the leads, he holding it by a wax handle; so the sparks, if the rod is electrified, will strike from the rod to the wire and not affect him."[17]

This famous "sentry-box experiment" was first performed in France on 10 May 1752, under the directions of a French scientist named Jean Dalibard (or d'Alibard), who had translated Franklin's book into French at the request of the great naturalist Georges de Buffon.[18] (King Louis XV had been so fascinated by Franklin's book that he ordered some of the experiments it described to be performed in his presence.)[19] The Franklin sentry-box experiment was soon repeated in England. Glowing testimonials to the Philadelphia scientist speedily increased in number. An enterprising British manufacturer advertised for sale a ready-made machine "for making the Experiment by which *Franklin's* new theory of Thunder is demonstrated." Franklin did not perform this experiment himself, apparently because he thought that a very high building would be necessary; he was waiting for the completion of the high spire of Christ Church in Philadelphia. After the book was published, but before he had heard from Europe of Dalibard's successful execution of the experiment, the kite project occurred to him as a good substitute and he carried it through instead.[20]

Franklin devised other experiments and instruments to test the charge of clouds, of which one of the most interesting was a pair of bells located in this study. One of the bells was grounded by a rod going into the earth and the other was connected to a rod ending in a point on the roof. A little ball hung between the bells. Whenever an electrified cloud passed overhead, the ball was set in motion and rang the bells. Franklin's careful studies soon showed him that clouds may be charged either plus or minus, and he concluded, therefore, that lightning probably goes from the earth to a cloud at least as often as from a cloud to the earth—an idea which has been confirmed only in our own time by such research as that of B.J.F. Schonland and his associates in South Africa.[21]

Franklin's studies of lightning and his invention of the lightning rod brought him universal fame, but the scientists even more impressed by his analysis set the seal to his scientific reputation. In the form in which the 18th century knew it, the condenser was a glass jar coated on the outside with metal foil and filled with either metal shot or water. It was fitted with a wooden cover into which a rod ending in a knob was inserted. From the lower end of the rod a metal chain depended, going down into the water or shot. This device, invented, in the late 1740's, was known as a "Leyden jar," because one of its several independent discoverers, Pieter van Musschenbroek, was a professor in Leyden. The essential feature of a condenser is the placement of an insulator or dielectric (*e.g.*, air, glass, wax or paper) between two conducting surfaces in close contact with it. In the first Leyden jar the inner conductor was water, the dielectric was the glass, and the outer conductor was a man's hand. Musschenbroek developed his version of it while carrying out some experiments with an electrical machine which charged a whirling glass globe by rubbing it against an experimenter's hands. The charge was transferred to a gun barrel, from the end of which hung a wire that was partly immersed in a round glass vessel filled with water. When Musschenbroek held the vessel in his right hand and attempted to draw a spark from the gun barrel with his left hand, he "was struck with such violence that my whole body was shaken as by a thunderbolt . . . in a word, I thought it was all up with me."[22]

The condenser was a wonderful instrument. By making it bigger and bigger, the shocks it could give were made stronger and stronger. Apparently, somehow or other electricity accumulated in it, and through some little-understood aspect of its construction, it could hold more electricity than anything else of its size. The electric fluids must, it was thought, be "condensed" in it. Musschenbroek wrote a letter describing this experiment which was published in the *Memories* of the French Academy of Sciences. It ended with the famous statement that he would never again receive such a shock, even if he were to be offered the Kingdom of France! For such ignorable sentiments he was publicly rebuked by Priestley, who called him a "cowardly professor" and contrasted him with the "magnanimous Mr. Boze, who with a truly philosophic heroism worthy of the renowned Empedocles, said he might die by the electric shock, that the account of his death might furnish an article for the memoirs of the French Academy of Sciences." Then, referring to a German physicist named Richmann, who had just been killed while performing a variation of Franklin's sentry-box experiment. Priestly concluded, "But it is not given to every electrician to die the death of the justly envied Richman."[23]

All the electricians of Europe wondered what made the Leyden jar work. "Everybody," wrote Priestley, "was eager to see, and, notwithstanding the terrible account that was reported, to *feel* the experiment." In France the new device provided a means of satisfying simultaneously the court's love of spectacles and the great interest in science. One hundred and eighty soldiers of the guard were made to jump into the air with a greater precision than soldiers of the guard displayed in any other maneuvers. Seven hundred monks from the Couvent de Paris, joined hand to hand, had a Leyden jar discharged through them all. They flew up into the air with finer timing than could be achieved the most gifted corps of ballet dancers. From one end of the world to the other, traveling demonstrators sought their fortunes by showing the public experiments of electrical phenomena.

Franklin's step-by-step analysis of the vexing problem of the condenser showed him to be a great master of the technique of scientific experimentation. He found that the charge on the inner conductor was always the opposite of the charge on the outer conductor and that the amount of charge given to both was the same in magnitude. In other words, by the "charging" of the jar, one of the two conductors gained the exact quantity of "electrical fluid" that the other lost. "There is really no more electrical fire in the [Leyden] phial after what is called its *charging*, than before, nor less a *discharging*." Franklin wrote the lead coating of a Leyden jar and placed it so that it was near the knob leading to the water inside the jar, but not near enough to produce a spark when the jar was charged. He then placed the jar on an insulating stand (a block of wax) and suspended a small cork on a string between the wire and the knob. The cork, he noted "will play incessantly from one to the other, 'till the bottle is no longer electrized." In other words, the cork carried the charge from the plus conductor to the minus until equilibrium was restored.

Most important of all, Franklin showed that "the whole force of the bottle, and power of giving a shock, is in the GLASS ITSELF." How would *you*, reader, go about finding "wherein its strength lay"? Every student knows today that the only way to proceed is to test the instrument one element at a time, and to find the role played by each. But this apparently simple rule was not taken for granted in the time of Franklin, as can readily be seen in the fact that none of his contemporaries made the kind of analysis that Franklin now proceeded to carry out.

He charged a Leyden jar that stood on glass and carefully drew out the cork with its wire that hung down into the water. Then he took the bottle in one hand, and brought the other hand near its mouth. "A strong spark came from the water, and the shock was as violent as if the wire had remained in it, which shewed that the force did not lie in the wire." If it was not in the wire, then perhaps it was in the water itself. Franklin recharged the Leyden jar, drew out the cork and wire as before, and carefully poured the water into an empty Leyden jar which likewise stood on a glass insulator. The second jar did not become charged in this process. "We judged then," Franklin wrote, "that [the charge, or force] must either be lost in decanting, or remain in the first bottle. The latter we found to be true; for that bottle on trial gave the shock, though filled up as it stood with fresh unelectrified water from a tea-pot." Apparently the essential element was glass, the insulator between the two conductors. But it still remained to be demonstrated whether "glass had this property merely as glass, or whether the form [of the jar] contributed anything to it."[24]

The next part of the experiment involved the invention of the parallel plate condenser.[25] Franklin sandwiched the large piece of glass between two square plates of lead, equal to each other in size but slightly smaller than the glass. When this condenser was charged, he removed the lead plates, which had but little charge, and noted that a small spark could be taken from the glass at almost any point that it was touched. When the two completely uncharged plates were put back in place, one on each side of the glass, and a circuit made between them, then, "a violent shock ensued." When we demonstrate this phenomenon to our students in physics classes today, we call it the experiment of the dissectible condenser. We explain it by stating that the dielectric, or glass, has been polarized during charging, *i.e.*, it has become an electret. There are certain types of wax that can be polarized in this way simply by being heated and then cooled. Such an electret will give off little or no charge by itself, but if we put a conductor on two sides of it, we have a charged condenser which can be then discharged like any other. Another fact about such condensers that we teach students today was also discovered by Franklin: the amount of charge is greater when the dielectric separating the two conductors is very thin than when it is thick.

Franklin's experiment of the cork that traveled back and forth between the two conductors contained, by the way, the germ of an important idea, although he did not realize it. We know today that a condenser never discharges in one complete stroke, but rather in a series of oscillations—a fact of great importance in radio and modern electronics.

Franklin's extraordinary experiments and his splendid theory marked the beginning of a new era in the subject of electricity. His theory showed its usefulness in many ways. Franklin discovered what is known today as the Faraday effect, namely that the charge on a hollow cylindrical condenser (or a hollow sphere) is on the outside surface only. At first he could not explain this. Later the answer came to him: the "electrical fluid" is self-repellent and the symmetry of the conductor causes it to distribute itself on the outside. From this explanation, Franklin's friend Joseph Priestley deduced that the law of electrical action must be an inverse square law similar to the law of gravitation. This deduction, although published, was overlooked and had to await rediscovery decades later by Charles Coulomb, when it became know as Coulomb's law.[26]

Yet another advantage of Franklin's theory was the ease with which it lent itself to the making of measurements, by concentrating attention on the amount of "electrical fluid" or charge which a body gained or lost. When working with two bodies, it did not matter which one was used because Franklin's law of conservation of charge meant that the quantity gained by one was exactly the quantity that the other lost. The first electricians to make quantitative measurements—such men as Volta, Bennet, Canton, Cavendish and Henley—built upon the convenient one-fluid theory of Benjamin Franklin and the law of conservation of charge which followed from it.

Of course, Franklin's experiments with lightning gave his general research program and his theory a spectacular fame. But this subject is not very well understood. The invention of the lightning rod did not just show that Franklin was practical minded; rather, this invention proved what every scientist since Francis Bacon and Rene Descartes fully believed, that the road to practical inventions lies in pure or disinterested or basic or fundamental research. Franklin did not "direct" his research so that it would lead to something useful, as a historian woefully ignorant of science once declared, but rather used the results of his research to produce something of practical use *after* the research had been completed and when he *then* saw that it might have some practical application. The lightning experiments caused Franklin's name to become known throughout Europe to the public at large and not merely to men of science. Joseph Priestley, in his *History . . . of Electricity*, characterized the experimental discovery that the lightning discharge is an electrical phenomenon as "the greatest, perhaps, since the time of Sir Isaac Newton." Of course, one reason for satisfaction in this discovery was that it subjected one of the most mysterious and frightening natural phenomena to rational explanation. It also proved that Bacon had been right in asserting that a knowledge of how nature really works might lead to a better control of nature itself; that valuable practical innovations might be the fruit of pure disinterested scientific research.

No doubt the most important effect of the lightning experiments was to show that the laboratory phenomena in which rods or globes of glass were rubbed, to the accomplishment of sparks, and induced charges and electrical shocks, belong to a class of phenomena occurring naturally. Franklin's lightning experiments proved that electrical effects do not result exclusively from man's artifice, from his intervention in phenomena, but are in fact part of the routine operations of nature. And every "electrician" learned from Franklin's investigations of the nature of the lightning discharge that experiments performed with little toys in the laboratory could reveal new aspects of one of the most dramatic of nature's catastrophic forces. "The discoveries made in the summer of the year 1752 will make it memorable in the history of electricity," William Watson wrote in 1753. "These have opened a new field to [natural] philosophers, and have given them room to hope, that what they have learned before in their museums, they may apply, with more propriety than they hitherto could have done, in illustrating the nature and effects of thunder; a phaenomenon hitherto almost inaccessible to their inquiries."[27]

Franklin's achievement of a highly successful career wholly in the field of electricity marked the coming of age of electrical science and the full acceptance of the new field of specialization. On 30 November 1753, awarding Franklin the Royal Society's Sir Godfrey Copley gold medal for his discoveries in electricity, the Earl of Macclesfield emphasized this very point: "Electricity is a neglected subject," he said "which not many years since was thought to be of little importance, and was at that time only applied to illustrate the nature of attraction and repulsion; nor was anything worth much notice expected to ensue from it." But now, thanks to the labors of Franklin, it "appears to have a most surprising share of power in nature."[28]

It is often said that Franklin was typically American in his approach to science—a utilitarian interested in science chiefly, if not solely, because of its practical applications. It is true that when he had discovered the action of pointed grounded conductors and proved that clouds are electrified, he applied these discoveries to the invention of the lightning rod. But he did not make these discoveries in order to invent a lightning rod.[29] Franklin's inventions were of two kinds. One type was pure gadgetry; in this class were his inventions of bifocal glasses, which required no recondite knowledge of optical principles, and of a device for taking books down from the shelf without getting up from one's chair. The lightning rod, on the other hand, developed from pure scientific research. If Franklin's approach to science had been strictly utilitarian, it is doubtful that he would ever have studied the subject of electricity at all. In the 18th century there was only one practical application of electricity, and that was the giving of electric shocks for therapeutic purposes, chiefly to cure paralysis. (Although Franklin on occasion participated in such therapy, he did not believe that the shock itself ever cured a case of paralysis. With shrewd psychological insight, he guessed that the reported cures arose from the desire of the patient to be cured rather than from the passage of electric fluid.)

Franklin studied nature because he wanted to discover its innermost secrets, and he chose electrostatics because chance brought him the instruments with which to study this subject, and because he quickly found out that this was a subject well fitted to his particular talents. In a spirit which might well be emulated by all men engaged in research, he wrote humbly at the end of one of his communications: "These thoughts, my dear friend, are many of them crude and hasty; and I were merely ambitious of acquiring some reputation in philosophy [*i.e.*, natural philosophy, or science], I ought to keep them by me, 'till corrected and improved by time, and farther experience. But since even short hints and imperfect experiments in any new branch of science, being communicated, have oftentimes a good effect, in exciting the attention of the ingenious to the subject . . . you are at liberty to communicate this paper to whom you please, it being of more importance that knowledge should increase, than that your friend should be thought an accurate philosopher."[30]

In fact, Franklin's story of electricity—though widely accepted and used—proved to have defects.[31] A major one arose in two ways. First of all, Franklin had assumed that neutral or nonelectrified bodies are composed of "common" matter and a "normal" quantity of electrical fluid. The electrical fluid was postulated to be composed of particles that repel one another and that mutually attract and are attracted by the particles of common matter.[32] In the case of two positively charged bodies, the excess electrical fluid in one will—according to the theory—repel the excess electrical fluid in the other, and hence the theory explains or predicts the mutual repulsion of two bodies, each of which has a positive charge or more electrical fluid than in the normal or uncharged state. Similarly, a body that has lost some of its electrical fluid (charged negatively) and a body with an excess of electrical fluid (charged positively) will attract one another. But what of two bodies that are both negatively charged? In fact, as Franklin reluctantly had to admit, they are observed to repel one another.[33] This defect in the theory was a serious one. An attempt to remedy the situation was made by Franz Ulrich Theodosius Aepinus in his *Tentamen theoriae electricitatis et magnetismi* (Essay on the theory of electricity and magnetism), published in St. Petersburg in 1759. Aepinus here added a postulate to the Franklinian theory, according to which the particles of common matter not only attract particles of the electrical fluid but also repel one another. At once, it follows that negatively charged bodies should repel one another just as positively charged bodies do.[34]

Aepinus did not, however, introduce his radical postulate primarily to take care of a fundamental deficiency in the Franklinian theory of electrical action, as has usually been alleged. Rather, that result was merely a major by-product of a logical and mathematical analysis of the Franklinian scheme amended. As Aepinus makes clear, and as R. W. Home sums up the situation, Aepinus's new electrical postulate (about particles of common matter repelling one another) was a product of logical analysis and clear thinking rather than having been simply "an ad hoc modification of Franklin's theory to enable it to account for the observed mutual repulsion between two negatively charged bodies." Rather, as Home puts the matter:

> With his skilled mathematician's eye, Aepinus perceived that if the principles Franklin had laid down were taken literally and their consequences

> rigorously traced out, they led to absurd conclusions. In particular, they led to the ludicrous proposition that two unelectrified bodies exerted electrical forces on each other. Hence Aepinus's additional postulate, or something formally equivalent to it, far from being a merely incidental modification of Franklin's theory, was absolutely essential if the foundations of the theory were to be rendered coherent. Only if this were done could the theory be reformulated in mathematical terms. In other words, Aepinus's innovation was an important step in the subjection of this particular branch of physical theory to mathematical analysis.[35]

Aepinus's theory was not widely accepted, although it won Franklin's support. Home has traced the stages of reception of Aepinus's ideas and suggests some possible causes for the lack of general acceptance. Many electricians of that day objected to the austere mathematical mode of thinking of Aepinus and others rejected a mathematical theory that was not based on a definite, certain, and established law of force. Furthermore, Aepinus's book was expensive and often difficult to obtain; the edition was small, limited to 650 copies. Franklin accepted Aepinus's conclusion that the impermeability of glass in condensers or Leyden jars was not related to unique aspects of glass (as Franklin had at first believed), but was a property of all non-conductors (or "electrics *per se*"); this became a feature of the Franklinian theory thereafter. Franklin strongly commended Aepinus's theory of magnetism. Aepinus had also shown that the Franklinian supposition "electrical atmospheres" (supposedly, the excess electrical fluid on positively charged bodies formed a kind of ethereal cloud or atmosphere surrounding such bodies) was untenable.[36] But Franklin was silent on the subject of the new postulate; we have no information as to whether he did not fully grasp its import or whether he did so but refused to believe that particles of common matter can repel one another.

Franklin's contributions to science were not limited to electricity; he concerned himself with such other branches of science as oceanography, meterology, general physics, and even medicine. Especially well known were his experiments to see whether oil spread on the surface of water would in fact still the waves. He made a spectacular demonstration of this phenomenon in Portsmouth harbor for the benefit of a group of Fellows of the Royal Society. He printed the first chart of the Gulf Steam and conceived of using a marine thermometer as an aid to navigation in relation to the Gulf Stream. He measured surface temperatures in the ocean during Atlantic crossings and devised a special instrument to measure ocean temperatures to a depth of 100 feet. He also was concerned to produce more efficient shapes for ships.[37]

Franklin was interested in meteorology and especially cloud formation and the electrification of clouds. He is generally acknowledged to have been the first scientist to report that northeast storms move toward the southwest, and he was a pioneer in observing convection phenomena in the atmosphere. He argued in favor of a wave theory of light, rejecting the strict Newtonian corpuscular theory. He was considered among the primary supporters of the wave theory.

Franklin tried to aply his doctrine of conservation, which had worked so well for electricity, to explain thermal phenomena. He assumed that there is a constant amount of heat, which is simply distributed, redistributed, conducted, and nonconducted, according to the kind of material in question. Interested in problems of heat conductivity, he designed a famous experiment, still performed in most introductory physics courses, in which a number of rods of different metals are joined together at one end and fanned out at the other, with little wax rings placed on them at regular intervals. The ends that are joined together are placed in a flame, and the "conductivity" is indicated by the relative speeds with which the wax rings melt and fall off. Franklin (in France) never had the occasion to perform the experiment, although he did obtain the necessary materials for doing so, and he suggested that Ingenhousz and he might do the experiment together. Ingenhousz, however, did it on his own. Franklin's experiments on heat were not fully understood until Joseph Black introduced the concepts of specific heat and latent heat.[38]

Franklin's only major contribution to the theory of heat is in the specific area of differential thermal conduction. The success of his fluid theory of electricity, and his writing on heat as a fluid, did, however, influence the later development of the concept of "caloric." Lavoisier wrote in 1777 that if he were to be asked what he understood by "matter of fire," he would reply, "with Franklin, Boerhaave, and some of the older [natural] philosophers, that the matter of fire or of light is a very subtle and very elastic fluid. . . ."[39]

Franklin was an advocate of fresh air and exercise. He invented (or perhaps reinvented independently) bifocal glasses and designed a flexible catheter. He wrote on a variety of medical subjects: lead poisoning, gout, the heat of the blood, the physiology of sleep, deafness, nyctalopia, infection from dead bodies, infant mortality, and medical education. He accumulated an impressive set of statistics in favor of the practice of inoculation and published them in a pamphlet (London, 1759), accompanying William Herberden's instructions on inoculation. Although Franklin gave electric shocks to patients suffering from "palsies," he believed that any temporary help was not due so much to the electricity as to "the exercise in the patients' journey, and coming daily to my house" or even—we may note with special interest today—the "spirits given by the hope of success, enabling them to exert more strength in moving their limbs." Franklin was a member of the Paris commission in 1787 to investigate the claims of Mesmerism to cure diseases by the manipulation of "animal magnetism." It is curious that neither Franklin nor the other members of the commission recognized the deep psychological significance of their conclusion that "the imagination does everything, the magnetism nothing."

None of these other scientific activities is in a class with the electrical research. Indeed, Franklin is sometimes described as the first scientist to have gained international fame for work wholly in this new branch of science. But Franklin's contributions to science in general include his aid in getting the work of other scientists published and his activities in founding the American Philosophical Society, our oldest scientific or learned society or academy.

With the discovery of electrons, protons and neutrons, many modern writers have argued about whether Franklin's one-fluid theory was or was not closer to the modern conception than the two-fluid theory of his rivals. To my mind, such debates are wholly without value. The value of Franklin's contribution to electricity does not lie in the degree to which it resembles our modern theory, but rather in the effect of his researches had in getting us along on the road to our modern theory.

At the time that Franklin undertook his studies, the world of science lay under the spell of Isaac Newton, whose great *Principia* had shown that the motions of the universe could be explained by simple mathematical laws. Newton thus convinced almost everyone that mathematics and mathematical laws were the only key to the understanding of nature. What many people forgot, however, was that Newton's success in applying mathematics to celestial and terrestrial mechanics was possible only because the facts had been accumulated and classified, and were in a state where his great genius could produce the general system of physics which became a paradigm for all other branches of science thereafter. But when it came to optics, Newton did not create a mathematical system of nature in the style that in the *Principia* had served so well for celestial and terrestrial mechanics, nor was he able to reduce his quantitative and qualitative discoveries to the form of general mathematical law.[40] In the field of optics, Newton was but one of the giants[41] upon whose shoulders some later mathematical physicist would stand so as to produce a mathematical system. In contrast with the austere *Principia*, whose motto was *Hypotheses non fingo* ("I frame [or feign] no hypotheses"), his *Opticks* contains a long set of "queries" in which Newton discussed the possible explanations that might be given to his observed facts. These resemble Franklin's speculations concerning electrical phenomena.[42] In Franklin's time, as with optics in Newton's time, the state of electrical science did not yet permit a full mathematical synthesis. What was required were "giants" to uncover the facts of charge, of induction, of grounding and insulation, of the effect of shapes of conductors and so on, giants to build a workable manipulative theory to unify these facts and to draw attention to essential elements that might be measured. Franklin's success paved the way for the mathematical theorists of the 19th century.[43]

But, even more, his mastery of the technique of experimentation, his successful and consistent explanations in terms of a simple physical conceptual scheme, and the many new and curious facts of nature he revealed, gave experimental science a new dignity in the eyes of his 18th-century contemporaries. The French philosopher Diderot wrote, in his essay on the interpretation of nature, that Franklin's book on electricity, like the works of the chemists, was the best teacher of the nature of the experimental art and the way to use the principles of experimental research to draw back the veil of nature without multiplying its mysteries. This was the sense, then, in which Franklin's contemporaries believed him to be the new Newton, and this was the first great contribution made by America to the mind of science. In this light, there can be no doubt of Franklin's stature in science, nor that he deserves to stand as the first American scientist.

Notes

1. These initial paragraphs repeat the argument in the introduction to my *Benjamin Franklin: Scientist and Statesman* (New York: Charles Scribner's Sons, 1975), pp. 11–14; the remainder of this essay is based largely on an article, "In Defense of Benjamin Franklin," *Scientific American*, August 1948, vol. 179, pp. 36–43.

2. On Franklin's introduction to electricity, see my "Benjamin Franklin and the Mysterious 'Dr. Spence': the Date and Source of Franklin's Interest in Electricity," *Journal of the Franklin Institute*, 1943, vol. 235, pp. 1–25 (reprinted, with revisions, in I.B. Cohen, *The Science of Benjamin Franklin* [New York: Neal Watson Associates, 1981], and my *Franklin and Newton* (Philadelphia: American Philosophical Society, 1956; Cambridge, MA: Harvard University Press, 1966 [revised reprint, 1981]. More recently, this topic has been discussed in Bernard S. Finn, "An Appraisal of the Origins of Franklin's Electrical Theory," *Isis*, 1969, vol. 60, pp. 362–69, and in John L. Heilbron, "Franklin, Haller, and Franklinist History," *Isis*, 1977, vol. 68, pp. 539–49. In particular, Heilbron has identified a source of Franklin's early knowledge of electricity in an article in *The Gentleman's Magazine* (1745, vol. 15, pp. 193–97), entitled "An Historical Account of the New German Experiments in Electricity," a translation from a French text by Albrecht von Haller.

3. Benjamin Franklin to Ingenhousz, 29 Apr. 1785.

4. Benjamin Franklin to Cadwallader Colden, 11 October 1750.

5. See the essay . . . by R.A. Millikan ["Benjamin Franklin As a Scientist," in *Meet Dr. Franklin*, ed. Roy N. Lokken (Philadelphia: Franklin Institute, 1981)] in which the discoverer of the electron pays a founder's tribute to the author of the first unitary theory of electrical action. Millikan even went so far to hail Franklin as the discoverer of the electron. For a balanced view of Franklin's achievement, see John L. Heilbron, *Electricity in the 17th and 18th Centuries* (Berkeley, Los Angeles, London: University of California Press, 1979).

6. Franklin's concept of a particulate electrical fluid arose from the Newtonian natural philosophy and was one of the "imponderables" used by eighteenth-century physicists; cf. my *Franklin and Newton* (cited in n.2 *supra*).

7. On the origins and background of the concept of conservation of charge, see Heilbron's book (cited in n. 6 *supra*), p. 330.

8. This experiment is described in Franklin's first letter on electricity to Peter Collinson (11 July 1747), printed in the later editions of Franklin's book under the date of 11 July 1974. See *Benjamin Franklin's Experiments: a New Edition of Franklin's "Experiments and Observations on Electricity,"* edited, with a critical and historical introduction, by I. Bernard Cohen (Cambridge, Mass.: Harvard University Press, 1941). A new facsimile of the first edition of Franklin's book (London, 1751–1753–1754), with introduction and appendixes by I.B. Cohen, is scheduled for publication in 1981 by the Dibner Library of the History of Science and Technology, Washington, D.C. On the dates of Franklin's letters, see I.B. Cohen, "Some

Problems in Relation to the Dates of Benjamin Franklin's First Letters on Electricity," *Proceedings of the American Philosophical Society, 1956*, vol. 100, pp. 537–42.

9. See my *Franklin and Newton*, ch. 8 & 10, and R.A. Millikan's essay (cited in n.5 *supra*).

10. These quotations concerning Nollet's theory come from John L. Heilbron's essay in the *Dictionary of Scientific Biography*, vol. 10 (New York: Charles Scribner's Sons, 1974), pp. 145–48. See, further, ch. 11 of Heilbron's book (cited in n.6 *supra*).

11. This quotation comes from the introductory comment by Jacques Barbeu-Dubourg's two-volume translation of Franklin's book on electricity. *Oeuvres de M. Franklin* (Paris, 1773).

12. Thomson, *Recollections and Reflections* (London: G. Bell and Sons, 1936), pp. 252–53.

13. See my *Franklin and Newton* (cited in n.2 *supra*), ch. 10; the experiments are described in Franklin's book (see n.9 *supra*).

14. As Franklin stated explicitly in the later editions of his book, this "power" of pointed bodies to "draw off" the electrical fluid was discovered by his Philadelphia coexperimentor, Thomas Hopkinson.

15. In a letter to John Lining, 18 March 1755, published in Franklin's book on electricity, an extract is given from Franklin's record book of experiments to show—as Franklin says—that the thought that the lightning discharge is an electrical phenomenon "was not so much 'an out-of-the-way one,' but that it might have occurred to any electrician." But the important difference between Franklin's thoughts on this matter and those of others is expressed in the final sentence of the extract, "Let the experiment be made."

16. Quoted from Franklin's "Opinions and Conjectures Concerning the Properties and Effects of the Electrical Matter . . . 1749," printed in Franklin's book on electricity. See, further, I.B. Cohen, "The Two-Hundredth Anniversary of Benjamin Franklin's Two Lightning Experiments and the Introduction of the Lightning Rod," *Proceedings of the American Philosophical Society*, 1952, vol. 96, pp. 331–66.

17. "Opinions and Conjectures . . ." (see n.17 *supra*), §21.

18. Buffon's interest in having Franklin's book translated into French was related to his active controversy with Reaumur, since the Abbe Nollet was a protege of Reaumur's and Franklin's book offered an alternative to Nollet's theory of electricity. See Heilbron's article (cited in n.2 *supra*) and his biography of Nollet (cited in n.11 *supra*).

19. Franklin described his reactions to the commendations of Louis XV of France in a letter to Jared Eliot, 12 April 1753.

20. See the article cited in n.17 *supra*, reprinted in *The Science of Benjamin Franklin* (see n.2 *supra*).

21. See Schonland's article in the issue of the *Journal of the Franklin Institute* devoted to the two hundredth anniversary of Franklin's lightning experiments (vol. 253, n. 5, May 1952); see also B.J.F. Schonland, *The Flight of Thunderbolts* (Oxford: Clarendon Press, 1950).

22. On the Leyden jar, see Heilbron's book (cited in n.6 *supra*) and his article. "A propos de l'invention de la bouteille de Leyde," *Revue d'Histoire des Sciences*, 1966, vol. 19, pp. 133–42.

23. Joseph Priestley, *The History and Present State of Electricity* (third ed., 2 vols., London, 1755), reprinted with an introduction by Robert E. Schofield (New York, London: Johnson Reprint corporation, 1966), vol. 1, pp. 107–8.

24. The analysis of the Leyden jar occurs in a letter to Peter Collinson, 29 April 1749, containing "Farther Experiments and Observations in Electricity, 1748," printed in Franklin's book on electricity.

25. Franklin observed in a note, "I have since heard that Mr. [John] Smeaton was the first who used panes of glass for that purpose."

26. On the discovery of the law, see Heilbron's book (cited in n.6 *supra*).

27. See my *Franklin and Newton* (cited in n.2 *supra*), p. 490.

28. *Franklin and Newton*, p. 490.

29. How could he have done so, since he could have had no prevision as to what his future discoveries would be?

30. Benjamin Franklin to Peter Collinson, 14 August 1747.

31. For example, Franklin used extensively the concept of "electrical atmospheres," clouds of electrical fluid or electrical matter surrounding positively charged bodies. The production of a condenser made of two parallel plates separated by air showed that this concept was untenable and had to be abandoned. See Roderick W. Home, *The Effluvial Theory of Electricity* (New York: Arno Press, 1981), and his article, "Franklin's Electrical Atmospheres," *British Journal for the History of Science*, 1972, vol. 6, 131–151. See also Heilbron's book (cited in n.6 *supra*), pp. 241–42, 262–63, 388–89, 414–18, 426–30.

32. See R.A. Millikan's essay, (cited in n.5 *supra*).

33. On Franklin's reluctance to admit that two negatively charged bodies mutually repel one another, see my *Franklin and Newton* (cited in n.2 *supra*), pp. 491–94, and also Heilbron's book (cited in n.6 *supra*). This phenomenon of repulsion was brought forcibly to Franklin's attention by his Philadelphia co-experimentor, Ebenezer Kinnersley.

34. See *Aepinus's Essay on the Theory of Electricity and Magnetism*, with an introductory monograph and notes by R.W. Home and a translation by P.J. Connor (Princeton: Princeton University Press, 1979).

35. *Aepinus's Essay*, pp. 119–20.

36. See n.32 *supra*.

37. See my *Benjamin Franklin: Scientist and Statesman* (cited in n.1 *supra*), ch. 6.

38. See, further, my *Franklin and Newton* (cited in n.2 *supra*), ch.8.

39. Antoine-Laurent Lavosier, *Oeuvres* (Paris: Imprimerie Nationale, 1862), vol. 2, p. 228.

40. See my *The Newtonian Revolution* (New York: Cambridge University Press, 1980).

41. See Robert K. Merton, *On the Shoulders of Giants: a Shandean Postscript* (New York: The Free Press; London: Collier-Macmillan Limited, 1965).

42. On the relation of Franklin's electrical theory to the tradition of experimental science associated with Newton's *Opticks*, see my *Franklin and Newton* (cited in n.2 *supra*).

43. On this topic, see the concluding section of Heilbron's book (cited in n.6 *supra*).

Religious Concerns

Franklin's Religion

Donald H. Meyer*

Why is it that Socrates did not invent the Franklin stove? Socrates was in as good a position as Benjamin Franklin to invent the fireplace that has been named after the famous Philadelphian; and people living in ancient Athens would certainly have benefited from the heating efficiency and comfort afforded by the Franklin stove as much as people living in eighteenth-century Philadelphia. Why did the human race have to wait over two millennia for an invention that is at once so simple and so basic to human well-being? This is the interesting question raised in 1929 by Joseph Wood Krutch in *The Modern Temper;* and the answer he gave to it provides us with an important clue in our effort to understand the religion of Benjamin Franklin. Centuries passed without any significant improvements in such elemental areas as heating, lighting, and transportation because it simply did not occur to people like Socrates or Aristotle or Aquinas that such improvements were a particularly worthwhile undertaking. The conception these men had of human nature and the human prospect did not include matters of "mere mechanical ingenuity" for the improvement of our material existence.[1]

Matters of religion, on the other hand, occupy only a small portion of Franklin's published writing, the bulk of which deal with science and invention, diplomatic and social issues, and scores of the day-to-day concerns that might interest an eighteenth-century man. The relatively scant attention Franklin gives to questions of what has been called "ultimate concern"[2] is itself worthy of note, for he represents a frame of mind that is fundamentally different from that of former ages, one that, in some ways, has more in common with what we call the modern secular consciousness than it does with all the centuries that preceded him. In looking into Franklin's religion, therefore, we are not only examining a man's attitude toward ultimate questions, but also his redefinition of the very meaning of "ultimate." We are, in other words, witnessing an important episode in the shaping of the modern sensibility.

*This essay was written especially for this collection and published here for the first time.

It is worth beginning with Franklin's remarkable stove in order to get some idea of the new mentality of which he is representative. It was, of course, a metal device, made of cast iron plates, designed to be installed in an ordinary brick hearth. Once the stove was properly set up in the fireplace, the smoke would be drawn up the chimney, and the room would be warmed not only by the radiant heat from the fire itself but also by convection currents of air circulating throughout the room after contact with the hot iron surface of the stove. In his lengthy, illustrated "Advertisement" of 1744 Franklin explained the basic principles on which the stove worked (complete with simple, do-it-yourself experiments), compared his device with other available stoves, answered possible objections to its use, and gave detailed instructions for its installation. Among the advantages of his stove, said Franklin, were comfort and convenience, cleanliness, decrease in air pollution, improved health, and fuel economy. Speaking particularly of the *"Publick Advantage"* in using such a fireplace, Franklin agreed to leave it to the *"Political Arithmetician"* to calculate.

> how much Money will be sav'd to a Country, by its spending two thirds less on Fuel; how much Labour sav'd in Cutting and Carriage of it; how much more Land may be clear'd for Cultivation; how great the Profit by the additional Quantity of Work done, in those Trades particularly that do not exercise the Body so much, but that the Workfolks are oblig'd to run frequently to the Fire to warm themselves: And to Physicians to say, how much healthier thick-built Towns and Cities will be, now half suffocated with sulphury Smoke, when so much less of that Smoke shall be made, and the Air breath'd by the Inhabitants be consequently so much purer.[3]

Referring to this episode much later in his *Autobiography,* Franklin recalled that he had turned down the suggestion that he patent his new invention. Since we regularly benefit from the inventions of others, he maintained, we should be happy to serve others in turn, and without compensation.[4]

The entire episode is instructive. From the basic physics involved, to the suggested experiments demonstrating the expansion and contraction of air, to the concern for convenience and comfort, to the computation of "publick advantage," to the breezy literary style of the descriptive pamphlet, we see a man who seems thoroughly at home in his world, and who is preoccupied with understanding its basic principles and using this understanding to increase the sense of earthly at-homeness. The Franklin stove involves more than a concern for economy or comfort. It involves a mode of attention, a way of seeing and studying the material world, of treating "things" as phenomena, and analyzing the phenomena into their basic properties to be "understood" through "Experiments." These experiments become possible only after we abstract from the blur of existence its physically manageable and quantifiable components.[5]

According to Krutch, Franklin, with his fireplace, represents a trade off that western people made somewhere in the early modern era. We purchased the new lamp of science and technology, with all that these have added to our understanding of the world and our comfort in it, but at the price of transcendence, a sense of cosmic comfort, the magic lamp of enchantment and spirituality.[6] We gained the world to lose, perhaps, even our souls. And Franklin has the dubious honor of serving as a symbolic figure in the transaction. Franklin, who personified the spirit of capitalism for Max Weber and snuff-colored philistinism for D. H. Lawrence, now becomes the modern Prometheus—forsaking and forsaken by the Heavens, once he stole their fire—forever marooned on the spiritually barren rock of the world, albeit with all his creature comforts. To speak of such a man's "religion" seems almost pointless; and those who do usually admit that one may "hardly claim reverence as one of [Franklin's] characteristics."[7] This becomes especially evident when we—as we inevitably do—place Franklin beside his great contemporary, Jonathan Edwards. While it may be true that both men "started from the same base, a very real and profound belief in the reality of God,"[8] the difference between them, even in this very real and profound belief, is astonishing. Edwards was driven by an intense God-hunger and, for all the empiricism of his theology, lived in a world in which the supernatural was as palpably real as the New England hills and forests. Franklin, for all his belief in God and in divine Providence, seems untroubled by real spiritual yearnings, indifferent to the supernatural, and unmoved by the Christian message of sin, atonement, and redemption. Once one has listed the things Franklin did not believe in, or did not appear to take very seriously, one is at a loss to say what is left in Franklin's religion.

The historian sometimes feels a little like a dangling cork in one of Franklin's famous electrical experiments, pulled back and forth between the positive and negative terminals of a charged Leyden Jar, unable to decide whether to linger with Franklin's affirmative Deism and Moralism or to fix on his opposition to dogma and "sect" and his apparently blasé indifference to the finer points of Christian theology. Which is the real Franklin? Is it the Franklin of the "Doctrine To Be Preached" and the Thirteen Virtues? Or is it the Franklin of the *Dissertation on Liberty and Necessity*, the defense of Samuel Hemphill, and the report on "A Witch Trial at Mount Holly." Are we to dwell on his somewhat vague affirmations or take at face value the good-natured indifference of the man who always gave his "mite" to every church's building program, and move on to more important, secular matters? The fact of the matter is, we must do both, for both men—together—are the "real" Franklin. And if Franklin's secularity informs his religion more than his religion transforms his secularity, this offers us no excuse to dismiss his professions of faith as too casual, bland, or vague to be of real interest or importance. Franklin represents not just secularity but the secularization of religious thought. Franklin's role as an agent of secularization both accounts for his originality and establishes his significance as an American philosopher. To understand this role we must examine Franklin's unique approach to religious matters as well as the content of his belief.

Franklin's approach to religion starts with a cultural heritage that includes Calvinist roots, his Boston background and "Leather-Apron" origins, and an intellectual milieu to which Franklin was extremely receptive. Although he was to become a diplomat, scientist, "founding father," international celebrity and all-around sage, Franklin never entirely transcended his identity as one of the "middling sort," who, starting out as a Boston printer's apprentice, was already engaged, as a teenager, in bitter disputes with that town's forever defensive Puritan establishment.[9] The man who consciously projected the self-image of order, moderation, and good-natured tolerance emerged from what seems a caldron of contradictions: Franklin was a vehemently anti-Puritan Puritan, a proud working man with terrible status anxieties, a freethinker with second thoughts, a Deist who (sometimes) believed in prayer, Providence, and public worship, a natural philosopher who never had the time to do what he really wanted to, an amiable and always humble inquirer who had some pretty strong opinions on "merely speculative" matters and was capable of an almost Old-Testament sense of outrage. Franklin gives new dimensions to the word "contrareity."

In his *Autobiography* Franklin speaks of an early propensity alike toward "handiness" and "bookishness."[10] It is easy to treat this admission casually, even though both qualities are well illustrated in the course of Franklin's life. Franklin's extraordinary experiments in electricity show him to be closer to Michael Faraday than to the Newton of the *Principia Mathematica* in his scientific style. It would seem that he was compensated for his lack of mathematical skill with a marvelous sense of the spacial, an instinctive trust in fact and a corresponding suspicion of mere assertion, and a knack for experimental precision that allowed him to transform the study of electrical phenomena from a curiosity into an exact science.[11] When Franklin proved the conservation of charge in a Leyden Jar (a primitive capacitor) with the cork suspended midway between the two oppositely charged poles, his combination of economy of detail and richness of concept stirs our admiration. Perhaps it is his idea of seriousness, or his redefinition of the serious, that puts Franklin in a different world from that of many of his contemporaries and of the great thinkers of the past. His is a definition of the serious that is based not on the results of logical argument and "bookish" learning only, but on something as mundane as "handiness" and an infinite caring for detail and meticulous mechanical procedure.[12] Franklin combined the craftsman's skill in handling things with the philosopher's ability to interpret new relationships, and herein lay his great intellectual strength.

It was in the period from the dawning of the Renaissance to the time of Francis Bacon, we are told, that the mechanic and the craftsman received more than condescending notice from the scholar, and the serious philosopher began to adopt the methods of the artisan—realizing that altering nature might be essential to understanding it, and that the understanding of nature as it actually works might be worthwhile.[13] It was no accident that God, in this period, was frequently described as a "clockmaker" and a master mechanic of the universe. The rise of modern science dates from this time and, in good measure, from this development. Franklin as scientist is surely within the tradition of the craftsman-scholar; and Franklin, as philosopher in the broader sense of that term, carries on in this tradition, applying new methods and a new way of seeing things to old questions. Cannot life be approached in the sensible, careful, and dependable way of the mechanical "arts"? Cannot life's "higher" concerns—even religious or "ultimate concerns"—be similarly treated and settled? The question sounds a little naive today. But Franklin lived in a time when many thinkers were starting to realize that for centuries the "Schoolmen," as Locke sometimes called them, had obfuscated and confused simple truths about religion, morality, and the nature of things in general. Theology, like natural philosophy, had been the province of men whose wisdom and judgment had been beyond questioning. But now any intelligent and "handy" person could understand the principles of the Leyden Jar or the Franklin Stove, and Franklin himself delighted in encouraging popular experimentation. An assertion that could not be submitted to this kind of public scrutiny was hardly to be taken seriously. One could quickly see the advantages of his new wood stove, Franklin had announced in 1744, by investigating the matter for oneself, come to understand the "Properties" and the "Principles" involved, examining them "separately and particularly," then make the necessary "comparisons." Why cannot something similar be done in the realm of faith? Has God hidden Himself like a prankish child, leaving clues that only a few close friends could ever figure out? Surely, such is not the God whose workmanship the great Newton had demonstrated to be so exquisitely orderly and rational! Why cannot religion be straightforward and rational, as everything else is? The real significance of this question lies in its second clause. It is only reasonable to suppose that the same kind of thinking that explains the physical universe would explain, equally well, the spiritual universe.

This attitude carried over to institutions. Franklin may have been a democrat "to the core,"[14] as some of his admirers contend, but he was a bookish handiman before he became a democrat, and his instinct for craftsmanship is as evident in his attitude toward social organization as it is in his approach to science and invention. Like physical things, institutions were subject to critical scrutiny, testing, alteration. They were to be judged, like conduct, on the basis of their utility, which involved both the nobility of their purpose and their efficiency in achieving it. Churches, like states, came within this category; and, for Franklin, the purpose that the churches were to serve involved mainly the public good and the general welfare.

In his defense of the Reverend Samuel Hemphill against the charge of heterodoxy by the Presbyterians, Franklin made it clear that the primary function of the preaching ministry is not saving souls—since church members are presumably saved already (Franklin was never much bothered by the difference between "true" Christianity and what Kierkegaard called "Christendom"—but in promoting socially beneficial conduct and right attitudes.[15] In his *Autobiography* he reports that he was inclined to respect the teachings of all "sects," at least insofar as these teachings set forth the "essentials of every religion," namely, the acknowledgement of a creator-deity who is providentially active in the affairs of men and who rewards (or punishes) our conduct in this world or the next. He added, however, that he regarded these different teachings with varying "degrees of respect" as he found them "more or less mixed with other articles which without any tendency to inspire, promote, or confirm morality, served principally to divide us and make one unfriendly to one another."[16] Franklin's rule in judging the doctrines of any sect was simple and broad, but inflexible. First, do they conform to the essential principles of every religion, principles which Franklin regarded as basic and universal? Second, insofar as they go beyond these basic principles, do they thereby encourage or undermine public morality and social tranquility? The utilitarian judgment is only half the test, applying only to those doctrines that claim more than the "essential" truths of religion. When the teachings of a sect go beyond the "truths" we all "know" they become matters of "speculation," and, as such, are to be handled not on the basis of truth or falsity but of social utility or worthlessness, perhaps mischief. In his public writings, like the *Autobiography*, Franklin liked to stress the positive side of his attitude, which makes him seem genially tolerant of just about anything. And, when dealing with a person's private convictions, Franklin probably really was this way. He had cordial relations with many among the Quakers, Dunkards, Moravians, and Baptists of Pennsylvania, and established a warm friendship with the great evangelist George Whitefield. But when convictions became institutionalized in a specific sect, and that sect managed to establish itself in a position to exert real social influence, Franklin's attitude could be considerably less tolerant.

His attitude toward the Presbyterians, at least until the last quarter of his life, is a case in point. He seems to have feared and distrusted his sect more than any other, mainly because the Presbyterians seemed to have more influence on the society he knew and were, therefore, capable of doing more mischief with their peculiar doctrines. Franklin claimed to have found the Calvinist doctrines of presdestination, election, and reprobation "unintelligible," sometimes "doubtful." In fact, he probably considered them quite mad—although beyond all proof or refutation. When people, holding such doctrines, form what amounts to a religious establishment they become a potential threat to the public good. It is little wonder that Franklin reacted with what seems at first glance uncharacteristic outrage when a heterodox preacher, like Hemphill—who, it turned out, was a plagiarist as well—was dismissed from his pulpit. Franklin was doing more here than speaking in behalf of better sermons or fighting for free speech: he was attacking what he considered a social menace—institutionalized ignorance equipped with the power to enforce its standards and its views on the wider society. The key to spiritual truth like the key to material progress is the open society, in which rational individuals can test conflicting claims for themselves, just as the prospective buyer of a Franklin stove might "make the Comparison" between the "old and the new Methods" of home heating. Any institution that has the power to prevent or restrict this kind of "Comparison" is dangerous. Franklin's tolerance applied to individuals, not to powerful social institutions.[17] Institutions were the machinery that ran society. They were to be studied, used, repaired when necessary, redesigned, even junked when the circumstances demanded it. Machines control things, but they must never be permitted to control people.

Machines should not control people, but Franklin's attitude of intelligent handiness applied to people as well as to things, ideas, and institutions. The problem here is that man, though rational, may be overcome by his emotions, which have to be kept under control. Franklin always wanted to write a treatise on the "Art of Virtue," not a philosophy, as we commonly understand it, dealing with ethical theory, but a book on method and technique. The often criticized discussion of the subject in his *Autobiography*, with its list of virtues, charts, job descriptions, progress reports, and schemes for behavior modification gives us some idea of what he had in mind. In a famous letter to Joseph Priestly of 19 September 1772, Franklin even tried to quantify the act of decision-making, as though to make our moral choices more rational and exact.[18] His plans for dieting and for the budgeting of time (time being money), even his measured surrender to "venery" for the sake of health or offspring, reveal a man anxious to control himself and direct his life in a rational, that is, workmanlike, manner—not denying his passions, but properly disciplining and mastering them. Like many of his contemporaries, Franklin condemned "zeal" and "enthusiasm"—excessive devotion to a cause and what Yeats would call "passionate intensity." In his defense of poor Hemphill, Franklin exhibited considerable passion himself in railing against "Ignorance and Error, Bigotry, Enthusiasm, and Superstition," condemning "the hellish Fires of furious Zeal and Party Bigotry," and accusing Hemphill's accusers of promoting "Enthusiasm, Demonism, and Immorality in the World."[19] Bigotry, Ignorance, Superstition, Error—these were clearly not the proper tools for arriving at the truth, either in matters of religion or of natural philosophy. We might differ in our "religious Speculation" as we do "in Astronomy or any other Part of natural Philosophy" in peace and "Brotherly Love," Franklin advised. We might then be able to achieve "those two invaluable Blessings, full Liberty and Universal Peace," that would in turn open up "the Ways of Truth," so that perhaps one day Christians might come to agree more than, as now, they differ.[20] The point here is not that Franklin could be zealous in his denunciation of zeal: to wax enthusiastic occasionally is as human as to practice occasional venery. What deserves our attention, rather, is his concern for opening the *ways* of truth. The enemy was anything that blocked these "Ways"—and the plural form is noteworthy—be they coercive institutions, "Party Bigotry," or "furious Zeal." The ways are many, and must be kept free and clear. Truth is one, but perhaps of less immediate concern to Franklin than keeping open the approaches to it. One can muddle along without the most efficient heating system, but as fully functioning human beings we cannot get along in a society where the possibilities of discovery are systematically denied or limited. That this commitment to openness might itself imply a judgment about ultimate truths—that free choice among "Ways" might itself determine "Truth"—perhaps never occurred to Franklin.

Franklin is usually pictured as a Deist—one who believes in a god, but who insists that this god is known primarily through reason and the study of nature, without recourse to special revelation; and who thinks of God not in personal terms, but more abstractly, as creator of the universe and, perhaps, its moral governor.[21] Everyone seems to agree, however, that Franklin is rather hard to pin down. In 1745, for example, commenting on the Massachusetts expedition against Fort Louisbourg, he could facetiously speculate on the efficacy of mass prayer, calculating the mechanical advantage of combined prayer power, and concluding that perhaps "works" count a bit more than "faith" when it comes to attacking fortified towns. Yet, during the Constitutional Convention in 1787, he proposed opening each session with a prayer in the conviction that "GOD governs in the Affairs of Men," and that, without God's help, the creators of the American republic would have no more success than the builders of the Tower of Babel.[22] Inconsistencies of this sort are frustratingly common in Franklin.

A simple but important reason for such inconsistencies is the fact that Franklin approached religion with the instincts of a layman and the mindset of a secular philosopher. As a layman, Franklin had no specialized training in the language and logic of theology: he was an amateur, though perhaps better acquainted with "polemic divinity" than he liked to admit. As secular philosopher, Franklin was committed to no particular doctrine, only to the search for truth regardless of where it led. To say that he was committed only to the "search for truth" makes it all sound quite smug, as though everyone else was practicing some kind of deception. Perhaps it would be more accurate to say that Franklin sought "truth" as opposed to "saving truth." He represents a relatively new phenomenon in western thought. The notion of the concerned layman, interested in religion as an intellectual problem, stems mainly from the Reformation and the growing conviction that religious thought is no longer the exclusive province of a handful of scholarly monks. The idea of the secular philosopher investigating something out of mere curiosity is older, of course; but the *combination* of concerned layman and secular philosopher turning his attention to matters of ultimate concern was relatively new to the West in Franklin's time. Now, no one, not even Benjamin Franklin, can shrug off his cultural background entirely. Franklin retained many of the prejudices and presuppositions of the Calvinist-Protestant heritage. But when he approched theological questions it was neither as what we today would call an "expert" nor as an apologist. He carried fewer pieces of theological baggage than any theologian, and he had less of a burden of pious concern than a lay believer. He could therefore afford to be flexible to the point of intellectual playfulness and rational to the point of irresponsibility if his curiosity, interest, logic, and whims led him in such a direction. Franklin represents western man entering a new era of intellectual consciousness.

Perhaps his most playful and scandalous theological work in his *Dissertation on Liberty and Necessity, Pleasure and Pain* (1725), which he published in England, at age nineteen, then later renounced as one of the "errata" of his life. In this early piece, Franklin took the basic assumptions of Deism and Lockean psychology and pushed them to their logical conclusions, denying free will, moral agency, and the very idea of moral distinction. The work, as Alfred Owen Aldridge rightly concludes, is implicitly atheistic, one might even say nihilistic.[23] In a clockwork cosmos of the kind young Franklin describes, everything is so perfect and thoroughly accounted for that, in the final analysis, nothing counts for anything. It is a world of right without wrong, Yin without Yang: it is morally frozen and existentially pointless. If there is a God, and that God is all-good, all-wise, and all-powerful, said Franklin, there is no freedom, no evil, no surprise. God has created a machine universe characterized by perfect "Order and Regularity" and little else. One may admire this universe for a while, then forget it entirely, since it will do what God intends it to do and nothing more. Franklin was being playful here, examining ideas and testing postulates mainly to see where certain assumptions lead. He may also have thought that this line of argument would provide one with a measure of metaphysical consolation, although his concluding remark to the effect that his idea might meet with an "indifferent Reception" and his homely advice that we cannot change geese into swans by wishful thinking suggest that our cosmic comfort was not uppermost in his mind.[24] In any event, Franklin soon repudiated these speculations as being, if not illogical, morally unrealistic. He used, in fact, the pragmatic test: supposing a proposition to be true, what would be the consequences of acting upon it? Franklin concluded that his theory, though possibly true, was not very useful.[25]

Franklin's *Dissertation* is itself an index of his secular rationalism. He felt no theological restraints in pushing his logic to its conclusion and in punctuating that conclusion with an exclamation point: "Our *Geese* are but *Geese* tho' we may think 'em *Swans*." But his renunciation of this conclusion is a clear mark of his empiricism: the empirical test of a moral proposition being its utility, Franklin found that as a philosophy of life the argument of the *Dissertation* was a failure. People actually making their way through the interrelationships of social life are, in fact, influenced by their moral cosmology and may behave the worse for believing their behavior counts for nothing.[26]

Franklin was already rewriting his theology on the tedious voyage back from England in the summer of 1726, and in 1728 he drew up his "Articles of Belief," in which he presented a revised version of the universe and of man's place in it. In the "Articles" one still has a sense of the immensity of the universe and of the puniness of humankind, but here Franklin's starting-point and his conclusions are different. In the *Dissertation* he started with God as the "First Mover," and reasoned deductively from that premise. In the "Articles" he also began by acknowledging God, the "one supreme, most powerful Being," but quickly shifted to the human perspective, looking up and out from "this little Ball on which we move," into the infinitude of deep space, finding his "narrow Imagination" quite overwhelmed by the cosmic prospect before him. His concern seems no longer cosmic description but basic comprehension, and he is less concerned with the workings of an enormous machine than with seeing himself emotionally in some kind of relationship with a vastness that seems beyond human conceptualization. His attitude is less one of curiosity than of awe and wonder. Still, Franklin was not the man to be entirely overwhelmed, even by cosmic emotion. A person is obliged to deal with the object of his wonder analytically, as he would deal with the problem of divine omniscience or of evil in the universe. But the question now is how we are to respond to something and not merely what we are to think of it. What is our personal relationship to God, and in what frame of mind do we properly approach the Creator of the Universe?

The "polytheism" of Franklin's "Articles of Belief" is a puzzle. Does it reflect his eighteenth-century devotion to classical thought and the ancient gods? Or is it an application of the idea of the Great Chain of Being, featuring subordinate gods to stand between the Supreme Being and man, just as the higher primates do between human beings and the lower animals?[27] Franklin's position is clear in any case. It is inconceivable that an infinite God could have much regard for "such an inconsiderable Nothing as Man," or feel any need for human devotion and worship. On the other hand, as rational beings, we feel the need, the "Duty," in fact, to pay homage "to Something." Franklin, apparently, felt ridiculous offering praise To Whom It May Concern, and yet he seems to have had no patience with or understanding of the Christian idea of God Incarnate in some time-space embodiment. He concludes, therefore

> that the Infinite has created many beings or Gods, vastly superior to Man, who can better conceive his Perfections than we, and return him a more rational and glorious Praise.

"It may be," he speculates, "that these created Gods are immortal; or it may be that after many Ages, they are changed, and others supply their Places." In any event, "I conceive that each of these is exceedingly wise and good, and very powerful," and each has his own sun and planetary system, of which he is creator and ruler. "It is that particular Wise and good God, who is the author and owner of our System, that I propose for the object of my praise and adoration." What seems significant here is not the source of Franklin's idea but his reason for and way for proposing it. "It may be," "I conceive that," "I propose." His tone is clearly hypothetical and conjectural, in line with the tactic of humility set forth in the *Autobiography,* but suggesting as well the tentative, deliberate approach of the experimental inquirer. And his reasoning lies clearly with economy of explanation: given the facts as we know them, what is the simplest, most sensible explanation available to us to account for them? Franklin proposes a kind of cosmic bureaucracy, a rationalized, well-organized chain of divine command with an Infinite Being acting through the agency of less-than-infinite deistic intermediaries. This explanation fits in well with Franklin's theistic premise, with the classical idea of a Chain of Being, and with good sense; and it is presented not with the urgency of a manifestation of the sacred but with the unflappable casualness of one proposing a better way of explaining an electrical discharge. Does this mean that Franklin was not serious about religion? Not at all. His statement of belief was followed by a service of adoration, petition, and thanksgiving, nothing in which suggests flippancy. It is just that Franklin had a different idea of religious "seriousness" from the traditional one. The feeling of awe and reverence that he experienced before the Great Mystery of Being was more controlled and subdued than that experienced by Moses at Sinai or Isaiah before God's Throne. It is the Holy scaled down to what Franklin would consider its proper proportions—met with fear and trembling, perhaps, but not ecstacy or any emotion beyond all controlling. Religion was too serious a matter to be permitted to drive one to distraction. Faith is too important to be left to the passions: we should serve it with our highest not our lowest proclivities.

The God who created and who governs our solar system is "vastly superior" to man in wisdom, goodness, and power, and yet is "not above" caring for us, being pleased by our praise and worship, and of being our "Friend." Since the time of Copernicus the universe had grown infinitely distant. Franklin's created, finite deity lived within human reach and was more like the God of Abraham, Isaac, and Jacob—in accessibility if not in transcendence. The Infinite God filled Franklin's intellectual need for a Creator of the Universe, a Prime Mover. The more finite God of this world system seems to have satisfied his more personal need for a friend behind phenomena, a deity we may address as "Thou" and recognize as our "Father." It is unclear whether Franklin needed to feel this in any deeply personal way. But it seems to have been important to his idea of human nature and the human condition, particularly when man is regarded not in his solitude but in his social life and moral relations. Franklin's "Articles of Belief" are followed by a prayer of "Adoration," then a "Petition," asking mainly for strength and guidance, and prefaced by a prayer that explicitly avoids any request for particular "Temporal Blessings" (since, in our ignorance, we cannot really know what is best for us), and instead begs help in "my Continued Endeavors and Resolutions of eschewing Vice and embracing Virtue."[28] One gets the impression that Franklin demands a nearby God who is a "Friend" not so much to console and support us in times of crisis, nor even to underwrite the moral order by punishing vice and rewarding virtue, but to inspire and cheer us in our noblest aspirations. Franklin's God relates to man primarily as a hope for transcendence, ever encouraging us to surpass ourselves in our moral life.

This moral life, furthermore, has to be understood in the broadest possible way. It is not to be narrowly identified with Franklin's list of specific virtues, for these were clearly instrumental virtues, enumerated only as a means or technique for improving one's attitude and conduct. It is, rather, our social existence regarded holistically, involving a network of human interrelationships, both public and private, in which we live to grow to the full measure of our humanity by always pushing beyond all measure, all limit. "Man's Perfection," Franklin said in 1731, "is in Virtue."[29] And, although he maintained, in his *Autobiography*, that he had developed a plan (albeit a "bold and arduous" one) for arriving at moral perfection, it seems clear that Franklin never regarded perfection as an attainable (*i.e.*, measurable) goal in life; not only because we always fall short or slide back into one vice while trying to overcome another, but because human perfection is by definition always one step beyond whatever measure has been attained. Franklin was empiricist enough to know that we can meaningfully evaluate our performance only if we establish a standard of measurable achievement. But he was Calvinist enough to realize that perfection is an open-ended concept that points beyond all measure, beyond all quantifiable limits. It is true that Franklin insisted that the idea of a "perfect Man" is no more absurd than that of a perfect horse or perfect oyster—defining "perfection" as the best something is capable of being.[30] Here he was arguing against Calvinists who insisted on human depravity and idealists who held up unrealizable standards. My point is simply that Franklin, in his more strenuous mood, did look beyond the actual, state-of-the-art best to see human life in terms of possibility and relentless striving. Religion offered Franklin not just reassurance for the moral status quo but hope for moral possibility in the making. He repudiated his own *Dissertation* for this very reason. The universe described therein saw to the punishment of horse thieves but offered no encouragement to the seeker after righteousness. To put it another way, the perfect man, unlike the perfect oyster, seeks always to outdo himself. For it is the built-in imperative of a moral nature that makes us human beings in the first place.[31]

In 1732 Franklin delivered an address to his Junto, "On the Province of God in the Government of the World." In it he argued that, on the basis of our knowledge of God's wisdom, goodness, and power, we may safely infer that, although God allows for free agency and the regular operation of the "Course of Nature," He is nonetheless free to intervene from time to time at His pleasure. Our sense of moral justice supports the belief in a God who is both able and willing to answer our prayers. Our faith in God's Providence is "the Foundation of all true Religion," serving as a "Powerful Regulator of our Actions," giving us "Peace and Tranquility within our own Minds," and rendering us "Benevolent, Useful, and Beneficial to others." The faith in Providence, in other words, provides a basis alike for socil discipline, moral inspiration, and spiritual comfort—all resting on the conviction that humankind is part of a larger pattern of conscious purpose and active concern in the universe.[32]

Franklin's thoughts on prayer and immortality tie in which his understanding of divine Providence. He put aside his early idea of a soulless, clockwork universe, but one suspects that he was never able entirely to shake off all the doubts expressed in the *Dissertation*. In any event, all his later utterances in behalf of prayer and immortality reveal as much doubt as faith, and seem more expressions of hope than of firm conviction.[33] Franklin wanted to believe in both the efficacy of prayer and the afterlife, again for spiritual as well as moral and social reasons. He longed for the feeling that the universe was somehow responsive to human needs and longings, and that human life had meaning that was not confined to earthly existence nor defined by biological description. If God be truly all-wise, good, and powerful, and if God be truly the "Author" of our life, then surely God must be concerned with His handiwork, attentive to its details, and prepared to correct and amend it one day, to produce "a new & more perfect Edition." This is the thrust of Franklin's famous epitaph for himself, which, in both its playful wording and hopeful tone, perfectly captures his temper of tough-minded but resolute optimism, of spiritual secularity.[34]

Franklin's attitude toward prayer appears to be a mixture of social pragmatism and spiritual instrumentalism. That is, he believed in public prayer and public worship as a basis for social unity and moral harmony among people, and in private devotion as a means of integrating one's spiritual energies. In making his proposal for public prayer before the American Constitutional Convention in 1787, Franklin evoked the image of the Tower of Babel and warned that, without God's help, the Americans will be "divided" by "little, partial, local interests," and their "Projects will be confounded."[35] In the 1770s Franklin had taken part in developing a *Liturgy on the Universal Principles of Religion and Morality*, the purpose of which was to provide "a form of social worship composed of the most enlarged and general principles, in which all men may join who acknowledge the existence of a supreme Intelligence and the universal obligations of morality," including Jews, Christians of all sects, and Mohammadens.[36] According to the organizer of this project, David Williams, Franklin had "with some emotion" declared that he "never passed a Church, during Public Service, without regretting that he could not join in it honestly and cordially. He thought it a reproach to Philosophy that it had not a Liturgy and that it skulked from the public Profession of its Principles."[37] Franklin's own private "Petition" of 1728, as we have seen, sought neither material things nor special circumstances but concentrated, instead, on the cultivation of desirable virtues and habits of mind—justice, generosity, tenderness, integrity, and the like. Prayer and worship, whether public or private, are treated as efficacious not in affecting events or provoking divine intervention in external affairs but, in the case of public worship, in drawing people together in a common bond of cosmic loyalty and humility, and, in the case of private devotion, summoning inner strength and resolve, and bringing one's spiritual energies to a focus. Our cosmic piety and cosmic loyalty inspire us in our highest endeavors and give us peace both within and among ourselves.

Franklin's views on the afterlife, like those on prayer and worship, have an "as if" quality to them. When formally declaring himself, as he did in his famous letter to Ezra Stiles a few weeks before his death, Franklin showed no hesitation in affirming "That the soul of Man is immortal, and will be treated with Justice in another Life respecting its Conduct in this."[38] Franklin expressed himself less formally and less confidently in a letter to George Whatley in 1785. There, after wryly noting the futility of our life's wishes, he yet observed that he had "some reason to wish" for improvement "in a future State." Observing God's economy in the natural world in both the proliferation of life and the conservation of matter, Franklin announced his inability to believe in the "Annihilation of Souls" and the "daily Waste of Millions of Minds." And, returning to his favored printer's metaphor, he declared that "with all the inconveniences human Life is liable to, I shall not object to a new Edition of mine."[39] Franklin's views on the afterlife are not consistent and are often quite tentative. He speaks, sometimes, in the conventional terms of rewards and punishments; yet he is capable of affirming universalism, the belief that all will be saved.[40] But the doubts of the *Dissertation* are never entirely dispelled. "My Esteem and Respect for you," he wrote Jan Ingenhousz in 1785, "will be everlasting"—concluding his lengthy letter on how to cure smoky chimneys—"if Consciousness and Memory remain in a future State."[41] The conditional qualification is important and characteristic of Franklin.

Recalling his early speculations about the nature of God and the universe, Franklin wrote Benjamin Vaughan in 1779 that the "great uncertainty I found in metaphysical reasonings disgusted me, and I quitted that kind of reading and study for others more satisfactory."[42] In 1757, having read a deistical manuscript submitted by a young man apparently hostile to Christianity, Franklin advised that the manuscript be burned and not even shown to another person. His reasoning offers no surprises. First, the manuscript denies the idea of specific Providence, that is, God's intervention in the world at His pleasure. To Franklin this amounted to an attack on all religion, for it removed all possibility of a real relationship with God, either in worship, in prayer, or in obedience through fear of divine wrath. Humankind cannot relate to a remote diety. Characteristically, Franklin refused to enter into any discussion of the truth or falsity of the writer's position: it was sufficient to observe that the work would win few converts and serve mainly to bring "Odium" upon its writer. Second, by implicitly denying religion, the work undermines morality among common folk who lack education and sophistication. For where is the motive (as far as most people are concerned) to seek virtue and shun vice once that of religion is removed?[43] Here we have both the key to Franklin's religion and a clue to his temper of mind in approaching religious matters.

The idea of divine Providence was central to Franklin's religious thinking, despite the many doubts he had about it. Franklin's God had to be more than an unmoved mover. He had to be in some way responsive to our entreaties, protective of our best interests, and moved by our efforts to do good. Franklin's God gave moral rationality to the universe and, as importantly, brought to it the warmth of personality. Beyond this Franklin was reluctant to go, for it lead into that realm of "great uncertainty" that so frustrated and "disgusted" him. Franklin's temper of mind here appears to resemble that of the agnostics of the nineteenth century who argued not only that *they* did not know the answers to the ultimate questions, but that such things were entirely unknowable by *anyone;* and that speculation about such matters was futile because no conclusive answers were possible.[44] Franklin allowed his own hopes and cosmic needs to take him so far and no further: he believed in all-powerful God who was benignly interested in His creation and both able and willing (occasionally) to intervene, notably in human affairs. Beyond this, speculation was useless.

It was worse than useless, in fact. For the great mass of people, religious faith was essential as a backstay for morality. Any speculation that served to undermine this faith might undermine morality as well, and with it the entire social order. This kind of reasoning seemed almost axiomatic to a large number of eighteenth-century thinkers beside Franklin. The social order stood at the top of a great pyramid, supported by public and private morality, and resting on the base of religious faith.[45] To chip away at the base was to risk toppling the entire structure.

Ultimately, we can only understand Franklin's religion by looking beyond it. To call him a "Deist" is fair enough; but it does not really explain very much, either about the man or about his age. Franklin's disgust at "metaphysical reasonings" and the "great uncertainty" surrounding them is as central to our understanding as his specific affirmations of belief—in

Providence, in prayer, in the afterlife. Religion, as Clifford Geertz has reminded us, is "never merely metaphysics," for it involves the entire conduct of life; but it is "never merely ethics either."[46] It is neither a body of "truths" to be believed nor a system of commands to be obeyed. It is, rather, a "world-view" by which "reality" is defined, in recognition of which and loyalty to which the people of a given culture perform the rituals, observe the rules, and acknowledge the symbols which give their lives significance. But what happens when this very complicated process starts to become self-conscious and when, because of social and cultural change, a people begins to observe its own beliefs and practices critically or from an entirely new point of view? And what happens when this "new point of view" is not just different, but actually raises to the level of a moral imperative the critical examination of all assumptions—not merely those involving the tenets of the faith itself, but the ontological presuppositions underlying those tenets? This is exactly the situation that faced the western world in the seventeenth and eighteenth centuries. Both the regulatory institutions and the reigning beliefs that had given order and purpose to western society and culture for hundreds of years were losing their legitimacy—the result of the Protestant Reformation, the rise of capitalism, global exploration, technological progress, and the Scientific Revolution that began with Copernicus. These are developments we have learned to connect with modernity, the first self-consciously cultural manifestation of which we identify with the eighteenth-century Enlightenment.[47] And it has long been customary to associate Franklin with the American Enlightenment, in perhaps its most dramatic manifestations.[48]

The word "Enlightenment" is, in a way, misleading, especially when we use it in connection with Franklin's religion. It suggests illumination, awakening, or instruction as opposed, presumably, to darkness, sleep, or ignorance. This, in fact, is how many eighteenth-century people liked to think of themselves. They saw themselves as putting aside the "supersitition," "mystery," and "ignorance" of the "Dark Ages" as they stepped into the "light" of "reason." We are left with images of children growing up, of blind men gaining their sight, or of prisoners released from a dungeon. And this invites the question raised by Krutch in his *Modern Temper:* just what have we "gained" with our "freedom"? Have we not lost more in our forsaken sense of purpose and our relinquished ability to transcend the world of things than we have gained in clarity, objectivity, and logical precision? In our mastery of means have we not lost sight of ultimate ends? It is perhaps more useful, if not more accurate, to think of modernity not so much as growing up or lighting up or coming forth, but as a lateral move from one world-view to another, a process of replacing one set of beliefs, values, and rituals with a different set.[49]

Eighteenth-century thinkers believed in truth no more passionately than those of the Middle Ages, and were no more opposed to superstition and corrupting influences than were their predecessors. But they were less committed to tradition and creeds, and they were more attached to the idea of simplicity and economy of explanation. Their idea of truth was more open-ended because they gave closer, more critical attention to the process by which "truth" was arrived at. This process they came increasingly to identify with the method of science and what David Hume called "the Experimental Method of Reasoning," which had been so successful in describing the physical universe by resolutely refusing to "go beyond experience."[50] By focusing on experience, systematically studied and critically analyzed, modern people developed the habit of equating the real with the material, and of regarding what is beyond the senses or immaterial as unreal. For medieval people, on the other hand, the unseen world could be every bit as "real" as the material world. Medieval people possessed what Carolly Erikson describes as a "visionary imagination," which allowed them to regard their world as "enchanted," the supernatural as "real," and the entire universe as part of a wider pattern of theological meaning.[51] When John Locke decided that the best way to approach the profound questions of religion and morality was not head-on but through an investigation of the meaning of knowledge itself—ultimately tracing knowledge to "sensations"—he not only revolutionized philosophy, but he also demonstrated how fundamentally the western imagination had shifted its focus. He showed how closely western people had joined truth "to temporal existence, to the world of individual variables."[52] All that was really needed was a system of thought to rationalize and describe the scope of the new imagination.

This new system of thought was taking shape in the eighteenth century. In the seventeenth and eighteenth centuries, according to Norman Fiering, western people moved from a theological to a moral universe—from an age dominated by the language and metaphors of theology to one that looked to moral philosophy to provide the basis for discourse and communication, the images and concepts by which people made sense out of their world. In the English-speaking world, says Fiering, we may trace the emergence of moral philosophy from its former status as a (rather suspect) branch of theology to independence, then to cultural dominance. And moral philosophy proved to be inseparable from *natural* theology—the effort to establish God's existence and attributes through the empirical study of the natural world—"since it invariably involved a kind of moral teleology of the universe."[53] This provided cosmic purpose and moral rationality to a universe being drained of spiritual meaning by science and, more fundamentally, disenchanted by a shift in mentality—in which the unseen became increasingly unreal, the supernatural was viewed with suspicion, and all "metaphysical reasonings" were plagued with "great uncertainty."

British and American moral philosophy owed much to Anthony Ashley Cooper, the Third Earl of Shaftesbury, for its central inspiration. Shaftesbury made the so-called moral sentiments central to his ethical system, in effect basing morality on human nature itself.[54] This meant that, just as natural theology allowed one to establish the existence and attributes of God, so moral philosophy allowed one to make a rational case for the moral order of the universe. If Franklin truly shifted his religious position from "scientific deism" to "humanitarian deism," no longer looking for proof of God in the physical universe, but searching instead into the human heart,[55] the shift was neither a fundamental nor an original one. Many, beside Franklin, realized that the "scientific deism" of natural theology needed the "humanitarian deism" of moral philosophy (including the emphasis it placed on man's moral nature) to make the case for value and righteousness in the universe. The indicative statements of physics cannot establish norms or duties: they describe a universe that is value free. Moral philosophy, on the other hand, probing into the deepest recesses of human nature—and doing so in an empirical or "experimental" way—finds here the most convincing proof of the morality of existence. As Franklin observed in his *Autobiography*, he became convinced:

> that vicious actions are not hurtful because they are forbidden, but forbidden because they are hurtful, the nature of man alone considered. . . .[56]

Franklin could not blindly accept the authority of revelation; nor could he find in the brute facts of the physical universe the germs of virtue. But in man's moral nature was the empirical link which, for Franklin, joined both the world of fact to the world of value and the method of science to the moral demands of religion. Franklin could, relieved, abandon the vagaries of metaphysical reasonings because moral philosophy ("the nature of man alone considered") joined world-view to ethos, translating the Divine Imperative into empirical terms. Together, natural theology and moral philosophy furnished the basis for a new way of interpreting experience—a new cosmic perspective to replace that which had formerly been provided by traditional theology and sustained by the visionary imagination of a vanished—or vanishing—age.

Benjamin Franklin—a self-made man in an age when the "self" (as distinct from society) had scarcely been defined—did not have a visionary imagination. Franklin's might be called a *graphic imagination*, an engineering, manipulative, hands-on approach to the world that could grasp the meaning of smokeless chimneys and improved heating devices, but was impatient with the fabulous, the theophanous, the unworldly. Yet, his graphic imagination could extend, by means of the new "experimental method of reasoning," to the invisible world of electrical "fluids," suggesting hypotheses, divising experimental situations to test them, and making intelligent inferences. Had he, like Newton, understood higher mathematics, Franklin might have explored the invisible world even more extensively. But the invisible world of the new physics was nothing like that invisible world to which the saints and martyrs of the past had consecrated their lives. It was a world of precise measurements, repeatable experiments, and public verifiability. The "miracles" of science were miracles only in a figurative sense; and herein lay a world of difference. The inventor of the Franklin stove participated in a universe of discourse in which science increasingly provided the standard of rationality, and reason was exalted as the proper instrument of good sense and clear thinking. This kind of thinking accompanied Franklin when he moved from science to religion. Franklin did not approach religion with the attitude of a scientist: he approached both science and religion with nothing more esoteric than the frame of mind of a no-nonsense workman who saw no reason why alert intelligence and solid common sense should not work as effectively on one area as in the other. And this frame of mind was not just a function of Franklin's snuff-colored mediocrity. It was an expression of his culture and its alteration in imaginative perception. To Franklin's way of thinking, what had been lost in making this move had probably not been worth having in the first place.

Notes

1. *The Modern Temper: A Study and a Confession* (New York and London: Harvest Books; Harcourt, Brace, Jovanovich, 1929, 1957), 126–30.

2. This useful term serves as Paul Tillich's basic definition of "faith." See his *Dynamics of Faith* (New York: Harper & Brothers, 1957), 1–4.

3. Leonard W. Labaree, et al., eds., *The Papers of Benjamin Franklin* (New Haven: Yale University Press, 1960), vol. 2, 421–46; quotation, 441. William B. Willcox took over the position of chief editor of this project in 1975, with volume 19. References henceforth will be simply to *Papers*.

4. Leonard W. Labaree, et al, eds., *The Autobiography of Benjamin Franklin* (New Haven and London: Yale University Press, 1964), 192 (hereafter *Autobiography*).

5. On Franklin's commitment to the "method of observation" see: Alfred Owen Aldridge, "Benjamin Franklin and the *Philosophes*," *Studies on Voltaire and the Eighteenth Century* 24 (1963): 54–55. See also I. Bernard Cohen, *Franklin and Newton* (Phildelphia: American Philosophical Society, 1956), 3–88, and Cohen's introduction to his edition of Franklin's *Experiments and Observations on Electricity* (Cambridge, Mass.: Harvard University Press, 1941; 1774), 3–138.

6. For a fascinating discussion of this see Morris Berman, *The Reenchantment of the World* (Ithaca, N.Y., and London: Cornell University Press, 1981), 27–132.

7. James Madison Stifler, *The Religion of Benjamin Franklin* (New York and London: D. Appleton & Co., 1925), 77.

8. Ibid., 46.

9. On the influence of Franklin's social background on his thought, see Paul W. Connor, *Poor Richard's Politicks: Benjamin Franklin and His New American Order* (New York, Oxford, London: Oxford University Press, 1965), 32–66. Franklin's part in the religious controversies both in Boston and Philadelphia is discussed by Melvin H. Buxbaum, *Benjamin Franklin and the Zealous Prebyterians* (University Park & London: Pennsylvania State University Press, 1975).

10. Laboree, *Autobiography*, 57–60.

11. On Franklin as scientist see, beside Cohen, *Franklin and Newton*, Carl Van Doren, *Benjamin Franklin* (New York: Viking Press, 1935), 156–73.

12. This kind of "caring"—a feature of modernity at its best—is one of the subjects of the excellent philosophical rhapsody by Robert Pirsig, *Zen and the Art of Motorcycle Maintenance* (New York: William Morrow & Co., 1974).

13. See Paolo Rossi, *Philosophy, Technology, and the Arts in the Early Modern Era*, Salvator Attanasio, trans., Benjamin Nelson, ed. (Harper Torchbooks; New York, Evanston, London: Harper & Row, 1970; 1962).

14. Stifler, *Religion of Franklin*, 77.

15. *Papers*, 2:31.

16. Labaree, *Autobiography*, 146.

17. On the Hemphill controversy of 1735 see Franklin's *Papers* 2:22–33, 37–126. This remarkable episode is discussed by Buxbaum, *Zealous Presbyterians*, 76–115, who also interprets Franklin's (nearly) life-long quarrel with the Presbyterians. See also: "Franklin on the Hemphill Trial: Deism Versus Presbyterian Orthodoxy," *William and Mary Quarterly* 10, ser. 3, no. 3 (July 1953):422–40.

18. *Papers* 19: 299–300. There is at least a scrap of evidence that Franklin actually used his "prudential algebra" himself. See *Papers* 20:336–38.

19. *Papers* 2:67, 85, 103.

20. Papers 2:85.

21. Franklin's Deism is most fully discussed in Alfred Owen Aldridge, *Benjamin Franklin and Nature's God* (Durham, N.C.: Duke University Press, 1967). This volume offers the most complete discussion of Franklin's religious views.

22. The two episodes are reported respectively in the *Papers* 3:26–27, and Albert Henry Smyth, ed., *The Writings of Benjamin Franklin*, vol. 9 (New York & London: Macmillan Co., 1906), 600–1 (hereafter Smyth).

23. *Benjamin Franklin and Nature's God*, 12–24. But compare this with Aldridge's earlier interpretation, "Benjamin Franklin and Philosophical Necessity," *Modern Language Quarterly* 12, no. 3 (September 1951):292–309.

24. *Papers*, 1:57–71.

25. Labaree, *Autobiography*, 114–15.

26. On Franklin's empiricism and its application to the moral life see I. Bernard Cohen, *Benjamin Franklin: His Contribution to the American Tradition* (Indianapolis & New York: Bobbs-Merrill, 1953), 48–67.

27. See Aldridge, *Nature's God*, 25–33.

28. *Papers*, 1:101–10.

29. "Doctrine to Be Preached," *Papers*, 1:212–13.

30. *Papers* 1:261.

31. Aldridge suggests this in his reference to Franklin's "humanitarian deism" (*Nature's God*, 81).

32. *Papers* 1:264–69.

33. Aldridge, *Nature's God*, 252–59.

34. *Papers* 1:111.

35. Smyth, *Writings* 9:601.

36. David Williams, "More Light on Franklin's Religious Ideas," *American Historical Review* 43, no. 4 (July 1938):803–13. It was in the same ecumenical spirit that Franklin revised the Lord's Prayer (Smyth, *Writings* 7:427–30) and offered, in 1773, an *Abridgement of the Book of Common Prayer* for the Anglicans.

37. Williams, "More Light," 810.

38. Smyth, *Writings* 10:84–85.

39. Ibid., 333–34.

40. See Franklin's letter to Mrs. Elizabeth Partridge, 25 November 1788, in Smyth, *Writings* 9:683.

41. Smyth 9:442.

42. Ibid., 412.

43. *Papers* 7:294–95.

44. See the famous "Reply to Dr. Lymann Abbott," in *The Works of Robert G. Ingersoll*, vol. 4 (New York: Dresden, 1909–1915), 463–64.

45. D. H. Meyer, *The Democratic Enlightenment* (New York: G. P. Putnam's Sons, 1976), 174–76.

46. Geertz, "Ethos, World-View and the Analysis of Sacred Symbols," *Antioch Review* 17, no. 4 (December 1957):421–37.

47. See Peter Gay, *The Enlightenment: An Interpretation*, 2 vols. (New York: Alfred A. Knopf, 1966, 1969), esp. 1:127–203, 322–419.

48. Henry F. May, *The Enlightenment in America* (New York: Oxford University Press, 1976), 126–32.

49. Carl Becker, *The Heavenly City of the Eighteenth-Century Philosophers* (New Haven: Yale University Press, 1932), made this suggestion, but tended to fix attention on the persistence of older forms—those of the Christian Middle Ages—in the new, "secular" context.

50. Hume, *A Treatise of Human Nature: Being an Attempt to Introduce the Experimental Method of Reasoning into Moral Subjects* (London: Oxford University Press, 1960, 1739), introduction.

51. Carolly Erickson, *The Medieval Vision: Eessays in History and Perception* (New York: Oxford University Press, 1967), 3–47, 213–19.

52. Ibid., 218. See also Locke, *An Essay Concerning Human Understanding*, 2 vols. (New York: Dover, 1959; 1690), "Epistle to the Reader," 1:7–24.

53. Norman Fiering, "President Samuel Johnson and the Circle of Knowledge," *William and Mary Quarterly* 28, ser. 3 (April 1971):213. See also Fiering's "Moral Philosophy in America, 1650 to 1750, and Its British Context" (Doctoral dissertation, Columbia University, 1969), and his published monographs, *Moral Philosophy at Seventeenth-Century Harvard* (Chapel Hill: University of North Carolina Press, 1981), 295–302, and *Jonathan Edwards's Moral Philosophy in Its British Context* (Chapel Hill: North Carolina University Press, 1981).

54. Fiering, "Moral Philosophy in America," 150–51. By the mid-eighteenth century Shaftesbury was being attacked by many American clergymen for his association with Deism. See Fiering, *Jonathan Edwards's Moral Philosophy*, 108–9.

55. Aldridge, *Nature's God*, 34–46, 81.

56. Labaree, *Autobiography*, 158. Cf. pp. 114–15.

Views from Abroad

[Introduction to *Franklin and His Contemporaries*]

Alfred Owen Aldridge*

As Voltaire in the eighteenth century stood as a symbol of the Philosophic Enlightenment and is now considered an intellectual precursor of the French Revolution, so his American contemporary Benjamin Franklin represented the Anglo-Saxon manifestation of the same spirit and ideals. Condorcet, who knew both men, regarded each as "the apostle of philosophy and tolerance" in his own hemisphere.[1] Franklin, like Voltaire, "had often used the weapon of humour, which corrects human folly, and teaches us to regard perversity as the most pernicious folly. . . . He had honored philosophy by the genius of silence, as Voltaire by that of poetry. Franklin succeeded in delivering the vast areas of America from the bondage of Europe, and Voltaire in delivering Europe from the ancient theocracies of Asia." Although few, if any, Frenchmen considered Franklin as a match for Voltaire as satirist, wit, or literary craftsman, most French contemporaries of the two *philosophes* admired Franklin as the more versatile genius. Franklin was heralded not only as a man of letters, but also as a scientist, as a practical moralist and master of economic theory, and as a diplomat respected by the entire court.

For this reason two dramatic meetings of Franklin and Voltaire became enshrined as popular anecdotes, resembling legendary tales of the gods and heroes of antiquity. Once Franklin visited Voltaire on his sickbed and asked for the blessing of the French sage upon his grandson; once at a public meeting of the Academy of Science the two men were called upon by a spontaneous demonstration of the assemblage to embrace *à la française*. Several versions of each incident exist, contributing to the fabulous nature of the encounters.

In February of 1778, Franklin, accompanied by his grandson William Temple Franklin, then eighteen years old, asked Voltaire to give the youth his benediction. In the presence of twenty witnesses profusely shedding tears of sensibility, Voltaire, according to his own statement, pronounced only the words, "Dieu et la liberté."[2] Another report has it that he said,

*Reprinted by permission from *Franklin and His French Contemporaries* (New York: New York University Press, 1957), 9–16, 239.

"Mon enfant! Dieu et la liberté,"[3] and it is possible that he added, as Condorcet asserted, "this is the only appropriate benediction for the grandson of M. Franklin."[4] La Harpe, drawing on the *Journal de Paris,* reported the benediction as, "Mon enfant, Dieu et la liberté; souvenez-vous de ces deux mots."[5] According to Condorcet, since the two sages had been speaking English, Voltaire pronounced the English words "God and Liberty."[6] It had been Voltaire, according to the *Journal de Paris,* who had chosen English as the mode of communication. His niece, feeling that the other spectators might wish to profit by the exchange of greetings, begged him to speak in French. "I ask your pardon," replied Voltaire; "I gave way a moment to the vanity of speaking the same language as Monsieur Franklin."[7] *Les Mémoires secrets,* a periodical collection of scandal and personalities, true to its sensational character, gave a caustic account of the episode, one of the few uncomplimentary pictures of Franklin in French letters. Franklin "by a base, indecent and puerile adulation, and, according to certain fanatics, by a derisive impiety, asked Voltaire to give his benediction to the child. The philosopher, playing out the scene no less thoroughly than the doctor, got up, placed his hand on the head of the little innocent, and pronounced with emphasis these three words, 'God, Liberty, and Tolerance!' "[8] Surely a touching scene played with a "little innocent" of eighteen years, an illegitimate son and illegitimate grandson, who seven years later was to become in his own right the father of an illegitimate son.

The histrionic overtones of the scene were emphasized in another contemporary account, spuriously attributed to the Marquise de Créquy. In her memoirs, Franklin's grandson is said to be four years old, and Franklin's request is interpreted as a species of ridiculous adulation. "The patriarch of Ferney, no less theatrical than the American philosopher, rose up with a hierophantic air; he placed his two hands on the head of the little man, and began to cry out at the top of his voice in tones of the devil with a cold, Liberté, Tolérance et Probité."[9]

As a result of the wide publicity given to this encounter, an admirer of Franklin wrote to him from Naples, suggesting that Franklin had introduced his grandson to Voltaire so that the young man might be able to say of Voltaire as Ovid had said of Virgil, "Virgilium vidi."[10]

The two sages met again April 29 of the same year at a public meeting of the Academy of Sciences. Although the name of neither is entered in the register of the Academy as being present that night, at least three eyewitness accounts leave little doubt that the encounter took place. A young student from the provinces in a letter to his father described the physical appearance of the two principals.[11] Franklin's simplicity stood out. He wore a plain suit of dull yellow cloth, a white hat, blending with his grey hair, and no adornments of any kind. He was quite corpulent in striking contrast to Voltaire, whose meagre bones were barely covered by a ghostlike skin, withered by eighty-four years of arduous living. Condorcet, in viewing the two patriarchs side by side, was struck by resemblances rather than contrasts.[12] Born in different worlds, each was respected for his age, his glory, and the employment of his talents, and each reflected with pleasure on the influence he had exercised on the century. As they embraced amid "noisy acclamation, one would have said that it was Solon who embraced Sophocles. But the French Sophocles had destroyed error and advanced the reign of reason; and the Solon of Philadelphia, supporting the constitution of his country on the immovable foundation of the rights of man, had no need to fear that he would see its uncertain laws during his own lifetime prepare chains for his country and open the door to tyranny." The analogy to Solon and Sophocles must have been commonplace, for it was used also by John Adams, future president of the United States, who, as joint commissioner with Franklin in Paris, was on the scene. He wrote in his diary:

> There was a general cry that M. Voltaire and M. Franklin should be introduced to each other. This was no satisfaction; there must be something more. Neither of our philosophers seemed to divine what was wished or expected; they however took each other by the hand. But this was not enough. The clamour continued until the explanation came out: *Il faut s'embrasser à la française*. The two aged actors upon this great theatre of philosophy and frivolity then embraced each other by hugging one another in their arms and kissing each other's cheeks, and then the tumult subsided. And the cry immediately spread throughout the kingdom, and I suppose all over Europe; Qu'il est charmant de voir embrasser Solon et Sophocle."[13]

The comparison was not inappropriate; apart from his incontestable reputation as a master of the classic theater, Voltaire himself maintained that his intellectual masters were Sophocles and Socrates.[14]

Voltaire's great reputation rested in some measure upon respect bordering upon fear. He had fought his way to popular esteem, not, to be sure, with the bludgeon force of his personality like Dr. Johnson in England, but with the rapier-like thrusts of his wit. Franklin's reputation rested upon love and affection. He had ingratiated himself into the hearts of the populace as well as the court; he was loved for his personal modesty and simplicity and for the simple ideas and appeal to common understanding in his literary works. This phase of his public personality was well expressed by Mme. Tussaud, creator of the famous London waxworks, who claimed to have known all of the most talented men in France before the Revolution. "Statesmen, authors, men of learning and science, metaphysicians, political enthusiasts, and even the populace," she wrote, "crowded to obtain a sight of the republican delegate; and the richest embroidered suit was an object of insipidity and passed unnoticed, whilst the simple garb of Franklin was the theme of admiration. 'He unites,' said the people, 'the deportment of Phocion to the wisdom of Socrates.' "[15] Both the disciples of Voltaire's philosophical iconoclasm and moral rationalism and the exponents of Rousseau's primitivism and social and psychological sentimentalism found in the work and personality of Franklin an expression of their cherished special beliefs.

The manifold accounts of the two interviews of Franklin and Voltaire and the impressionistic terms in which they are described illustrate a major difficulty in tracing Franklin's career. As the deists said about conventional religions, when there are so many conflicting accounts and portrayals of the attributes of god, how can we be sure that any one is true? Since nearly all modern versions of the meetings of Voltaire and Franklin derive from the accounts of John Adams and Condorcet, an air of authenticity surrounds these episodes; yet all that can be assumed about them is that they represent fictitious elaborations containing varying degrees of truth and embellishment. Other anecdotes of Franklin may be purely apocryphal. It is almost impossible to reach conclusions concerning the relation to historical fact of incidents which Franklin does not allude to in his own writings. In estimating Franklin's reputation, however, truth is of no more consequence than fiction. We are as much interested in learning what his contemporaries thought he said, did, or represented, as we are in knowing the true facts of his career.

Franklin's glory survived in France long after his death. As late as 1864, a French critic gave vivid testimony to the tremendous extent and duration of his reputation.[16]

> A strange thing, that such an enthusiasm, which in France ordinarily has the duration and the éclat of a fuse, should be prolonged from year to year, should be maintained and solidified, so to speak, to such a point that even today Franklin exists as a demi-god. He represents for everyone more or less the type and the model of all human virtues—antique simplicity, good faith and sincerity. What is there in such a conglomeration of truth or of exaggeration, of sincerity or of artificiality?

The answer to this question is to be found in the works of Franklin's contemporaries. The hundreds of references to the century's most famous American reveal that two, or possibly three, Franklins existed in French letters: first, the legendary Franklin, whose traits of character were based on his *Way to Wealth* and on a calculated pose that Franklin consciously adopted in Paris to create the impression that he was a rural philosopher or primitive patriarch. This pose he adopted in part because it suited the role he wished to play at court and in part because the French public expected him to conform to the character of Father Abraham in *The Way to Wealth*. From this pose developed, secondly, the purely imaginary Franklin, the character adopted by authors of fiction and drama from the legend which Franklin had helped to create. Finally, the actual Franklin is revealed by means of the recollections, memoirs, and eulogies of his close friends and associates. Parallel to these in their effect upon Franklin's

French reputation are the products of Franklin's own pen in France, particularly a group of light essays—some of which were composed in the French language—written for the amusement of his Parisian friends. Equally important is his autobiography, a large part of which was written at Passy and the major part of which was published in French translation before an English version appeared in print.

From another perspective we may speak of Franklin portrayed by the scores of journalists, critics, essayists, and dramatists who knew him only slightly or not at all and Franklin portrayed by the much smaller number of intimate friends who were able to describe his opinions, personality, and character from firsthand observation. Nearly all the writers of any consequence who discussed Franklin, those including Turgot, d'Alembert, abbé Morellet, Condorcet, du Pont de Nemours, La Rochefoucauld, and Cabanis, belong to the category of friends and close associates. Apart from the abbé Raynal, Cerutti, and Marmontel, who may be considered authors of some distinction, the group who wrote about Franklin without an intimate acquaintance were by and large literary hacks and propagandists or well-meaning poets and dramatists of minor talents.

Those who presented purely fictitious accounts of Franklin were obviously writers who lacked personal contact, and conversely those who portrayed the real Franklin were associates who knew him intimately. But both groups to some extent perpetuated the legend of Franklin—his pose of a primitive moralist. Barbeu Dubourg and du Pont de Nemours, to cite two examples of philosophic friends who corresponded extensively with Franklin and lived on intimate terms with him in Paris, both stress the patriarchal (to them almost avuncular) phase of Franklin's personality and consider *The Way to Wealth* as the serious expression of moral and economic ideals.

The mass of facts, records, impressions, and feelings that combined to form Franklin's total reputation derives from both his legendary and his actual character. No previous attempts have been made to separate these two threads. Indeed the only works which have hitherto touched on the subject of Franklin's reputation in France are histories of his diplomatic negotiations and full-scale biographies, works in which Franklin's reputation has been merely an incidental concern. It is a commonplace that Franklin had great influence upon his French contemporaries, but the extent of this influence in thought and literature has never been traced. One or two anecdotes and newspaper fragments have been continually quoted and the obvious literary products, such as elegies, have been known as titles, but no attempt has been made to show the extent to which Franklin's name appeared in contemporary French letters or to suggest the spirit in which French authors approached their subject.

It is possible to extract from biographical and historical materials a completely new picture of Franklin's Gallic reception. We see that some of the opinions he expressed concerning his host country were widely disseminated and that constitutional theories attributed to him had a fundamental influence upon the French Revolution. His reputation through several clearly-defined stages. At first he was considered exclusively as a scientist, later as an economist, moralist and primitive philosopher, and finally as a shrewd diplomat and distinguished statesman. Although he eventually came to be regarded as a composite of these characters, the progress in individual steps may be clearly traced. His reputation as a scientist preceded his actual appearance in France, and during the course of his first visits in 1767 and 1769 he became known as a moralist and economist. The physiocrats, his original friends and sponsors, helped to crystallize this conception by the publicity they gave to his portrayal of Indians and to kindred moral pieces. Franklin's early journalistic work, which created for him the role of primitive philosopher, became in French translation the basis of the pose he semiconsciously adopted throughout his later extended sojourn in France during the American Revolution. During this latter period, French journalists and historians gave full testimony to the respect they felt for his diplomatic abilities and political principles. Propaganda pieces that he himself inspired served further to spread his fame as statesman and journalist. Both complete strangers and literary friends and acquaintances contributed to the portrayal of this phase of his personality in French letters. Depictions of Franklin in his public character comprise a combination of the real and the assumed, his concrete activities blended with his subconscious pose and legendary attributes.

The portrayals of Franklin in belles lettres derive exclusively from his legendary character; even his Polly Baker sketch contributed to the French conception of Franklin as an exemplum of primitive rationalism. In France the double discovery was made that the sketch was a hoax and that Franklin had perpetrated it. Had French authors not taken it up, it would probably have been lost to the literary world; certainly Franklin would otherwise never have had occasion to admit his authorship. The French authors who wrote about Polly without knowing that she was Franklin's creation fostered notions concerning the primitive reason and simple morality of the American milieu out of which the Franklin legend was constructed.

Of the host of writers who celebrated Franklin in fiction, poetry, drama and allied forms, only Turgot knew him well. Turgot's tribute, a Latin epigram, is in itself graphic proof of the force of the Franklin legend. Five words elevate Franklin to epic stature. Although his achievements are compared to exploits of classical deities, his unassuming, human personality still predominates. He is a man invading the realms of supernal power and autocratic privilege for the benefit of his fellow men.

> Eripuit coelo fulmen, sceptrumque tyrannis.
>
> (He seized the lightning from the sky, and the sceptre from tyrants.)

Turgot found the legend of Franklin already formed; his epigram gave it unalterable and external character. Literally scores of poets imitated Turgot's line in French verse, and others turned their hand to original pieces.

Authors of fiction presented Franklin almost exclusively either in caricature or in allegory. Propagandists against the American Revolution played up the ludicrous aspects of his diplomatic negotiation; court satirists ridiculed the superficial aspects of the legend surrounding him—his alleged rural background, simplicity of manners, and humble demeanor. Allegorists and dedicators, on the other hand, eulogized him as the symbol of the political liberty of the new American nation. On the stage during the French Revolution, Franklin appeared as a stereotyped symbol of liberty and reason.

We have said that the real Franklin is to be seen in his bagatelles, his memoirs, and in the recollections of his friends. These works present as close an approximation to the real Franklin as literary works may conceivably attain, but still they represent approximations. We cannot be sure that any one of Franklin's friends—no matter how intimate or how observant—captured the essence of Franklin's personality. Nor can we be sure even that Franklin in his own work revealed his fundamental nature—his motives, impulses, desires, or opinions. Even if he were himself aware of all aspects of his nature—a doubtful assumption to make about anyone—he obviously made a careful choice of the elements to present to the public. His entertaining anecdotes concerning actual events in his early life, for example, may not have been consistently presented in their proper perspective. Certainly in his reminiscences elements of the Franklin pose are imperceptibly interwoven with historical fact. This explains the apparent paradox that most of his bagatelles seem to be the work of a facetious, somewhat critical wit; the autobiography, the work of a serious, somewhat parsimonious moralist. The recollections of Franklin's friends illustrate a similar paradox. All exhibit his private rather than his public or official behavior, but some reveal his frailties, his facetiousness; others his intellectual curiosity, his moral earnestness. The personalities of the authors themselves as much as the manifold aspects of Franklin's character explain these variations.

The eulogies appearing after Franklin's death exhibit similar variety. La Rochefoucauld presented a crisp, unemotional record of the major events in Franklin's life; the abbé Fauchet limited himself to Franklin's moral and religious opinions and his legislative career; Condorcet stressed Franklin's ideology; Vicq d'Azyr covered all phases of Franklin's career including his scientific achievements. But all eulogists agreed with Mirabeau, who had made a dramatic oration in the National Assembly announcing Franklin's death, that Franklin was the symbol of the new order in France and America which he had in large measure helped to create—the new order of political organization in which eminence is based not upon the accident of birth, but upon service and merit.

Notes

1. (Œuvres de Voltaire, ed. Beuchot (72 vols; Paris: J. Didot, 1827–1829), I, 289. All translations of French texts in this book are my own with the exception of the passages from Soulavie's *Mémoires historiques,* which are from the London edition of 1802.

2. Letter to the abbé Gaultier, 21 février 1778. (*Œuvres de Voltaire,* LXX, 450. Voltaire became acquainted with Franklin as early as 1767. He wrote to A. M. Mariott, 26 février 1767: ". . . Si vous voyez M. Franklin, je vous supplie, monsieur, de vouloir bien l'assurer de mon estime et de ma reconnaissance." (*Œuvres complètes* (52 vols.; Paris; Garnier frères, 1877–1885), XLV, 137.

3. "Extrait d'une Lettre de Charles Villettte sur Voltaire," *La Bouche de Fer.* No. X. Octobre, 1790, p. 149.

4. *Vie de Voltaire,* in (*Œuvres de Voltaire,* I, 290.

5. Lettre LXXXIII, *Correspondance Littéraire* (6 vols.; Paris: Migneret imprimeur, 1801–1807), II, 210–11.

6. *Vie de Voltaire,* ±, 290.

7. Lettre LXXXIII, *Correspondance Littéraire,* II, 210–11.

8. 22 février 1778.

9. *Souvenirs de la marquise de Créquy,* ed. Maurice Cousin, Cte de Courchamps (10 vols.; Paris: Garnier frères, 1903), VI, 8.

10. François Astori to Franklin, March 13, 1779. *Calendar of the Papers of Benjamin Franklin in the Library of the American Philosophical Society,* ed. I. Minis Hays (5 vols; Philadelphia: Printed for the American Philosophical Society, 1908), II, 42.

11. Letter of Etienne Catherine Baillot, May 1, 1778. Ernest Choullier, *Voltaire et Franklin à l'Académie des Sciences* (Troyes: imp. de P. Nouel, 1898), p. 4.

12. *Vie de Voltaire,* I, 290.

13. "Autobiography," *Works by John Adams* (10 vols.; Boston: Little, Brown, 1850–1856), III, 147.

14. Hays, ed., *Calendar,* IV, 241. Voltaire to Mme. Duboccage. November 2, 1777.

15. Francis Hervé, ed., *Madame Tussaud's Memoirs and Reminiscences of France* (London: Saunders & Otley, 1838), p. 56.

16. George de Cadoudal, *Les serviteurs des hommes* (Paris: C. Dillet, 1864), p. 24.

Franklin and the Imperial Court

Kimura Ki*

1. PRE-MEIJI KNOWLEDGE OF FRANKLIN

The American literary figure whose name was earliest known to Japan was Franklin. Strictly speaking, he cannot be referred to merely as a literary man, but his position in the history of American literature and philosophy makes it logical to classify him under this category. Also an industrial-

*Reprinted by permission from *A History of Japanese-American Culture Relations (1853–1926)* (Tokyo: Obunsha, 1957), 2:115–24.

ist, scientist, politician, and moralist, he may well be compared to such Japanese figures as Ninomiya Sontoku (1787–1856) and Fukuzawa Yukichi.

At the end of the Tokugawa and in the early Meiji period the *Hōtoku-sha* movement, based on the moral and economic teachings of Ninomiya, and the teachings of Fukuzawa Yukichi, both of which emphasized practical science, came into the foreground. Up to this time the official government-supported philosophy had been the Chinese Confucianist ethical and social concepts which lacked any means of practical application, being primarily abstract discussions. Opposed to these concepts was the practical science which had first been developed from the teachings of Ninomiya Sontoku. Ninomiya did not himself advocate a specific practical science, but through the influence of various teachers of economics, culminating in Yokoi Shōnan (1809–1869), specific practical proposals for reform were set forth. Fukuzawa Yukichi turned towards nineteenth century Europe and contributed positivistic learning to the new Japan. It was Franklin who fit perfectly into Japan's search for new values.

At this period of her emergence from feudalism Japan was not prepared to appreciate a refined, pure literature. Thus Franklin, not being a true man of literature but rather a writer with marked practical leanings, quickly attracted the attention of the Japanese.

In 1825, Japanese scholars of the West first heard of the history of the American Revolution and of President Washington from the German scholar, Von Siebold, who had come to the Dutch trading station at Nagasaki. It is probable that they learned also of Franklin, although no documentary evidence remains to confirm this. In 1854 a work entitled *America sōki* (General Outline of America), a partial translation of the Chinese work by Lin Tse-yü, *Kai-koku t'u-shih* (Illustrated history of Foreign Nations) was published by Hirose Chikuan. A reprint of a work by the American, Bridgman, who had gone to China and learned to write in Chinese, appeared, annotated for Japanese reading by Mizukuri Gempo, under the title *Rempō shiryaku* (Brief History of the United States). These works gave a chronological history of the United States, but failed to mention Franklin because he had not served as President. However, a brief biography appeared before the Meiji era in a book by Mizukuri, *Gyokuseki shirin* (Miscellaneous Histories), which was a translation of an article which had appeared in the 1855 edition of the *Hollandische Magajiyn*.

2. FRANKLIN'S "VIRTUES"

Franklin's autobiography was imported in the early Meiji period and was the topic for lectures by Motoda Eifu at the school for Members of the Imperial Family in the palace. How deep an impression it made may be measured by the fact that the Meiji Empress (Later the Empress dowager Shōken) composed a series of twelve poems to accompany Franklin's "Virtues." These poems caused Motoda to reply with his own series of twelve poems. They were written sometime between 1872 and 1876, most probably in 1875. Not only is this of interest as the first impact of American literature upon Japan, but it is also of importance in that it should have been made upon no less a person than the Empress of the country and upon her lecturer. It is significant that common morality, the ethics of a democracy, should have entered into the court of Whitman's "Venerable Asia." The comparison may be somewhat far-fetched, but it was something akin to the infiltration of Christianity into the Roman court, where the letters of Paul of Tarsus were read in secret by the women of Nero's court. It was a fresh breeze blowing amid the moldy air of the two thousand years of the Imperial Court.

For example, to accompany Franklin's injunction on Temperance, "Eat not to dullness; drink not to elevation," the Empress wrote:

> Hana no haru momiji no aki no sakazuki mo
> Hodo-hodo ni koso kumamahoshikere
>
> When flower-viewing in spring and admiring the maples in autumn,
> It is best to drink only in moderation.

To which Motoda replied:

> Ippyō nomitarite yokan ari
> Haru wa baika nao imada takenawanarazaru ni ari
> Tashō ningen kōraku no koto
> Jūbun wa shikazu hachibun no yasuki ni
>
> One goord gives sufficient pleasure
> Plum blossoms are best just before they are in full-bloom,
> When people go on an outing,
> It is best to enjoy, without becoming fully sated.

To accompany the virtue of Silence, "Speak not but what may benefit others or yourself; avoid trifling conversation," the Empress wrote:

> Sugitaru wa oyobzarikeri karisome no
> Kotoba mo ada ni chirasazaranan
>
> Do not speak too much,
> It serves no purpose, speak not even insignificant words

And Motoda replied:

> Kiku o itō chōchō bummei o toku o
> Shikazu chinsen shite mazu makoto o yashinawan ni
> Tōri mono yū naki mo nanzo iro o genzen
> Mankei no kōsai ni jinkō muragaru.

I dislike hearing much talk of civilization,
Better to introspect and nurture the truth.
Even though the peach and dansom say nothing, their
beauty does not fade,
And people crowd the roads to see their brilliance.

These abstract moral tenets cannot be described as literature. In Christianity there are parables and moralistic verse teaching the moral tenets which are scarcely worth the trouble of reading. But the poetic techniques of those who created such verse must, to a certain extent, be taken into consideration, and the ability of the Empress in this capacity was indeed extraordinary.

In reading these "Virtues" from Franklin's autobiography, two questions arise. The first is that Franklin mentions thirteen virtues, which poses the question as to why only twelve are given in the Japanese version. The virtue of chastity has been omitted, probably because it was either completely deleted in editions prepared for use by the young, or else merely mentioned and briefly explained. It is probable that an edition of this type was used at the Imperial Court. The other question which arises is the order in which these virtues are listed. The Japanese version, as found in the poems of the Empress and Motoda, varies greatly from the original. This was because Motoda arranged them in what he thought was a fitting order of importance for use by members of the court. In addition, some of the more easily explained virtues were listed first since they might more readily be described poetically.

3. *FUJIN KAGAMI* OR A MIRROR FOR WOMEN

One of the most significant characteristics of the Emperor Meiji was his extreme interest in moral education. In the early fall of 1879 he ordered Motoda Eifu to compile a work for education in general morals for the young. The result was *Yōgaku kōyō* (Essentials of Child Education), published two years later. An Oriental version of Smiles' *Self-Help*, it was a collection of twenty moral anecdotes based on Chinese and Japanese morality. Originally it had been planned to include western moral tales, but these were later deleted. It is unknown whether they were omitted because their inclusion would make the work too large, or whether the existence of Smiles' work, which was known as the "Emperor's Bible" made it superfluous, or whether the Confucianists wondered if the oriental virtues were perhaps not superior to the Occidental.

Next Motoda, again at the Emperor's behest, composed a work for the education of young girls, the *Fujin kagami*. Fortunately, Western stories were not excluded from this work. In the fourth part *(kan)* of the work the story of Sarah Bache and how she sewed clothing for the Revolutionary

Army is contained. Once again Franklin enters the picture, for Sarah Bache was his child.

The Emperor Meiji was fully satisfied with both works and frequently called together the young female members of the Imperial Household in his private chambers, and took pleasure in lecturing to them. Thus the Emperor must frequently, in the course of these lectures, have talked of Franklin.

Seventy years later, when Mrs. Vining came as tutor to the Crown Prince, a biography of Franklin was used during his instruction. This is not written of in her widely read work, *Windows for the Crown Prince,* but mention of it was made in articles she wrote for American newspapers. When the Crown Prince returned from participating in the Coronation ceremonies for Queen Elizabeth, he stopped in Philadelphia and was photographed standing before Franklin's statue. Franklin has long been associated with the education of the members of the Japanese Imperial Family.

4. KAJIN NO KIGO (CHANCE MEETING WITH TWO BEAUTIES) AND FRANKLIN

Franklin's appeal to the Imperial Court was limited to the early Meiji period, when the spirit expressed in the fifth article of the Emperor's oath, "to seek learning widely throughout the world," was at its height, and during the postwar period under the Occupation. In the intervening years little attention was paid him. However, for the most part, Franklin was readily understood by Japanese and was cordially received and accepted as a person of universal appeal.

Franklin is mentioned three times in Nakamura Keiu's (1832–1891) translation of Smiles' *Self-Help* and twice discussed in Fukuzawa Yukichi's translation of Chambers' Moral Class Book. Both books were widely read, so that Franklin's name became known throughout Japan. However, these were translation only, so that neither the translators' reactions to Franklin nor how they judged him were critically expressed.

Perhaps the first instance in which a direct critical judgment of Franklin is made is in Shiba Shirō's (1852–1922) *Kajin no kigū.* This work was a political novel, the first volume of which appeared in 1885. In the interim period between the decay of Tokugawa period light literature and the emergence of the Meiji novel, the political novel, although unrefined, was to some extent a fresh stream in the literary production of the time. However, most Japanese novelists followed the pattern set by Disraeli; Shiba's work, however, differed entirely, and was the product of his own imagination.

It was partly autobiographical in nature and told of the adventures of one Tōkai Sanshi, which was a pseudonym used by the author. As was the author himself, the hero is born in Aizu, and with his clan's defeat at the time of the Restoration, he determines to go to America. There he meets a daughter of Spanish royalty and a girl who has been forced to flee her native Ireland. Both women are superlative in beauty and patriotically grieving at conditions in their homelands. The three are joined by a Chinese working for the restoration of the Ming dynasty, who has come to America as a cook.

The novel depicts events throughout the world and concerns itself largely with modern history in which weak nations are oppressed by the stronger. Described first as oppressors are Britain, followed by Russia, France, and Germany. The United States, being deemed a country of freedom, is not included. America is described in the opening pages of the book, making this perhaps the first Japanese novel of any importance in which the American scene is depicted. The author tells of Tōkai Sanshi's visit to Independence Hall in Philadelphia, where he sees the Liberty Bell, reads the Declaration of Independence, and encounters, but does not speak to the two beauties with whom he is to share continental adventures. The hero soon falls ill, but being unable to bear the solitude of bed, pays a visit to Franklin's tomb where he reads a Chinese poem bespeaking the American's virtues.

The novel was printed on indigo paper, and it is said that the students of the time carried it about, reciting the verses contained. Perhaps the poem at Franklin's grave was one of those recited.

The author, Shiba Shirō, was elected to the diet when the parliamentary system was introduced to Japan, and served as a parliamentary undersecretary in the Foreign Office in the Okuma cabinet.

5. DISSATISFACTION OF KUNIKIDA DOPPO

Perhaps the first version of Franklin's autobiography to appear as a single volume was *Meika no yokun* (Fragrance of Departed Blossoms). Published in 1887, it was translated by Mitarai Masakazu, of whom all that is known is the information to be found on the colophon, which states that he was of a samurai family in Shizuoka Prefecture. The first sixteen chapters are a translation of the autobiography, and the remaining chapters contain a rendition of supplementary material concerning Franklin. A comparison with the original reveals that certain minor details have been omitted, but that, on the whole, it is a faithful translation. It may be that Mitarai based it on an American or English abridged edition.

The preface, by Nakamura Keiu, the translator of Smiles' *Self-Help*, is of interest, for it compares Franklin's autobiography with Arai Hakuseki's *Oritaku shiba no ki*. Not only do the two works resemble each other, but the two men themselves have many points of similarity.

Some fourteen or fifteen years later Franklin's autobiography was widely used as a textbook in the teaching of English in schools throughout Japan, with the result that a large number of commentaries appeared in magazines and in book form. When the present author was attending school prior to matriculating in the literature department at Waseda, the teacher of English composition, frequently corrected the students papers with the comment that a certain grammatical usage was to be found in the autobiography. Thus, it became customary for the students to memorize portions of the biography in order to strengthen their English composition.

In 1896 the Min'yū-sha publishers issued a series of biographies of famous men for use by young people. The first volume was a work on Franklin's younger days. The author's name was not given in the work; however, it was none other than Kunikida Doppo (1871–1908), who has been compared by some with Chekov as a writer of short stories. This was his first work, a pot-boiler, written because he was in need of money so that it need not be taken into consideration when evaluating his work.

In his diary Doppo records the impression that Franklin made upon him. He appraises him as a man without religious insight, but possessed of common sense reasoning, intrepidity, business acumen, and an advocate of common morality. He found him not a man of religious genius capable of moving people, but rather a great example for the citizens of America. He was struck by Franklin's common sense and by his successful harmonization of public and private life. However, his criticism of Franklin's religious attitude marked the first time that a Japanese had found something unsatisfactory in Franklin's character. Doppo himself, being somewhat self-centered and unrestrained by nature, found it difficult to adjust to society, and admired Franklin's ability to contain himself within the restrictions of actual living.

6. NATSUME SŌSEKI AND MASAOKA SHIKI

Masaoka Shiki (1867–1902) when ill in bed, read the autobiography with extreme interest. Shiki, a poet who did not customarily read western books, wrote in his *Byōshō Rokushaku* (Six-foot Sickbed) of how the work had impressed him. Writing one year after he had read the work, he remarks how he laboriously made his way through the fine print, and how he felt that this work, although widely read by Japanese, had made a more than usually deep impression upon himself.

Shiki, who effected a great change in the writing of *haiku* poetry, was a realist by nature. In the works of Tsubouchi Shŏyō, whose *Shōsetsu Shinzui* (Essence of the Novel) first nurtured realism in Meiji literature, and in those of Tayama Katai, who produced works of daring naturalism, there is evidence of a transplanting to a Japanese setting of western literary theories and plots. Shiki alone infused Meiji literature with a realism that was all his own. Maudlin sentimentality and hollow idealism are not to be found in his works, so that Franklin, the advocate of scientific management, held great appeal for him. Two and a half weeks before his death Shiki wrote of the great impression that Franklin's autobiography had made upon him.

Natsume Sōseki, a close friend of Shiki's, in his well-known novel, *Bot-*

chan, speaking through one of his characters, looks down upon the Franklinian concept of "pushing to the front." This criticism of Franklin was made, however, in reference to the wide distribution of his works as textbooks.

This was the death knell for the popularity of Franklin. After the Russo-Japanese war, naturalism, and in a broad sense, modernism swept the literary and intellectual world. At the same time the old American morality was received with deep scepticism and looked upon with extremely critical eyes. The common peoples' morality of Franklin was no longer acceptable.

Accompanying the socialism which arose with World War I, this type of morality was not only denied, but also considered as representative of nineteenth century capitalist morality.

However, Franklin, no matter how the times have changed, has unique and eternal virtues, so that it was quite appropriate that interest in him should have been revived following World War II.

Franklin in the American Mirage of the Risorgimento

Antonio Pace*

Eighteenth-century Italians necessarily saw America through a mist of illuministic prejudices. Although somewhat less inclined than some other European groups to overlook history and reality,[1] the Italians of the age of Montesquieu, Voltaire, and Rousseau were concerned primarily with the same universal philosophical problem of defining in rational terms man and his earthly lot. The issues of liberty, equality, and fraternity were thus debated habitually from a broad, humanitarian point of view. The American Revolution seemed the spearhead of a great crusade destined to bring about the terrestrial paradise envisoned by the philosophers; and the various Jacobin governments set up in Italy in the wake of the French Revolution were animated in the main by ideals of universal justice and brotherhood.

Notwithstanding the global propensities common to Enlightenment thought, recent historical investigation has found in the eighteenth century many of the roots of the Risorgimento, that movement through which Italy achieved national self-consciousness, and, after a crescendo of political and military action, identity as a unified, sovereign nation. It is therefore not surprising that Italian interest in the events of the American Revolution should furnish significant clues to the first stirrings of the patriotic spirit. The Italians at first stood aghast at the spectacle of the Americans locked in combat with England, idolized as the least decadent of European nations.

*Reprinted by permission from *Benjamin Franklin and Italy* (Philadelphia: American Philosophical Society, 1958), [167]–83, 343–44, 422, 430–31, 438.

Gradually the realization dawned that the Americans, far from sacrificing themselves for universal ideals, were fighting for their own lives, their own homes, their own values; and that one had to go back to the Catos, Brutuses, and Fabiuses of antiquity to find an analogue for their moving spirit. Here and there a perspicacious commentator glimpsed the truth—the anonymous reporter, for example, who observed in the Roman *Literary Ephemerides* in the year 1776:[2] "A people arises from the depths of the New World, who, sustained by this true feeling of patriotism which is not even understood among us, will be able to renew the example of those ancient nations which, sustained by this animating spirit, were capable of everything." Implicitly or explicitly, Franklin had his place in such considerations. A Milanese, writing on the subject *Concerning the Love for One's Country* shortly after the end of the American Revolution,[3] cited Frankin as an example to illustrate for his compatriots the spirit he was discussing: "He, taking his leave to return to Philadelphia, answered gracefully the polite exhortations of French gentlemen to remain under their sky: 'Gentlemen, if I did not have a country, I would not leave Paris.' " On the brink of the nineteenth century, the transitional political thinker Melchiorre Gioia, in a famous plea for a united republic entitled *Which of the Free Governments Is Most Suitable for the Happiness of Italy*, called for the spirit that had snatched the scepter from the hands of the tyrant of America.[4]

Eighteenth-century Italian historians of the American Revolution were among the first to perceive patriotic motives in the colonial uprising. The fact that Italians were the earliest historians of the momentous rebellion[5] must be attributed in good part to circumstances in the peninsula sensitizing them to national issues at stake in the conflict between the Americans and the British. The war was scarcely begun when the Florentine litterateur Vincenzo Martinelli, an old friend of Franklin's in London, expanded his previous history of England to include the American colonies.[6] In the midst of typical eighteenth-century hallucinations (Pennsylvania, for example, figures in Martinelli's account as the "sojurn of that Golden Age which the poets have so ingeniously pictured for us"), there is no lack of more realistic considerations, some of them doubtless colored by direct contact with Franklin. Particularly worthy of remark is the manner in which Martinelli took stock of colonial resources and interests to prophesy for England either "shameful losses, or lamentable victories even unto the third and fourth grandsons of the present generation." To judge from the tone of the single letter to Franklin that has survived, a notable awareness for the patriotic motives underlying the American Revolution animated the proposal made in 1783 by another Tuscan, L. J. Grobert,[7] to "transmit to posterity the most remarkable event of this century" in a history composed in the Italian language as "the most proper by its richness and energy to trace it."

Keen disappointment with the results of the French Revolution caused the Italians to turn their eyes more resolutely than before across the Atlantic in the nineteenth century. As their nationalistic fever rose, they became increasingly prone to view the American Revolution possessively in some sort as an emergency of the *pietas* of their own Roman forbears. The anonymous author of an unpublished history of the American Revolution dated 1804[8] exclaimed fervently at the end of his account:

> Here is that Nation which emulated the forum and the Capitolium of ancient Rome. If the latter had, too, at its birth its Ciceros, its Catos, and its Cincinnatuses, may provident Heaven watch over the former land, that there not be born there Catilines, Sullas, Caesars. Therefore, you illustrious Americans, do not degenerate from what your Fathers were, and keep untarnished and complete the sacred palladium which Washington and Franklin have deposited in your hearts and in your minds.

The American-Roman adumbrated by this passage was readily made into an Italian patriotic ideal, and the American Revolution itself became a complete paradigm of the Risorgimento. The parallels were obvious. Both the United States and Italy began as agglomerations of separate states dominated by foreign powers and weakened by internal dissent. The conditions of victory seemed the same in both instances: indomitable patriotic zeal, brilliant, though necessarily limited, military action against the oppressor, and an astute international diplomacy to neutralize the opposition and enlist the support of friendly powers. Just as Washington, the American Cincinnatus, eventually represented the ideal military leader, the vital need for manipulating rival foreign powers in the diplomatic arena evoked the figure of the classically wise, virtuous, and tactful Franklin.

At the same time the older concept of the palingenetic role of America reappeared, strengthened by new philosophic and patriotic overtones. Cesare Correnti, in his militant almanac *The Nephew of the Vesta-verde*,[9] envisioned America as the locus of a new level in the great chain of being: "The New World, as is the law of germs destined to initiate a more perfect form in the chain of creation, gathered all the best elements of the Old World," with the result that the "New World of nature becomes now the New World of humanity." Correnti then held America up mystically as the ideal homeland of his readers: "America . . . perhaps more than your country . . . is the country of all those who look for one." Carlo Cattaneo, the outspoken champion of the federalist ideal, argued long and loudly[10] that unity and liberty for his country could be reconciled only in a United States of Italy modeled after the archetypal United States of America. Vincenzo Gioberti, on the other hand, used Hegelian thesis and antithesis to establish the connection between the Old World and the New and to justify the conclusion reached in his influential *Civic Renewal of Italy* (1851)[11] that America would lead Europe to republican forms of government. The success of the American experiment was for Gioberti incontrovertible proof that a republic combines better than any other form of government the "two parts from which is derived the perfection of the civil dialectic—that is, stability and motion, the conservative principle and progress." The revolution that would bring about the victory of the republican order had its beginning in America, in accordance with "the geographical law governing human civilization"—namely, the "interrelated dialectic of two opposing motions, one of which is a flowing from east to west, and the other a reflux from the latter to the former, like the flux and ebb and the opposing currents that carry the sea back and forth." Although the Europeans were in many respects still superior to the Americans, "no one can deny that in regard to government we receive the model from them rather than give it." This political reflux meant to Gioberti that Europe was already on the road to republicanism. And just as the French Revolution had been animated by "the doctrines of Benjamin Franklin and by the glorious deeds of George Washington," so the subsequent revolutions that had travailed Europe were in good part inspired by the accounts of American democracy given by such writers as Carlos Botta and Tocqueville.

Giorberti's reference to Carlo Botta was deliberate, because the latter's *History of the War of Independence of the United States of America* published in Paris in 1809[12] is, despite its early date, the most successful Romanized palingenetic interpretation of America. The work had grown out of a conversation held one evening in the year 1806 at the home of Alessandro Manzoni's mother,[13] the daughter, incidentally, of the famous criminologist Cesare Beccaria. The talk having turned at one point to a discussion of what modern event would make the most suitable theme for a heroic poem, all agreed that the American Revolution was the best subject. Botta's history of the Revolution, suggested to him by that conversation, was a multifaceted patriotic achievement. Modeled linguistically with conscious pride after the style of the best sixteenth-century writers and developed with Livian drama and grandiloquence, it exploited every opportunity to excite the nationalistic aspirations of the Italians and to suggest analogies with Italy's past and contemporary history.

Franklin clearly symbolized for Botta Roman-like poise and virtue in statesmanship. He appears at two glorious moments in the Turinese historian's account of his political career—the examination before the House of Commons[14] and the arrival in Paris to assume the vital charge of representing the rebellious American colonies.[15] Before the English Parliament, Franklin, "a man esteemed above all others at that time," bore himself with the gravity and distinction of a Roman senator in the Forum. "The fame of this person, the candor of his mind, along with the memory of the things accomplished by him both in matters of state to the advantage of his country as in physical matters to the advantage of the human race, kept the minds of everyone in suspense; and on that day the House was crowded with spectators, all eager to hear him speak on an affair so important." Franklin's well-known depositions, proffered "with great gravity and greater acumen of intellect," follow in sober indirect speech, contrasting with the subsequent orations, in direct discourse, of the prime minister George Grenville and William Pitt.

The Parisian assignment furnished an opportunity to draw a warm portrait of the venerable old man who, in order to plead the cause of the colonies before the Europeans, had faced all the natural dangers of the Atlantic crossing, as well as the risk of being captured and put to death as a spy by the British. "For a long time no man had come to this city who more than this one was both worthy of veneration and was venerated, whether out of consideration for his age, which had already exceeded seventy years, or for the excellence of his genius, or the vastness of knowledge, or his reputation for virtue." Nor did it escape Botta how Franklin, settled at Passy "with a certain simplicity which derived from that of the ancient philosophers," cleverly used his personal appeal to political advantage in winning the active support of the French.

An episode of minor importance in Botta's narrative, but one which frequently inspired the efforts of nineteenth-century illustrators of his history, was Franklin's presentation of the commemorative sword decreed for La Fayette by the grateful American Congress. Botta, who knew La Fayette personally and made use of his papers in writing the history of the American Revolution,[16] was able to report in full the details of the occasion, even to the engraving on the sword itself—a waxing moon standing for America, accompanied by the motto *Crescam, ut prosim.*

Two other historians, C. G. Londonio and Giuseppe Compagnoni, rendered notable service in keeping America before the eyes of the Italians as a mirror of their own Risorgimento. In the three volumes of the former's *History of the English Colonies in America from Their Founding up to the Establishment of Their Independence,*[17] published in Milan in the years 1812–1813, there is no direct mention of Franklin, since the author prudently limited himself to unfolding the "remote causes" of the American Revolution. There can be no doubt, however, that in tracing the evolution of the institutions to which he attributed the marvelous maturation and robustness of America Londonio was strongly influenced by what he knew of Franklin. The figure of Franklin as a bourgeois ideal unmistakably underlies Londonio's conception of frugality, love of labor, and "that golden mediocrity which is the most comfortable and happy state"[18] as forces that molded America's greatness. Furthermore, without Franklin, America might not have so strongly impressed Londonio as dominated by a characteristic "noble sentiment that urges man to sacrifice his private interest to public utility."[19] The voluntary collaboration of Americans in "the establishment of hospitals, academies, colleges, the building of roads and canals, the founding of societies destined to encourage commerce and agriculture," praised by Londonio as a factor of prime importance in the development of America,[20] is obviously a generalization from Franklin's career. When Londonio implicitly identified this strong public-spiritedness of the Americans with "that love of country for which the inhabitants of English America are famous and which alone could accomplish such marvels as it did later,"[21] the lesson was clear for his compatriots.

The comments of Londonio point to a new concept of Franklin in Risorgimento thought—namely, his contribution as a bourgeois in crystallizing certain underlying forces in the American Revolution. As Londonio was writing his history of pre-Revolutionary America, Franklin, in the guise of Poor Richard, had already begun to symbolize to Italy the economic and moral metamorphosis she would have to undergo before she could hope to emerge as a modern sovereign nation. Implied is an important new dimension in the idea of America as paradigm of Italian evolution and revolution.

The Lombard journalist and historian Giuseppe Compagnoni also shared the beatific vision of America and helped to communicate it to his countrymen. Although his *History of America*[22] came after the works of Botta and Londonio, Compagnoni is more a child of the eighteenth century than either of his fellow historians. His picture of nature and man in the Western Hemisphere subscribes to well-established clichés. The unsophisticated Indian substantiates innate goodness, affability, and sincerity. The transplanted human seed of Europe, purified in the Lethe of American skies, again rises to pristine dignity, virtue, and love of liberty. Compagnoni's account reaches its crisis in the momentous revolution "through which not only did England lose her control over these great colonies of hers, but the whole world underwent a shock whose oscillations will last for quite some time."[23] Tacit aspirations for his own country can be felt in his concluding tableau of conditions in America toward the end of the first quarter of the nineteenth century,[24] wherein the United States are praised "for such political institutions which, although not devoid of imperfections which seem inevitable in human works, compared to whatever has been glorified as most illustrious in like matters, are the ones which have provided best for the welfare of men." And it obviously seemed to the author somehow prophetic of things to come, as well as symbolic of things past, that the city of Washington should rise from "a hamlet whimsically called Rome by its founder."[25]

In Compagnoni's great historical panorama of America, Franklin appears as the moving spirit of the crucial colonial revolution. His message from London to his compatriots that "the sun of liberty had set"[26] heralded the imminent break with England. His command "Arm yourselves," supported with secret information regarding the plans of the English ministers, finally touched off the insurrection. Where Botta had remained faithful to the facts in keeping Franklin unobtrusively in the background of the Declaration of Independence, Compagnoni transforms him into an effervescent advocate of separatism, putting into his mouth an inflammatory Livian speech to counter the dissuasive arguments of John Dickinson:[27]

> You have unsheathed the sword, and with good success. They are afraid of you. . . . If you do not want to be treated very soon as rebels,

> declare yourselves independent. The King of Great Britain aims only to make slaves of you. . . . And do not be concerned with frightening, by the bold resolution that I suggest to you, the part that is favorable to you in England, because the uselessness of the efforts that it has made for ten years have embittered it and makes it fearful of seeing born once more days of oppressions. If you yield, it will succumb; nor will there be any longer English liberty if there is not an American liberty. . . . The present Ministers, confused in their dispositions and measures, will expiate the conflagration that they have awakened and the devastation that they have brought to our peaceful regions. Other ministers will recognize our independence, sustained and assured by victory. Already France and Spain, in order to help our cause with their armies . . . , wait only to hear that you have declared yourselves independent. . . . Fight then with all the advantages that your situation grants you; or else stop fighting.

These "words of fire," Compagnoni assures his readers, driven home by the gravity of their content and by "the authority of the one who uttered them," preluded the official consideration of the Declaration of Independence by the Revolutionary Congress assembled at Philadelphia. In keeping with the Italian historian's intent to make his countrymen see Franklin as the prime mover behind the Declaration, the latter's name is made to lead the list of those who brought before the Congress "this act, one of the weightiest that have ever been noted in the annals of the world, and whose consequences will perhaps be felt down to most distant posterity."[28] Transported soon thereafter to Paris, the venerable Franklin, because of his "hoary age, excellence of genius, vastness of knowledge, and fame for virtue," remained a constant force in winning decisive European good will and material support.

The nimbus that lingered about the name of Philadelphia until long after Washington had become the capital of the United States is due largely to the imperishable prestige of the colonial metropolis's most famous citizen. Italian capers associated with the name of Philadelphia continually disturbed the authorities. Police records make note of efforts to control the activities of a widespread revolutionary sect who called themselves "Philadelphians," akin, no doubt, to other groups known as "American Huntsmen" and "American Marksmen."[29] The use of Philadelphia in false imprints for clandestine publications[30] must also have helped to keep the police busy. Usually, however, this preoccupation with Philadelphia and all that the name suggested came to the surface in disguised form. The esoteric meaning of Philadelphia in the ideology of the first part of the nineteenth century is perhaps best illustrated by information from the city of Turin, in itself a fact of some weight if one recalls that Piedmont was later to lead the militant Risorgimento. What is more, viewed in the light of nineteenth-century events, the extraordinarily keen interest in Franklin which we have already noted in eighteenth-century Turin becomes a significant detail in what the eminent modern Piedmontese historian Carlo

Calcaterra has identified as "Our Imminent Risorgimento."[31] We need only mention at this point the remarkable exchange between Giambatista Beccaria and Franklin, the contacts of numerous pupils and associates of Beccaria with the great American, and the active group of the Turinese Academy of Sciences, of which Franklin was made a charter member.

The feverish attention given by the Turinese to Franklin's scientific academy, the American Philosophical Society, is in good measure a venting of patriotic impulses. The exchange in the name of science with the academy in Philadelphia served as an expression of solidarity with America in much the same way that the various Italian scientific congresses of the first part of the nineteenth century substituted for national unity.[32] No Piedmontese had succeeded in being named to membership in the American Philosophical Society in the eighteenth century, although Franklin seems to have promised to nominate Beccaria. But the Restoration inspired the Turinese to such a furious compensatory exchange with the American Philosophical Society that five of them were made members by 1830.[33] The first to be elected was, appropriately, Carlo Botta, in 1816. The 1823 Gaspard Deabbate, the Piedmontese ambassador to the United States, was admitted. Lorenzo Martini, a physiologist, and rector of the University of Turin, was made a member in 1830, after having deluged the American Philosophical Society with his writings. The following year the Society took into its ranks Prospero Balbo, the favorite pupil of Giambatista Beccaria, and Giacinto Carena, scientist and lexicographer.

Of the Turinese elected to the American Philosophical Society at this time, Martini was the most outspoken, and his attitudes were doubtless shared by his less demonstrative compatriots. "To belong to that scientific body which possessed a Franklin," notes a eulogist who knew him personally,[34] "seemed to him a great good fortune." In almost the same breath, our biographer remarks pointedly that "The glory of Italy formed the principal object of his [Martini's] every thought." The facts, as they can be reconstructed, bear out the statements and implications of this eulogist. Raised to a high pitch of elation by his admission into the American Philosophical Society, Martini, to show his appreciation for the honor done him, set out to inform his fellow academicians beyond the Atlantic of the progress of letters, sciences, and arts in Italy. This project, taking the form of essays under the general title of *Philadelphia Discourses*,[35] was, however, little more than an outpouring of the author's nationalistic feelings. The opening words of the first discourse set the tone of the book and betray Martini's real purpose. Especially noteworthy are Martini's sense of communion with his American colleagues and the pride with which he pointed to Franklin's relations with Beccaria, still fresh in the memory of every Turinese:

> In my most verdant years, Honored Academicians, I heard resound the names of Franklin and Washington. Their virtue inspired within me

> a feeling of reverence near to religion for your country. Hence I eagerly sought out everything that concerned your past, and your glories filled my soul with honest exultation. My heart took special delight in the thought that between America and Italy, and more particularly between the United States and Piedmont, there was a close and ancient alliance. A Christopher Columbus, Ligurian, discovered your continent; and Americus Vespucci, Tuscan, gave it his own name; a Giambatista Beccaria, Piedmontese, shares with the immortal Benjamin the honor of having expanded electrical science; finally, a Carlo Botta, another Piedmontese, undertook to narrate with Livian grandiloquence your brilliant, nay more, marvelous deeds.

Martini explained that his book grew out of a royal assignment to instruct Piedmontese youth in "the science of the physical man." The volume was at the same time a "treatise to smooth the way" for his teaching, a "monument to his love for his native land," and a way of expressing his gratitude for election to the Society by "revealing the merits of Italy to the good Americans." Just as Cicero had attached the adjective "Tusculan" to certain of his disputations from the fact that he composed them in Tusculum, so Martini entitled his book *Philadelphia Discourses* because he conceived them as personal conversations with his American colleagues.

Martini's head was still in the clouds when he wrote his *General Pathology* two years later,[36] dedicating it to the American Philosophical Society with the explanation that "Being called to belong to a group in which one day Franklin sat could not fail to fill me with joy. . . ." Despite repeated protestations of unworthiness, he was still rejoicing at the honor of membership, and again, as in the *Philadelphia Discourses*, imagined himself in person among his confreres as he discussed his ideas on pathology.

The restlessness of the Italians in the post-Restoration years provoked such rigid control of the expression and communication of thought that, as in the earlier Jacobin period, forthright declarations of faith in the American mirage are not common. Furthermore, since the writers who dealt with Franklin were, in the nature of things, usually moderates who rarely transgressed reasonable limits, the task of identifying political overtones becomes no less piquant for the modern historian than it was vexatious for the contemporary censor. Now and then the distillation of political intentions is not difficult. The Batelli and Fanfani *Series of Lives and Portraits of Famous Persons,*[37] compiled in the period right after the fall of Napolean, went a bit beyond the bounds of discretion in its comments on the American scientist and statesman:

> Franklin found the secret of rendering lightning innocuous; Franklin did everything to establish America in the dignity of an independent nation. The discoverer, the conquerer of electrical matter, the upholder of American glory has perpetual right to the homage of whomever venerates

> and loves the sublime inventions of science, the liberal institutions of peoples. Praise therefore to this sublime genius of the New World. . . .

Such an allusion as Federico Giunti's to *Poor Richard's Almanack* in his 1830 Franklinian miscellany[38] as a "notable service which Franklin rendered to his country" is cautious enough; but no one could have mistaken Cesare Correnti's purpose in the critical year 1848 when he presented Franklin in the initial volume of his *Nephew of the Vesta-verde* as "the true model of *galantuomini,* and who preached economy and thrift to the people not to inspire tenacity and niggardliness in their souls, but to open to them the way to true independence." Other writers shook off momentarily their inhibitions. The Milanese educator Giuseppe Sacchi, reviewing Thouar's translation of Mignet's *Life of Franklin,*[39] pointed out that the latter part of the book "depicts for us the statesman in Franklin, and shows us how one's country should be loved and served." The freely adapted *Way to Wealth* published by the Turinese "Free Propaganda" in the year 1850 contains an editorial remark deprecating war that furnished the opportunity to add:[40] "Among the wars to be condemned one must not count those for independence and for making ourselves masters of our own homes—wars which must be continued stubbornly until they are won." The last line of this version of *The Way to Wealth* puts into Father Abraham's mouth the apocryphal plea: "Love your country above everything, because if she is free and fortunate, the days of your life will be happy and contented."

A more subtle form of disguised patriotism, and one sometimes countenanced by the censor, was the use of Franklin to betoken the part that ideas would have to play in the regeneration of Italy. Franklin thereby appears within the pattern of the New World mirage as the Philosopher of Revolution. Although no one dared suppose that the Italians could act as altruistically as the Americans, the implication was obvious that Italian progress and independence were functions of reactivated ideals and impulses once exemplified by the Ancients, now by the Americans. The poet Cesare Arici, for example, in a biography first published in 1815 by the Risorgimento printer Niccolò Bettoni,[41] pictured Franklin as a model of enlightened patriotism and the guiding intelligence behind the American Revolution. To this "citizen philospher," Arici informed his readers, America owed almost exclusively her "priceless treasure of . . . liberty and independence." The colonies, led by this "modern Phocius" and "trained by Franklin's ideas," succeeded in breaking the power of the British oppressors. Nor did Frankin's love of country cease to move him after independence had been won. Having returned to the "land of his compatriots" torn by dangerous dissensions, the aged Franklin, in a "wise and liberal constitution put to the vote of the assembly, laid the fundamental bases for the future greatness and happiness of the Americans."

A remarkable meditation of the youthful Vincenzo Gioberti,[42] smacking strongly of eighteenth-century primitivistic notions, but, like Arici's biographical essay, conceiving Franklin as a model repository and shaper of this country's elemental moral energies, has come down to us intact, thanks perhaps to the happy circumstance of its having remained unpublished until after Italian unification:

> The modern age seemed no longer capable of producing those singular men of ancient wisdom who presided at the origin of nations, and whose names are almost confused with those of the demigods in ancient writings. Benjamin Franklin is one of the exceptions. Such a man, if he had been born and had lived in Europe, could doubtless have been just as wise and virtuous, but he would not have been so novel and rare in his life and writings as he was. He had to be born in another world, in a nation segregated from European refinement, and full, in the midst of a still virgin nature, of the vigor and simplicity of adolescence. His origins had to be humble, and his education limited to that of a happy nature; and little by little, with no effort whatsoever, he had to rise from private obscurity to public light, and be called by Providence to the rare office of helping in every way a new and uncorrupt nation in need of wisdom and perfection. Franklin, placed in the midst of all these circumstances, set an example entirely his own and renewed a spectacle missing for many centuries. In short, whether one looks at his life, his deeds, all bent to the welfare of his country, or indeed at his moral and political conduct and the brief writings which dropped from his pen on many points of economy and morality, at his useful discoveries in natural things, one can find nothing comparable outside of those ancient sages of Greece and Asia who united moral and political action with the wisdom of life and helped their country with the excellence of their knowledge, with institutions, and with inventions. Do we not see in the short writings of Franklin the image of that life full of simplicity and candor which Plutarch has depicted in the life of the ancient sages?

It is very probable that Gioberti, though barely out of his teens, had some premonition of the part he was to play in laying the philosophical bases for Italian unity and independence, and envisoned himself already in a role similar to that of the philosopher of America.

Other writers held Franklin up as a paragon of the patriotically inspired educator. In 1835 the Bolognese popularizer Salvatore Muzzi[43] declared Franklin "a model . . . of the magnanimous patriarchs of the New World" who, by means of his didactic opuscules, "in a short time infused good customs into all Pennsylvania and removed . . . arrogance and uncouthness, rehabilitating her to love, morality, and civilization." The Milanese writer Antonio Cattaneo, in his biographical sketch of Franklin of the year 1842,[44] gave him credit for America's "education, civilization, and all those civic and military virtues which make states flourish." Three years later an anonymous writer in the Luccan *Friend of the People*[45] explained to his readers how Franklin, after having assured his own material future, "did not abandon himself to slothful repose, but recalling that he was a citizen, dedicated himself with more ardor to collaboration in behalf of the future of his country." His most effective contribution was his writings composed in the conviction that "the beginning and base of every social improvement is popular education." At the very middle of the century, the biography distributed by the "Free Propaganda" group of Turin[46] construed Franklin's moral and educational activity in America as an indispensable prelude to his political role: by virtue of the effort made to enlighten his fellow citizens through his newspaper and almanac, Franklin "became one of their principal educators before being one of their most glorious liberators."

Realizing that they were playing a dangerous game, the purveyors of Franklinism rarely gave the authorities any excuse to intervene. From time to time, however, some fact or episode reveals the deterrent hand of the censor. About the year 1837 the Austrian censorship issued orders that no more biographies of Franklin were to be printed.[47] In 1838 the Austrian police confiscated from the shop of a bookdealer in Pavia a number of copies of a work on the life of Franklin published without permission.[48] Certainly the presence of Franklinian writings in Guerrazzi's *Livornese Indicator* and Lorenzo Valerio's *Popular Readings* could not but have contributed to the quick suppression of those propagandistic magazines.[49] Little is known, unfortunately, about the collection of *Moral Opuscules of Benjamin Franklin the Printer* published by a "Typography of the Patriot" in Leghorn in the year 1848.[50] The inflammatory, and doubtless fictitious, name given to the press, as well as the fact that only one copy seems to have survived the nineteenth century, suggests that the publication was clandestine.[51] Moreover, the censor could never have given his imprimatur to such pieces as a note of Colletta's on the Neapolitan revolution of 1820, an essay by Armani on "National Feeling in Italy," or the anonymous biography of Angelo Brunetti, the Roman popular hero executed by the Austrians—all found in the little book cheek to jowl with such writings of Franklin as *The Way to Wealth*, the "Hints to Those That Would be Rich," "The Whistle," and the famous program for arriving at moral perfection.

A woman's political ingenuousness brought on the only outright clash with the censor recorded in the nineteenth century. In 1837 the Parmesan lady Antonietta Tommasini, friend and comforter of the romantic poet Giacomo Leopardi and wife of Giacomo Tommasini, one of Italy's most distinguished physicians, published in Milan a collection of Franklin letters under the title of *Moral and Literary Correspondence of Benjamin Franklin.*[52] For some years, she confessed in her preface, she had been reading Franklin's letters for her own instruction. The conviction gradually grew upon her that the correspondence of the famous American was not well enough known to Italians, and she decided to translate at least those letters "most fitting for the education of youth." She dedicated the slender little volume to her husband, "because the more I progressed in my undertaking, the more manifest to my eyes became the analogy of your character with that of the immortal American, an excellent father and husband."

Antonietta's dedication of the book to her husband would in itself have been enough to cause the censor to prick up his ears. Giacomo Tommasini had been a marked man since 1831 because of his active participation in subversive activities. Even the Piedmontese police knew[53] that he displayed "scorn for Sovereigns, and more markedly for the Pope." In any case Antonietta's naive decision to submit her translation for approval under the title *Political and Literary Correspondence of Benjamin Franklin* precipitated a crisis with the Austrian censorship in Milan.[54] The censor made her change the "Political" of the title to "Moral." Her introductory notice on the life of Franklin was at first flatly rejected, because, in the words of Defendente Sacchi, a patient of her husband's and her mediator in Milan, it contained "too much savory talk of what Franklin did for independence and liberty, hydras for our censorship." Furthermore, the censor insisted upon changes and expurgations in the Franklinian texts themselves. The unhappy Antonietta would have gladly withdrawn her book from publication, but commitments with the printer had gone too far. The volume finally did appear, the introduction "cruelly mutilated," to use the anguished wording of Sacchi's report, and with the cuts in the text specified by the censor, involving in some instances the suppression of whole letters. The inconsistent dating—1837 on the title page and 1838 on the original paper jacket—remains a mute reminder of the unexpected embroilment with the censor.

The loss of the censorship records of the State Archive of Milan removes that source of information regarding official strictures on Antonietta Tommasini's book. However, a comparison of the published work with the three manuscript copies preserved among the personal papers of Antonietta Tommasini in the Palatine Library of Parma reveals both the innocence of the authoress and the sensitivity of the censor. The deletions from the introductory biographical study indicate that the censor was intent upon blotting out Franklin as a political symbol. Near the beginning of the essay Antonietta Tommasini indiscreetly opened a long section on Franklin's career as a statesman with the words:

> . . . If Benjamin Franklin wanted his fellow citizens to be educated, and active, sober, and friends of justice, he also wanted them to be defenders of their own rights and American independence. That was why he promoted those *voluntary associations* for the defense of his country which later contributed so much toward upholding her rights and establishing her liberty.

The censor's pen went to work at once. Expunged likewise were the references to Franklin's opposition to the Stamp Act, to the failure of his wise attempts at reconciliation with England, and to his part in the ensuing struggle. There could be no question about the fate of the casual, but unwise, sentence with which the authoress concluded her brief discussion of Franklin's political career: "It is well known how much his prudent counsel, foresight, and firmness contributed to the magnanimous undertaking, which, after several years of courageous resistance and heroic virtue, freed that part of America from English dependence and made of the united Provinces a free people." At the very end of the biography the censor obviously objected to the exalted, romantic tone of Antonietta's remarks on the passing of Franklin:

> The tombs of great men who have died remind us with a sense of wonder of their heroic deeds. But we are more delicately touched and moved by the memory of those virtues derived from loftiness of mind conjoined with goodness of heart. This immortal man, this man beneficent beyond all mortal custom, will always bring a tear of sorrow to our eyes whenever it occurs to us to recall that he, too, succumbed to the final common destiny.

The changes in the text of Antonietta Tommasini's selections need no explanation. Franklin's letter of 1 May 1776 to Samuel Cooper describing European enthusiasm for the American cause and the colonial constitutions was eliminated. The same fate understandably befell the letter of 4 May 1779 to Thomas Viny expressing Franklin's aspiration of joining his friend in enjoyment of American "Peace and Plenty, a good Government, good Laws, and Liberty, without which Men lose half their Value," and containing the fervent prayer that the terrible struggle with England be rewarded with "Freedom in the new World, as an Asylum for those of the Old, who deserve it." The relentless censor's pen was equally harsh with an extract from the letter of 4 December 1789 to David Hartley voicing the hope that France would find peace under a good constitution and ending with the words: "God grant, that not only the Love of Liberty, but a thorough Knowledge of the Rights of Man, may pervade all the Nations of the Earth, so that a Philosopher may set his Foot anywhere on its Surface, and say, "This is my Country." Inasmuch as a two-headed eagle adorns the Austrian escutcheon, it is no wonder that the censor removed from the letter of 26 January 1784 to Mrs. Sarah Bache the part containing the objection that the eagle, being a wicked, predacious, lazy, and cowardly bird, was "by no means a proper emblem for the brave and honest Cincinnati of America, who have driven all the *Kingbirds* from our Country."

Certain correspondences in the great paradigm equating the American Revolution and the Risorgimento came into clearer relief as the moment of independence approached. If Garibaldi was the Italian Washington, the parallel between Franklin and Cavour was not less patent. What is more, there is good reason to suppose that the similarity was an actively cultivated one. Cavour admitted on his deathbed to having been a "passionate admirer of the Americans."[55] Americanism had, in fact, been an important ingredient in the fierce liberalism that characterized Cavour's outlook from early youth. We have the testimony of a childhood classmate that at the tender age of fourteen Cavour often talked of Franklin. To those who urged him to develop his marked talent for mathematics in order to make of himself a second Lagrange his answer was that political economy was more important than mathematics, and that he hoped to see Italy under a constitution. And already he was speculating on the possibility of becoming prime minister.[56] In February, 1851, speaking as Piedmontese Minister of the Navy, Agriculture, and Commerce, Cavour cited the name of Franklin[57] to prove the utility of diplomacy in rebuttal of a leftist proposal to suppress the Sardinian Ministry of Foreign Affairs and all its functions for the sake of economy. Cavour's life aim appears to have been realized in the years after 1852 when, not as a Lagrange, but as Premier of Piedmont in a role analogous to Franklin's, his adroit maneuvering of foreign powers, especially France under Louis Napoleon, broke the power of Austria in the peninsula.

The spirit of Franklin also attended the most brilliant military operation of the war for Italian freedom—the campaign of Garibaldi's "Thousand" which freed southern Italy from the Spanish Bourbons. The wooden sidewheeler that carried Garibaldi across the strait of Messina to Calabria on 20 May 1860 to launch the famous attack on the Kingdom of the Two Sicilies was called the "Franklin." The encouragement given his men by Garibaldi's determination to remain with the "Franklin" even after a dangerous crack was opened in the hull by a traitor[58] was probably an important factor in the success of the daring invasion of the mainland. Nor did the spirit of Franklin desert Garibaldi and his men after the debarkation. Among the many willing helpers whose efforts accelerated the swift march of the "Thousand" upon Naples was a Nicola Mignogna, for many years a busy conspirator against the Spanish rulers of southern Italy. The signal for the invasion of the "Thousand" had been the news transmitted to Garibaldi that he, along with Cesare Albini, controlled Potenza, the capital of Basilicata, and that the Redshirts could count upon military aid on the mainland.[59] A part, at least, of Mignogna's preparatory work had been done as member of a "carbonico-military" sect in which he veiled his identity under the alias of "Franklin."[60]

The fear of consequences obviously kept the Italians from expressing openly their thoughts on Franklin as an ideal of political behavior. The outburst of tribute that followed immediately the act of unification gives some idea of how intensely the Italians had felt their repression. Nevertheless, the evidence from the Risorgimento years, tenuous though it be on the whole, proves clearly that Franklin was an important inspirational element in the American mirage as seen by the Italians laboring for national regeneration. As the pattern of the Risorgimento evolved and the Italians saw in the rise of the United States the shape of things to come for their country, Franklin, too, was remade in their own image. The concept of him as the sage who molded the mind and character of his compatriots to fit them for independence signified the importance of education as the basis for Italian freedom. His role as the statesman whose wise moves in the alien courts of

Europe made victory possible must have in some measure suggested the strategy of international counterpoise and gambit from which Italy salvaged her autonomy.

Abbreviations

CtY—Yale University Library

MB—Boston Public Library

PPAP—American Philosophical Society

PPHi—Historical Society of Pennsylvania

Hays—I. Minis Hays, *Calendar of the Papers of Benjamin Franklin in the Library of the American Philosophical Society.* 5 vols. Philadelphia: American Philosophical Society, 1908.

Notes

1. Recent writers on the Italian Enlightenment who call attention to its indigenous features are L. Salvatorelli, *Il pensiero politico italiano dal 1700 al 1870*, Turin, Einaudi, 1949; G. de Ruggiero, *Il pensiero politico meridionale nei secoli XVIII e XIX*, 2nd ed., Bari, Laterza, 1946; B. Brunello, *Il pensiero politico italiano del Settecento*, Milan-Messina, Principato, 1942; G. Natali, *Il Settecento*, 3rd ed., Milan, Vallardi, 1950.

2. See D. Visconti, *Le origini degli Stati Uniti d'America e l'Italia* (Centro Italiano Studi Americani, ser. 2, 1), 85, Padua, CEDAM, 1940.

3. Visconti, ser. 2, 1, 85.

4. Salvatorelli, 134.

5. Natali, 579.

6. *Istoria del governo d'Inghilterra e delle sue colonie in India, e nell'America Settentrionale* . . . , Florence, Cambiagi, 1776.

7. Hays, 3: 50.

8. Ms. in the Clements Library of the University of Michigan.

9. *Il nipote del Vesta-verde* 7: 54–55, 1854.

10. Cattaneo, *Stati Uniti d'Italia* (ed. N. Bobbio), Turin, Chiantore, 1945.

11. *Del rinnovamento civile d'Italia* 2: 248 ff., Bari, Laterza, 1911.

12. *Storia della guerra dell'indipendenza degli Stati Uniti d'America*.

13. C. Dionisotti, *Vita di Carlo Botta*, 138–39, Turin, Favale, 1867.

14. Bk. ii.

15. Bk. vii.

The fact that Felice Foresti, a political exile who taught Italian at Columbia University after Lorenzo Da Ponte, chose Botta's account of Franklin in Paris as a passage for a reader he compiled in 1846 (Bibl., No. 8) is some indication of the Piedmontese historian's efficacy.

16. G. Mazzoni, *L'Ottocento*, 2nd ed., 97, Milan, Vallardi, 1944.

17. *Storia delle colonie inglesi in America dalla loro fondazione fino allo stabilimento della loro indipendenza*.

18. Londonio, 1: 124–25.

19. Londonio, 1: 288.

20. Londonio, **1:** 289.

21. Londonio, **1:** 289.

22. *Storia dell'America in continuazione del compendio della Storia universale del sig. conte di Segur,* 14 v., Milan, Fusi, Stella, 1820–1822.

23. Tome xxvi, 125.

24. Tome xxviii, 250.

25. Tome xxvii, 60.

One of the tracts included within the limits of the original city of Washington was in fact called "Rome"; furthermore an adjacent inlet of the Potomac bore at the same time the name "Tiber" (see W. B. Bryan, *A History of the National Capital,* 53, New York, Macmillan, 1914).

26. Tome xxvi, 156.

27. Tome xxvii, 64–66.

28. Tome xxvii, 74.

29. *Carte segrete e atti ufficiali della polizia austriaca in Italia dal 4 giugno 1814 al 22 marzo 1848* **1:** 92, 406; **2:** 10, 89, 92–93, Capologo, Tip. Elvetica, 1851–1852. *Cf.* O. Dito, *Massoneria, carboneria ed altre società segrete nella storia del Risorgimento italinao,* 308, Turin-Rome, Roux & Viarengo, 1905.

30. *Cf.* M. Parenti, *Dizionario dei luoghi di stampa falsi, inventati o supposti in opere di autori e traduttori italiani con un'appendice sulla data "Italia" e un saggio sui falsi luoghi italiani usati all'estero, o in Italia, da autori stranieri,* 83–85, Florence, Sansoni, 1951.

Parenti's entries under "Filadelfia" are far from a complete list.

31. *Il nostro imminente Risorgimento,* Turin, SEI, 1935.

32. *Cf.* Bibl., No. 14, p. 402 ff.

33. Pace, 400–1.

34. S. Berrutti, *Saggio sulla vita e sugli scritti del professore cavaliere Lorenzo Martini,* 31, Bologna, Tipografia Camerale alla Volpe, 1847.

35. *Discorsi filadelfici,* Turin, 1831.

The American Philosophical Society possesses a copy donated by the author.

36. *Patologia generale,* 2 v., Capolago, Tipografia e Libreria Elvetica, 1834.

37. Bibl., No. 2.

38. Bibl., No. 3, **1:** xvii.

39. Bibl., No. 10.

40. Bibl., No. 11, p. 23.

41. Bibl., No. 1.

42. Bibl., No. 15.

43. Bibl., No. 4.

44. Bibl., No. 6.

45. Bibl., No. 7.

46. Bibl., No. 11, p. 26.

47. Bibl., No. 13, p. 275.

48. Bibl., No. 13.

49. *Cf.*, for the *Indicatore livornese,* C. Carocci, *Prose e poesie di Sansone Uzielli con un saggio critico,* xxii–xxiii, Florence, Seeber, 1899; for the *Letture popolari,* see M. Robba, Le *Letture popolari* del Valerio, *Levana* (Florence), **3:** 635–58, 1924.

50. Bibl., No. 9.

51. Luigi Rava probably examined the copy he described (Bibl., No. 12, p. 21) in the

municipal library of Leghorn. If so, he may have been the last person who will ever see the work, because the volume owned by the Biblioteca Labronica, the only copy known to me, was destroyed in World War II.

52. Bibl., No. 5.

53. A. Manno, *Aneddoti documentati sulla censura in Piemonte,* 114, Turin, Bocca, 1907.

54. Bibl., No. 12.

55. W. de la Rive, *Le Comte de Cavour: récits et souvenirs,* 440, Paris, Hetzel, 1862.

56. P. Villari, La giovinezza del Conte di Cavour, in *Scriti vari,* 427, Bologna, Zanichelli, 1894.

57. Cavour, *Discorsi parlamentari* (ed. A. Omodeio), 3: 62, Florence, "La Nuova Italia" Editrice, 1932.

58. M. Rosi, *Dizionario del Risorgimento Nazionale* 7: 399–400, Milan, Vallardi, 1931.

59. G. Pupino-Carbonelli, *Nicola Mignogna nella storia dell'unità d'Italia,* 204, Naples, Romano, 1889.

60. *Cf.* C. Pisacane, *Epistolario* (ed. A. Romano), 483 ff., and *passim,* Milan, Albrighi, Segati, 1937.

Years later, writing in his autobiography about the selfless sacrifice of Luigi Carniglia, a faithful follower, Garibaldi could think of no higher tribute than to place him in the company of Franklin as an example of true nobility in humble garb, to be contrasted with the empty pretensions of the upper class, "which generally works for no one and consumes for many" (*Memorie, nella redazione definitiva del 1872,* 45–46, Bologna, Cappelli, 1932).

Bibliography

1. Vita di Benjamino Franklin scritta da Cesare Arici, in *Vite e ritratti di cento uomini illustri,* Padua, Bettoni, 1815 (unpaginated). (PPAP)

   Only twenty-five fascicles of the original prospectus were completed, which were reprinted in 1822, and again in 1823, as *Vite e ritratti di venticinque uomini illustri,* Padua, Tipografia della Minerva [Bettoni].

   The *Vita di Benjamino Franklin,* n.p., n.d., by Arici in the Library of Congress (Rare Book Collection E302.6 F8 A7) is a stray fascicle from this Bettoni repertory of *Vite e ritratti.*

2. Beniamino Franklin, in *Serie di vite e ritratti de' famosi personaggi degli ultimi tempi* 1, Milan, Batelli e Fanfani, 1815–1816 (unpaginated).

3. *Saggi di morale e d'economia privata estratti dalle opere di Banjamino Franklin: prima traduzione italiana.* 2 v. Pisa, Nistri, 1830. (CtY; PPHi; PPAP)

4. S. Muzzi: Franklin, in *Storie e ritratti di uomini utili benefattori della umanità* 1, Bologna, Tipi Governativi della Volpe al Sassi, 1835. (Bologna, Archiginnasio)

   Unpaginated, but with biographies arranged chronologically according to date of birth.

   There was also another edition, in a single volume, entitled *Storie e ritratti di uomini benefattori della umanità di tutti i paesi e di tutte le condizioni,* Bologna, Tipografia Governativa della Volpe al Sassi, n.d. (PPAP)

   The Muzzi fragment in the Biblioteca Apostolica Vaticana (Ferraioli III. 2013. it. 34; PPAP, microfilm) is a separate fascicle from one of these collections.

   For a notice of Muzzi's biography of Franklin, see the *Giornale arcadico* (Rome), 76: 212–13, 1838.

5. *Carteggio morale e letterario di Beniamino Franklin* (tr. A. Tommasini). Milan, Omobono Manini, [1838].

   Elenchi lombardi, 1838, No. 41 (January): edition of 650 copies. (MB; PPAP; Florence, Biblioteca Nazionale Centrale)

   Antonietta Tommasini's dedicatory letter to her husband is dated 15 October 1836, the original cover of the volume bears the date 1838, and the title page is dated 1837. This discrepancy in dates is doubtless owing to the embroilment with the censor (see No. 12 below). The evidence of the *Elenchi lombardi* indicates that the book was actually published at the beginning of 1838.

6. A. Cattaneo: Cenni su la vita di Beniamino Franklin, *Biblioteca di farmacia, chimica, fisica, medicina, chirurgia, terapeutica, storia naturale, ecc.,* (Milan), 35: v–xlvii, 1842.

   Elenchi lombardi, 1842, No. 235 (January): edition of 200 copies.

   Reprinted separately as *Cenni su la vita di Benjamino Franklin del dottor Antonio Cattaneo giureconsulto e professore d'economia rurale ecc. ecc.,* Milan, Presso la Società degli Editori degli *Annali universali delle scienze e dell'industria,* nella Galleria Decritoforis sopra lo scalone a sinistra (Tip. Lampato), 1842.

7. Racconti storici—Le veglie di Maestro Biagio: Beniamino Franklin, *L'amico del popolo* (Lucca), 1: 66–67, 77–79, 1845–1846.

8. C. Botta: Benjamino Franklin a Parigi, in *Crestomazia italiana: a Collection of Selected Pieces in Italian Prose Designed as a Class Reading Book for Beginners in the Study of the Italian Language* (ed. F. Foresti), 18–20, New York, Appleton, 1846.

9. * *Operette morali di Beniamino Franklin stampatore.* Leghorn, Tipografia del Patriotta, 1848.

   Rava, p. 21, outlines the contents of the collection.

10. *Vita di Franklin ad uso di tutti, operetta di M. Mignet della Sezione di Storia Generale e Filosofica: prima traduzione dal francese per cura di P. Thouar.* Milan, Libreria di Educazione e d'Istruzione di A. Ubicini (Tip. Bernardoni), [1850]. (PPHi; Florence, Biblioteca Nazionale Centrale)

    Reviews by G. Sacchi in *Letture di famiglia* (Florence), 2: 71–72, 1850; and in *Annali universali* (Milan), 104: 5–6. 1850.

    The Thouar translation of Mignet's biography was apparently reprinted: Pagliaini reports the date Turin, Paravia, 1850; and Rava, p. 21, indicates a reprinting by Ubicini in 1869.

11. *Vita di Franklin.* [Turin,] Arnaldi (A spese della Libera Propaganda), 1850. (PPAP; Turin, Biblioteca Nazionale)

12. A. Boselli: Beniamino Franklin, Antonietta Tommasini e la censura austriaca di Milano, *Rassegna storica del Risorgimento* (Rome), 19(4): 265–81, 1932.

    Also reprinted separately, Rome, Proja, 1933.

13. A. Pace: The American Philosophical Society and Italy, *Proceedings of the American Philosophical Society* 90: 387–421, 1946.

14. V. Gioberti: Beniamino Franklin, in *Meditazioni filosofiche inedite . . . pubblicate dagli autografi della Biblioteca Civica di Torino da E. Solmi,* 413–14, Florence, Barbèra, 1909.

    Composed apparently in the period 1822–1825.

Franklin: An Idol of the Times

Horst Dippel*

While Washington, in the eyes of the German bourgeoisie, was primarily the expression of the heroism and virtue of the American Revolution, Franklin was looked upon as the embodiment of American social and cultural ideals. In Germany, in contrast to America,[1] Franklin's fame outshone Washington's. Even before the beginning of the War of Independence, Franklin had enjoyed great respect in all of Europe. This reputation, resting on his fame as a scientist and moral philosopher,[2] was enhanced by his journey to Göttingen in 1766 and his election to membership in the Göttingen Akademie der Wissenschaften.[3]

Franklin's prestige as a scientist[4] was based in part on his identification with the American Philosophical Society, whose "president is the famous Mr. Benjamin Franklin."[5] The great esteem in which Franklin was held in Enlightenment circles during those years was expressed by an invitation to the margrave of Baden's court late in 1774: "He invites you to Germany upon that principle which seems to have actuated your whole life, I mean, the benefit of mankind in general and his subjects in particular."[6]

Franklin's image as represented here is that of a scientist and a sage only. His political activities and the role he played in the growing conflict with England were scarcely mentioned, although some details concerning his position had been published in Germany, including his interrogation in the House of Commons on the Stamp Act.[7] German contemporaries did not become aware of Franklin as a revolutionary leader until, having arrived in France at the end of 1776, he tried to recruit active support there for the Americans' fight for independence. Now, suddenly, sectors of the bourgeoisie saw the great scientist and exponent of the Enlightenment in a political setting. Because of the increasing sympathies for the patriots, he was at once extolled as an eminent statesman and champion of the ideals of the American Revolution.

The letters written to Franklin during the time he was in Paris express clearly the character of the German enthusiasm for him. They display the mood of the age, invoking Franklin's fame in ever new terms. Writers were convinced that Franklin was "the most renowned man of these times,"[8] something like their spiritual father, "the prime source of all that is good,"[9] "the great man, the American Orpheus, the extent of whose merits astonishes Europe,"[10] and who had so decisively contributed "to break the chains of an oppressed people."[11] In these statements were merged Franklin's image as a sage and scientist—whose thoughts and ideas benefited all mankind—and his new identity as a spokesman of the American Revolution and its principles.

Admiration for Franklin and devotion to the patriots' ideals were, as a rule, closely allied in the bourgeois mind, bringing about the immense re-

*Reprinted by permission from *Germany and the American Revolution, 1770–1800*, trans. Bernhard A. Uhlendorf (Chapel Hill: University of North Carolina Press, 1977), 248–56.

spect in which he was held all over Europe. Franklin, even more than Washington, was the best vehicle for the articulation of revolutionary enthusiasm,[12] and he came to symbolize the American Revolution and its ideals. His popularity was due not to his participation in the event, but rather to his position as the most eminent exponent of the Enlightenment in the New World who had thrown his whole moral weight on the side of the patriots. This also made Franklin a focal point for the appraisal of these events. The aura that emanated from him gave his public advocacy of the insurgents a powerful influence on the European judgment of the Revolution. In 1795 Franklin's biographer, Christian Jakob Zahn, reduced to a simple statement the probable interrelation between Franklin's image and the people's appraisal of the Revolution: "The question of the legality of the American Revolution and that of Franklin's moral righteousness in taking part in it are one and the same. If a discussion should end in a judgment against the Americans, Franklin would also be condemned, and vice versa."[13] It is evident from such interpretations and from Franklin's immense popularity in Europe that his share in the Revolution was much overemphasized by the German bourgeoisie.[14]

Franklin's concrete influence on German evaluation of the American Revolution can be verified in the case of many people whose former political prototype was liberal England. Jan Ingenhousz, the court physician in Vienna, is an excellent example, having been on close terms with Franklin ever since the latter's stay in England as the colonies' representative. Ingenhousz was probably the only person in the German-language area who could truly call himself Franklin's friend. Ingenhousz commonly called England his spiritual homeland. But affection for Great Britain and sympathy with the American patriots could exist harmoniously side by side for only so long; after the war broke out, he had to make a choice.

His correspondence with Franklin furnishes the key to an explanation of his final decision. Franklin had broadly expounded to Ingenhousz his motives, as well as all the consequences thereof, and this caused Ingenhousz to make up his mind. The American had convinced him; Ingenhousz now condemned English policy and told his friend: "I am fully persuaded that you act according to your best judgment for the good and the dignity of your country."[15] In a report Ingenhousz made to Empress Maria Theresa he put Franklin's moral authority in the foreground: "If Mr. Franklin, whose moderate and gentle temperament is beyond question among noted Americans as well as among those who, like myself, have been associated with him in sincere friendship, is so violently turned against the old government, then we are constrained to believe that the majority of his compatriots, who have always listened to him as the most clear-sighted among them, very much share his enthusiasm."[16]

Even in the 1790's, after Franklin's death, numerous Germans were of this conviction. Johann Gottfried Herder wrote of him as one of his "favorites," whose "sense of humanity" he especially valued: "The greater part of the English nation knows well enough that he was no insurgent, that he made the most sensible proposals for peace and reconciliation." According to Herder, Franklin had not started the war with England; there was rather a "star of peace" shining in him.[17] At the end of the century Samuel Baur saw even more clearly this direct relationship between the justification of the American Revolution and Franklin's morality: "Franklin did everything possible to get the ministers' assent to changing their policy. . . . In vain! They did not listen to his wise council, but blindly pursued their own plans, leaving the colonists a choice only between unconditional submission and active resistance. The former was not compatible with the principles of liberty, which the colonists had been brought up to revere; thus, in the end, they were forced to have recourse to the latter."[18]

Interpretations like these were quite in keeping with the personalized idea of history popular at that time. Numerous bourgeois representatives obviously shared the view that the Revolution was even more justified because one of the best-known exponents of the Enlightenment took part in it.[19] We may assume that Franklin's visit to Göttingen similarly affected some individuals, especially in view of the friendly words used by the orientalist Johann David Michaelis and the professor of constitutional law Johann Stephan Pütter when reminiscing about this event in the 1790s.[20]

Georg Forster is another case in point. He visited Franklin in Paris before he ever made any meaningful statement on the American Revolution. He returned from Paris at the age of twenty-three, full of idealism and deeply impressed by this illustrious person.[21] He took a benevolent stand on the American Revolution only in later years, but his admiration for Franklin never left him, and as late as 1791 he described Franklin as "the most venerable name ever pronounced by the eighteenth century."[22] Johann Reinhold Foster, who was influenced by England more than his son, made a similar remark: "It is one of the most pleasant memories of my life to have met the great Franklin in person."[23]

The above remarks did not ignore or reject Franklin the statesman; rather, they integrated this side of the man into the overall image. He appeared to be "a genius with few equals anywhere, equally great as philosopher and statesman."[24] And this was by no means the last stage the Franklin legend was to attain with an enthusiastic bourgeoisie. Even Johann Christian Schmohl, a usually clear-headed apologist of the American Revolution, contributed to the myth: "Franklin is the father of science and of all sound philosophy and politics in America."[25] Knowledgeable Germans could read the appraisal of Franklin by the popular Italian poet and liberty enthusiast, Vittorio Alfieri, in his ode "L'America libera": ". . . father, advisor, soul, mind / of nascent liberty."[26] A less eminent German colleague of Alfieri's, Johann Jakob Meyen, sang of Franklin a little later:

> My song is for the sage who brought the light of science
> To new-discovered lands across the northern ocean.

His country he has freed of tryants who oppressed it.
By nature chosen, he assumed the leader's duty
When Indian woods and huts gave way to provinces.
Ennobling the spirit of liberty through his art and wisdom,
The essence of his gentle nation he created
And with it the foundation of his state.[27]

The obituaries at Franklin's death seemed to justify in every way John Adam's fears regarding the overemphasis of Franklin's role in the American Revolution. In a long necrology Friedrich Schlichtegroll praised the American's "cleverness and deftness in his dealings with France" and then concluded: "Adding to this his first efforts to disseminate lofty principles among his fellow countrymen, we can appreciate how rightfully Franklin deserves to be called the father of American liberty."[28]

Obviously, antagonists of the American Revolution did not agree with these eulogies. These individuals can be divided into two distinct groups. Those adherents of the Enlightenment ideal of liberty who were largely under the influence of England respected Franklin as a scientist and an exponent of Enlightenment philosophy while they condemned the rebel in him. This was the position of Georg Christoph Lichtenberg, for example. When Franklin died, Lichtenberg could not resist making the remark: "They should have put crape on the lightning rods to commemorate Franklin's death."[29] The Göttingen mathematician Abraham Gotthelf Kästner seems to have had similar views; on Franklin's death he wrote to Christoph Gottlob Heyne: "Franklin concerns us as a scientist. I do not think it proper to praise him as the originator of American liberty. To me the Americans are merely rebels who were successful. But even if I thought differently, I would not voice his praise in the king's German countries."[30]

Those among the American Revolution's antagonists who rejected the Enlightenment and its civic ideals of liberty and equality saw no reason to differentiate between the natural philosopher and the rebel. They thought that Franklin's siding with the patriots branded him as an outlaw rebel against England. When Johann Georg Sulzer told the Hanoverian court physician Johann Georg Zimmermann about his anger at Franklin's taking part in the Revolution, he got the following answer: "You should never have taken old Franklin for a good man."[31] But Zimmermann, too, took a different stand later on; in 1791 he wrote to his friend Christoph Girtanner: "Mirabeau, Europe, America, and you have very nobly mourned Franklin's death. But only an idiot, a scoundrel, or a fool like Klopstock could ever wear a mourning band for Mirabeau in Germany!"[32] The bourgeoisie in Germany, devoted to the Enlightenment and to liberty, had so strikingly recorded Franklin's role in the American Revolution that even his adversaries made no attempt to change this.

One question still remains: What was the attitude of the several German governments toward Franklin? Franklin's stay in Britain had drawn government attention to him, and his departure for America in 1775 was duly recorded, but the governments had not formed any clear ideas about his political tasks and achievements. The diplomats ordinarily talked about the old man with a certain feeling of sympathy, fearing, however, that "the famous Dr. Franklin" might side with the rebels.[33]

In December 1776 "the famous Franklin" suddenly turned up in France, and still the German emissaries in the western countries clearly felt benevolent toward him.[34] But at the same time, their reports expressed an astonishing misconception of the purpose of his journey, which they of course conveyed to their governments. Hans Moritz Graf von Brühl zu Martinskirch, the chief of the Saxon mission in London, no less than Thulemeyer at The Hague,[35] recognized and reported Franklin's true intentions, but the minister in Dresden disagreed with him,[36] and put into words what most of the politicians and diplomats were merely assuming at the time: Franklin is simply leaving the sinking ship and looking in France for a place of repose in his old age.[37] Prince Wenzel Anton von Kaunitz was also convinced that Franklin's motives were philosophical rather than political in nature. According to the English envoy in Vienna, "Prince Kaunitz . . . could by no means be brought to suppose that Franklin could be so foolish (as he called it) as to come to Paris with any prospect of inducing the French ministry to take a part in the American quarrel. The Prince seemed fully persuaded that Franklin sought for nothing more than a philosophical retirement in the French king's dominions."[38]

But when the diplomats, too, recognized the true intentions of Franklin and the American patriots, their praise and admiration for the venerated figure vanished. However, they did remain largely neutral and avoided open condemnations of Franklin, although a few critical remarks were made of his open allegiance to the insurgents' cause.[39] Nevertheless, when the war was over, Franklin became the "celebrated doctor" again, even in diplomatic circles.[40]

This attitude shows that the German diplomats, who believed themselves unable to assent more than minimally to the rebels' actions, were considerably influenced by Franklin's personality. In the 1780s Franklin's character was likely to arouse sympathies that in turn could affect individual attitudes toward the American Revolution. Franklin's image apparently influenced the German bourgeoisie's assessment of the American Revolution much more than did Washington's. When the enlightened bourgeoisie in Germany, enthusiastic about liberty and America, recorded their interpretations of the Revolution, they mythically glorified Franklin as a "kind of saint to every good man."[41]

Abbreviations

AAW, Göttingen-Archiv der Akademie der Wissenschaften

DZA, Merseburg-Deutsches Zentralarchiv

GSA, Weimar-Goethe-und Schiller-Archiv
GStA, Munich-Geheimes Staatsarchiv
HHStA, Vienna-Haus-, Hof-und Stantsarchiv
LB, Karlsruhe-Landesbibliothek
NB, Vienna-Nationalbibliothek
PRO, London-Public record Office
StA, Dresden-Staatsarchiv
StA, Marburg-Staatsarchiv
SuUB, Göttingen-Staats-und Universitätsbibliothek

Notes

1. Marcus Cunliffe, *George Washington: Man and Monument* (New York: New American Library, 1960), 20–23; Louis Hartz, *The Liberal Tradition in America* (New York: Harcourt, Brace, Jovanovich, 1955), 51.

2. E.g., Emilio Goggio, "Benjamin Franklin and Italy," *Romantic Review*, XIX (1928), 302–8; Antonio Pace, *Benjamin Franklin and Italy* (Philadelphia: American Philosophical Society, 1958), 17–48, 120–43.

3. It may be noted that in 1793 some members of the Akademie objected to the expulsion of Georg Forster with the argument that the Royal Society had not excluded Benjamin Franklin during the American war (Pers. 66, nos. 1, 2, AAW, Göttingen).

4. E.g., George Christoph Lichtenberg, *Aphorismen*, ed. Albert Leitzmann (Berlin, 1902–1908), aphorism K.A. 16 (c. 1770).

5. "Präsident der berühmte Hr. Benjamin Franklin": Albrecht von Haller in a review of the first volume of the *Transactions of the American Philosophical Society* in *Göttingische Anzeigen von gelehrten Sachen*, Zugabe, Jan. 29, 1774 (see Haller's ex libris copy in the Stadtund Universitätsbibliothek, Bern). See also [Benjamin Franklin], *Merkwürdiger Americanischer Haushaltungs Calendar* (Boston, i.e., Germany, 1771) (first German translation of the *Way to Wealth*).

6. P. P. Burdett to Franklin Dec. 15, 1774 (Franklin Collection 1, 25, Pennsylvania Historical Society, Philadelphia).

7. Olef Torén, *Reise des Herrn Olof Toree nach Surate* . . . [ed. Carl von Linné] (Leipzig, 1772), 143–238.

8. "l'homme le plus renommé de ces temps": Framz Streinsky to Franklin, Prague, Sept. 12, 1781 (Franklin Collection, II, 40, Pennsylvania Historical Society, Philadelphia).

9. "la première source de tout le bien": Franz Anton Freiherr von Seyffertitz to Franklin, Sept. 13, 1778 (Franklin Papers, IX, 135, American Philosophical Society, Philadelphia. Hereafter Franklin Papers).

10. "der grosse Mann, der amerikanische Orpheus, der diesen Umfang der Verdienste hat, welcher Europa in Erstaunen setzt": Johan Jakob Meyen to Franklin, June 28, 1788 (Franklin Papers, LIX, 29).

11. "à briser les chaines d'un peuple opprimé": August Friedrich Wilhelm Crome to Franklin, Mar. 4, 1783 (Franklin Papers, IX, 1).

12. Among the numerous letters to Franklin see especially those by Nikolaus Paradis, Lt. Wommrad, Ludwig Friedrich Gottlob Ernst Gedike, Bek, Baron von Welffen, Johann Valentin Embser, and also those by Jean Rodolphe Vautravers (all Franklin Papers, IX, 164).

13. "Die Frage also von der Rechtmässigkeit der amerikanischen Revolution ist eine und eben dieselbe mit derjenigen von Franklins Moralität in Absicht auf seine Mitwirkung

zu derselben. Fiele das Resultat der Erörterung gegen die Amerikaner aus, so wäre auch Franklin verdammt, und umgekehrt": [Zahn], *Dr. Benjamin Franklins Leben* (Tübingen, 1795), 220.

14. Cf. Esmond Wright, *Benjamin Franklin and American Independence* (London, 1966), 90–161; Roger Burlingame, *Benjamin Franklin: Envoy Extraordinary* (New York, 1967), 121–22; also Michael C. Kammen, *A Rope of Sand: The Colonial Agents, British Politics, and the American Revolution* (Ithaca, N.Y., 1968), 240–52, 273–81.

15. Ingenhousz to Franklin, June 28, 1777 (Franklin Papers, VI, 83), American Philosophical Society, *Proceedings*, Philadelphia.

16. "Si Mr. Franklin dont le tempérament modéré et doux est hors de question chez tous les Américains de note comme à tous ceux qui ont vécus dans une étroite amitié avec lui, comme moi, est si violemment exacerbé contre l'ancien gouvernement, il y a bien de croire, que la plupart de ses compatriotes, qui l'ont toujours écouté comme l'homme le plus clairvoyant parmis eux, participent beaucoup de son enthousiasme": May 18, 1777 (NB, Vienna).

17. "Lieblinge . . . Sinn der Humanität. . . . Dem bessern Teil der englischen Nation ist es bekannt genung, dass er kein Aufrührer gewesen, dass er zum Frieden und zur Aussöhnung die einsichtvollesten Vorschläge getan habe. . . . Friedenssstern": Herder, *Briefe zu Beförderung der Humanität*, 10 vols. (Riga, 1793–1797), I, 10–11, 37–38.

18. "Franklin liess nichts unversucht, die Minister zu bewegen, ihre Einwilligung zu veränderten Massregeln zu geben . . . Umsonst! Sie hörten nicht auf seinen weisen Rat. Blind verfolgten sie ihre eigenen Pläne und liessen den Kolonisten nur die Wahl zwischen unbedingter Unterwerfung und tätigem Widerstande. Jene vertrug sich nicht mit den Grundsätzen von Freiheit, in deren Verehrung sie erzogen waren: sie sahen sich also am Ende, wiewohl ungern, genötigt, ihre Zuflucht zu dem letztern zu nehmen": Samuel Baur, *Geschichtserzählungen*. . . . (Leipzig, 1978), II, 101, cf. 118–19. See also *Das graue Ungeheuer*, VII (1786), 252; Benjamin Franklin, *Kleine Schriften*, trans. from the English by Georg Schatz, 2 vols. (Weimar, 1794), I, [3–4] (foreword by Schatz).

19. E.g., Iselin to Jean Rodolphe Frey, July 28, 30, 1778 (Nachlass Iselin, LVI, 146, 151, StA, Basel); Isidor Bianchi, in Carli, *Briefe über Amerika*, I, ix–x; Georg Friedrich Palm, *Adel der Menschheit* (Leipzig, 1798), 327–47; Karl August Schiller, *Gallerie interessanter Personen* (Berlin and Vienna, 1798), 264–69); *Der Unglickliche Walter oder Leiden und Verfolgungen eines Deutschen in Amerika* (Vienna and Prague, 1798), 142–46; also Benjamin Rush, *Untersuchungen über den Einfluss körperlicher Ursachen auf die Moralität*, trans. from the English (Offenbach, 1787), 93.

20. Johann David Michaelis, *Lebensbeschreibung* . . . (Leipzig, 1793), 110–11; see also his letters to and from Jean Le Rond d'Alembert, June 17, Sept. 6, 1780 (Nachlass Michaelis, CCCXX, fols. 21v, 22v–23, SuUB, Göttingen); Johann Stephan Pütter, *Selbstbiographie*, II, (Göttingen, 1798), 491.

21. Georg Forster, *Tagebücher*, ed. Paul Zincke and Albert Leitzmann (Berlin, 1914): 25–26 (entry of Oct. 9, 1777).

22. "der ehrwürdigste Name, den das achtzehnte Jahrhundert ausgesprochen hat": G. Forster, *Ansichten vom Niderrhein* (1791), ed. Gerhard Steiner, in his *Werke*, ed. Deutsche Akademie der Wissenschaften, IX (Berlin, 1958), 194. See also his considerations on Franklin in his *Erinnerungen aus dem Jahr 1790* (Berlin, 1793), reprinted in his *Kleine Schriften*, VI (Berlin, 1797); Kahn, "George Forster and Franklin," *Proceedings of the American Philosophical Society*, 102 (1958), 1–6.

23. "Es gehört zu den angenehmsten Erinnerungen meines Lebens, dass ich den grossen Franklin persönlich gekannt habe": J. R. Forster in a note to his translation of Brissot de Warville, *Neue Reise*, Berlin, 1792), 105. Cf. Brissot de Warville's own remarks, *Neue Reise*, 94.

24. "ein Genie, dérgleichen wenige gefunden werden, gleich gross als Philosoph und Staatsmann": Johann Zinner, *Merkwürdige Briefe und Schriften. . .*, (Augsburg, 1782), 137.

25. "Franklin ist Vater der Naturkunde und aller gesunden Philosophie und Politik in Amerika": Johann Christian Schmohl, *Über Nordamerika und Demokratie, . . .* ([Königsberg], 1782), 204.

26. ". . . padre, consiglio, anima, mente / Di libertà nascente": Vittorio Alfieri, *L'America libera* (Kehl, 1784), 27.

27. "Den Philosophen besingt mein Lied, der dem neueren Weltteil / Jenseits des Mar del Nort' das Licht der Wissenschaft brachte, / Und sein seufzendes Vaterland von Tyrannen befreite, / Von der Natur gesandt, als Wälder und Hütten der Wilden / In Provinzen verwandelt, einers Führers bedurften, / Der den Geist der Freiheit durch Weisheit und Künste veredelt, / Den Nationalgeist bildet, und mit sich höher emporhebt / Die Grundfeste des Staats": Johann Jakob Meyen, *Franklin der Philosoph und Staatsmann* (Alt-Stettin, 1787), 5–6.

28. "die Klugheit und Geschicklichkeit, mit welcher der Philosoph sein Geschäft in Frankreich betrieb. . . . Nimmt man dies und seine ersten Bemühungen, den Samen grosser Grundsätze unter seinen Landsleuten auszustreuen, zusammen, so sieht man, mit wie vielen Rechte Franklin den Namen des Vaters der amerikanischen Freiheit verdient": Friedrich Schlichtegroll, *Nekrolog auf das Jahr 1790,* I (Gotha, 1791), 295. For similar remarks see [Johann Georg Heinzmann], *Gemälde aus dem aufgeklärten Jahrhundert,* 2 vols. (Bern and Leipzig, 1786), I, 201–2; [Friedrich Samuel Mursinna], *Leben und Charaktere berühmter Männer* (Halle, 1792), 69; C. Milon, *Denkwürdigkeiten zur Geschichte Benjamin Franklins* (St. Petersburg, 1793), 31, 56–58, 110; Henry Wansey, *Tagebuch einer Reise* (Berlin, 1797), 132; Johann Gottfried Grohmann, *Neues Historisch-biographisches Handwörterbuch,* 10 vols. (Leipzig, 1796–1808), III (1797), 325–27; Karl Ludwig Woltmann, *Geschichte der Europäischen Staaten* (Berlin, 1797–1799), I, 310; see also Kenneth N. McKee, "The Popularity of the *American* on the French Stage During the Revolution," *Proceedings of the American Philosophical Society,* 83(1940)., 479–91.

29. "Bei Franklins Tod hätte man sollen Flöre an die Blitzableiter hängen": Georg Christoph Lichtenberg, *Aphorismen,* ed. Albert Leitzmann (Berlin, 1902–1908), IV, 71 (c. 1790), cf. the aphorisms J 412 (c. 1790), J 503 (c. 1791), J 840 (c. 1792), and J 1125 (1793). See also Lichtenberg to Schernhagen, Nov. 25, 1779, and to Ernst Gottfried Baldinger, Nov. 1784, in Lichtenberg, *Briefe,* ed. Leitzmann and Carl Schüddekopf (Leipzig, 1901–1904), I, 336, III, 251.

30. "Franklin geht uns als Gelehrtr an. Den Urheber der amerikanischen Freiheit würde ich nach meiner Empfindung nicht loben, weil ich die Amerikaner nur für Rebellen, denen es geglückt ist, erkenne. Indessen, wenn ich auch anders dächte, so würde ich doch dieses Lob in des Königs deutschen Landen verschweigen": Dec. 1790 (Chron. 23, no. 49, AAW, Göttingen). See also Georg Friedrich Brandes to Heyne, June 24, 1776 (Nachlass Heyne, CXXVI, fol. 48, SuUB, Göttingen); Schlözer in his *Briefwechsel,* I/i (1777), 49; Historisches Portefeuille, June 1785, 726–27, Nov. 1785, 674; Stöver, *Unser Jahrhundert,* I, 26, 505, 507, 533.

31. "Den alten Franklin soll mann nie für einen guten Mann gehalten haben": J. G. Zimmermann to Sulzer, Feb. 23, 1777, in Zimmermann, *Leben und Briefe,* ed. Bodemann, 262. See also Sulzer to Zimmermann, Jan. 19, 1777, in Zimmermann, 261. For similar opinions see J. F. C. E. Freiherr von Linsingen, "Beschreibung der Reise von Stade nach Quebeck" (1778), fol. 6 (L B, Karlsruhe), and the rather low-level polemics in the anti-Franklin satire, *Franklins freier Wille, ein Wink für denkende Menschen über die Macht des Zufalls* (Leipzig, 1787).

32. "Sehr edel haben . . . Mirabeau, Europa, Amerika und Sie für Franklin getrauert. Aber nur ein Idiot, ein Schurke oder ein Narr wie Klopstock konnte in Deutschland für Mirabeau die Trauer anlegen!": to Christoph Girtanner, Nov. 18, 1791 (G S A, Weimar).

33. "le célèbre Dr. Franklin": Hans Mortiz Graf von Brühl zu Martinskirch to Sacken, Mar. 24, 1775; cf. Brühl's dispatch of Apr. 28, 1775 (Locat 2685, conv. XI, fols. 122r–v, 167v / 170, StA, Dresden). For more critical remarks see especially the Prussian minister to London, Maltzahn, in his letters and dispatches to Frederick II, Feb. 4, 1774, July 7, 1775, and to his colleague Thulemeyer, Mar. 21, 1775 (Rep. 96, 35A, vol. IX, fols. 42v–43v, 35B, vol. X, fols. 130r–v, Rep. 92 Thulemeier, no. 10, vol. V, D Z A, Merseburg).

34. "le fameux Franklin": Seinsheim to Haslang, Dec. 29, 1776 (Bayer. Gesandtschaft: London, no. 255, GStA, Munich). See also Seinsheim to Maximilian Emanuel Freiherr von Eyck, Dec. 28, 1776 (Bayer. Gesandtschaft: Paris, no. 36, GStA, Munich); Johann Adolph Graf von Loss to Sacken, Dec. 20, 1776 (Locat 2747, conv. XXII, fols. 6r–v, StA, Dresden); Belgiojoso to Prince Wenzel Kaunitz, Dec. 20, 1776 (Staatskanzlei, Stattenabteilung: England, K. 118, fol. 60v, HHStA, Vienna); Mr. S. to Haenichen, Dec. 15, 1776 (I Alt 22, no. 1505, XIV, StA, Wolfenbüttel); more critical, Maltzahn to Frederick II, Dec. 17, 1776 (Rep. 96, 35C, vol. XI, fols. 312r–v, DZA, Merseburg), and Baron von Boden to the cabinet at Kassel, Dec. 28, 1776 (4 f Frankreich, no. 1716, StA, Dresden).

35. To Frederick II, Jan. 3, 1777 (Rep. 96, 41D, vol. XVI, fol. 2v, DZA, Merseburg).

36. Brühl to Sacken, Jan. 7, 1777, Sacken to Brühl, Jan. 12, Feb. 2, 1777 (Locat 2685, conv. XIII, fols. 17r–v, II, 42r–v, StA, Dresden).

37. E.g., Bernhard Wilhelm Freiherr von der Goltz to Frederick II, Dec. 19, 1776 (Rep. 96, 28C, vol. IX^b, fols. 160v–161, DZA, Merseburg); Seinsheim to Haslang, Feb. 8, 1777 (Bayer. Gesandtschaft: London, no. 255, GStA, Munich); Boden to landgrave, Dec. 11, to the cabinet, Dec. 15, 1776 (4 f Frankreich, no. 1717, fol. 10, no. 1716, StA, Marburg); Mr. S. to Haenichen, Dec. 12, 1776 (I Alt 22, no. 1505, XIV, StA, Wolfenbüttel). For an opposing, retrospective view see Christian Wilhem von Dohm, *Denkwürdigkeiten meiner Zeit oder Beiträge zur Geschichte vom lezten Viertel des achtzehnten und vom Anfang des neunzehnten Jahrhunderts 1778 bis 1806*, 5 vols. (Lemgo and Hanover, 1814–1819), II, 102–3.

38. Robert Murray Keith to Suffolk, Dec. 30, 1776 (S. P. 80 / 218, PRO, London).

39. E.g., Boden to landgrave, Mar. 24, 1779 (4 f Frankreich, no. 1718, fols. 8 2r–v, StA, Marburg); Schönfeld to Stutterheim, Aug. 4, 1780 (Locat 2748, conv. XXV, fol. 211, StA, Dresden); Mercy d'Argenteau to Kaunitz, Mar. 18, 1780 (Staatskanzlei, Staatenabteilung: Frankreich, K. 162, fol 9v, HHStA, Vienna).

40. "célèbre Docteur": Brühl to Stutterheim, Oct. 1, 1782 (Locat 2686, conv. XVIII, fol. 296, StA, Dresden).

41. "jedem guten Menschen gewissermassen ein Heiliger": *Genius der Zeit*, May 1794, 72. Cf. *Genius der Zeit*, Oct. 1794, 245–46. Also, *Neue Bunzlauische Monatsschrift*, July 1790, 207–11; *Deutsche Monatsschrift*, Sept. 1790, 3–9; Daniel V. Hegeman, "Franklin and Germany: Further Evidence of His Reputation in the Eighteenth Century," *German Quarterly*, XXVI (1953), 189; Gilbert Chinard, "The Apotheosis of Benjamin Franklin, Paris, 1790–1791." *Proceedings of the American Philosophical Society*, 99(1955), 440–73.

INDEX

Adams, John, 82, 84, 89, 109, 171–72, 205
Adams, Matthew, 23
Affaires de l'Angleterre et de l'Amérique
Aldridge, Alfred Owen, 10, 12
Alembert, Jean Le Rond d', 3, 173
Alfieri, Vittorio, 204
Almanach des muses, 3
L'America libera, 204
Angoff, Charles, 9
Answer to the Plot, An, 1
Aquarone, Bartolomeo, 4
Arici, Cesare, 192–93

Bache, Benjamin Franklin, 24
Bache, Sarah, 6, 179–80, 196
Bancroft, Edward, 89–90
Beccaria, Giambatista, 190
Becker, Carl L., 111–12
Benjamin Franklin and His Ass Return to Boston, 8–9
Benjamin Franklin, 12
Botta, Carol, 186–88
Boucher, Jonathan, 2
Bradford, William, 22
Brühl zu Martinskirch, Hans Moritz Graf von, 206
Buffon, George de, 133
Burnet, William, 23

Cabanis, Pierre Jean Georges, 173
Calcaterra, Carlo, 189–90
Calendrier de Philadelphie par l'année M DCC LXXVII, 3
Carmichael, William, 89–90
Carteggio morale e letterario di Beniamino Franklin, 194–96
Cattaneo, Antonio, 193
Cavour, Camillo Benso di, 196–97
Cerutti, Joseph-Antoine-Joachim, 173
Choiseul, Duc de, 86
Clark, Ronald W., 12
Cohen, I. Bernard, 8
Collins, John, 72
Compagnoni, Giuseppe, 187–89
Condorcet, Marie Jean Antoine Nicolas, 169–73, 175
Conyngham, Gustavas, 90
Cooper, Samuel, 90–91

Dalibard, Jean, 133
Dartmouth, Earl of, 103, 105, 109
Deane, Silas, 83–84, 86–89, 92
Decow, Isaac, 23
Denham, Thomas, 23
Dennie, Joseph, 5
Dialogue entre Pasquin et Marphorio, 3
Diderot, Denis, 143
Dole, Nathan Haskell, 7
Doppo, Kunikida, 182
Duane, Russell, 8
Duane, William, 6
Dubourg, Jacques Barbeu, 2–3, 173
Du Pont de Nemours, Pierre Samuel, 112, 173
Duyckinck, Evert Augustus, 5
Duyckinck, George Long, 5

Edwards, Jonathan, 149
Eifu, Motoda, 177–79
Electricoram libri VI, 2
Emphémérides du Citoyen, 112

Fauchet, Claude, 175
Feutry, Aimé Ambroise Joseph, 3
Fisher, Sydney George, 6
Fleming, Thomas, 10–11
Forster, Georg, 204
Foster, Johann Reinhold, 204
Franklin, Benjamin
  and St. Augustine, 4
  contrasted to Thomas Paine, 5
  controversy over, 1–12, 41–80, 203–5
  defeated in election for Pennsylvania Assembly, 1

as a diplomat, 81–110
and Timothy Dwight, 8
as an economist, 111–27
elusiveness, 1
and the Great Depression, 7–8
identified with Andrew Carnegie, 7
identified with Poor Richard, 4–7, 41–60
identified with John D. Rockefeller, 7
identified with Theodore Roosevelt, 7
and Cotton Mather, 8, 26–27, 64
and Pennsylvania Germans, 1
and Pennsylvania politics, 1–2, 97
as a philosopher, 103, 109, 112, 149–50
religious views and deism, 4–5, 7, 100, 147–67
reputation in France, 169–76, 205
reputation in Germany, 200–210
reputation in Italy, 183–99
reputation in Japan, 176–83
scientific interests and invention, 101–2, 129–45, 147–49
and surrogate fathers, 19–41
as a typical American, 7, 28, 41, 45, 49, 51, 55–56, 59–60, 138–39
and the Walpole Company, 99–100, 107, 119

WRITINGS OF:
"Advertisement" (for stoves, 1744), 148
"Advice to a Young Man," 20
"Advice to a Young Tradesman, Written by an Old One," 20
Art of Virtue (unpublished), 19, 26, 31–33, 73–75, 153
"Articles of Belief and Acts of Religion," 156–58
Autobiography, 3, 19–80, 148–50, 152–53, 158, 164, 177–79, 181–82
Dissertation on Liberty and Necessity, Pleasure and Pain, 149, 155–56, 158, 160
"Doctrine to Be Preached," 149
Dogood Papers, 63–68
Experiments and Observations on Electricity, 129
Modest Enquiry into the Nature and Necessity of a Paper Currency, A, 115–16, 118–19
Observations Concerning the Increase of Mankind, 28
On the Price of Corn, 112
Poor Richard's almanacs, 66–72, 74, 76
Remarks and Facts Concerning American Paper Money, 116–17
Rules by Which a Great Empire May Be Reduc'd to a Small One, 103
Speech of Miss Polly Baker, 174
Way to Wealth, 69–71, 74, 78, 100, 172, 192
"Witch Trial at Mount Holly," 149

Franklin, Deborah, 6
Franklin, James, 21–22, 64
Franklin, Josiah, 19–41
Franklin, Sarah ("Sally"). *See* Bache, Sarah, 6, 179–80, 196
Franklin, William, 6, 10, 24, 83, 97, 99
Franklin, William Temple, 24, 90, 169–70
Friend of the People, 193–94

Galbraith, John Kenneth, 116
Garibaldi, Giuseppe, 196–97
Gioberti, Vincenzo, 192–93
Giunti, Federico, 4, 192
Greene, F. B., 6
Griswold, A. Whitney, 8
Guggenheim, William, 7

Hamilton, Andrew, 23
Hawke, David Freeman, 11–12
Hemphill, Samuel, 11, 149, 152–54
Herbert, Eugenia, W., 11
Herder, Johann Gottfried, 203–4
Hewson, Margaret, 24, 97
Heyne, Christoph, 205
Hillsborough, Earl of, 109
History of America, 188–89
History . . . of Electricity, 137–38
History of the English Colonies in America . . ., 187–88
Hughes, Thomas, 5
Hulbert, Charles, 4
Hume, David, 103, 112, 117–18, 163
Hunt, Freeman, 5
Hutchinson, Thomas, 104–8

Ingenhousz, Jan, 130, 141, 160, 203

James, Abel, 19, 25, 29–31
Jay, John, 24, 84–85

Kästner, Abraham Gotthelf, 205
Kajin no kigū, 180–81
Kant, Immanuel, 102
Kaunitz, Wenzel Anton, 206
Keimer, Samuel, 22–23, 72–73
Keith, William, 22, 35, 73
Ketcham, Ralph L., 10

Keynes, John Maynard, 112, 117, 121–22, 124–25
Krutch, Joseph Wood, 147–49, 162

Lafayette, Marquis de, 84, 187
Laurens, Henry, 24
Laurens, John, 89
La Rochefoucauld d'Enville, Louis Alexandre, 173, 175
Lawrence, D. H. (as subject), 9, 60–80, 149
Lee, Arthur, 29, 87–88, 90, 108
Lee, Charles, 93
Lee, William, 87
Lichtenberg, Georg Christoph, 205
Life of Franklin, 1
Lingelbach, William E., 7
Liturgy on the Universal Principles of Religion and Morality, 159–60
Londonio, C. G., 187–88
Lopez, Claude-Anne, 11
Loughry, Joseph Bolton, 9–10
Louis XV, 133
Lyons, William, 23

M'Neile, Hugh, 5
Malthus, Thomas, 121
Mangasarian, M. M., 7
Mandeville, Bernard, 23
Man Who Dared Lightning, The, 10–11
Marmontel, Jean François, 173
Martini, Lorenzo, 190–91
Martinelli, Vincenzo, 184
Marx, Karl, 111, 115, 117–18, 123
Mather, Increase, 26–27, 64
Matthews, Brander, 5–6
Mazzelarri, Giuseppe Maria, 2
Meiji Emperor, 179–80
Meiji Empress (Empress dowager Shōken), 177–79
Meika no yokun, 181
Meredith, Simon, 23
Meyen, Johann Jakob, 204–5
Michaelis, Johann David, 204
Mickle, Samuel, 23
Mifflin, Thomas, 24
Mignogna, Nicola, 197
Morellet, André, 173
Miles, Richard D., 9
Miller, Perry, 9
Mitchell, Donald G., 6
Modern Temper, The, 147–49, 162
More, Paul Elmer, 7
Morris, Richard B., 10, 21
Morris, Robert, 83, 85
Morse, John Torrey, 5
Muzzi, Salvatore, 193

Nephew of the Vesta-verde, 192
Newton, Isaac, 23, 142, 150–51, 164
North, Lord (Earl of Guilford), 83, 102, 108
Norton, John Nochols, 5

Oliver, Andrew, 105–8

Paine, Thomas, 25, 91
Palmer, Samuel, 23
Pancoast, Henry S., 6
Papers of Benjamin Franklin, 10
Parton, James, 5
Paxton Boys, 85
Pemberton, Henry, 23
Penn, Thomas, 1–2, 97
Petty, William, 115
Philadelphia Discourses, 190–91
Port Folio, The, 5
Presbyterians, 1, 152
Priestly, Joseph, 135, 137–38, 153
Principia Mathematica, 142, 150
Principles of Trade, 114
Proprietary Party, 1
Pütter, Stephan, 204

Quakers. *See* Society of Friends, 1, 152

Raynal, Guillaume, 173
Report of Trade, 116
Rousseau, Jean Jacques, 3, 172

Sacchi, Giuseppe, 192
Salvadori, Massimo, 112
Schlichtergoll, Friedrich, 205
Schmohl, Johann Christian, 204
Scribbler, The, 2
Series of Lives and Portraits of Famous Persons, 191–92
Shaftesbury, Third Earl of, 163–64
Shiki, Masaoka, 182
Shipley, Jonathan, 19, 189
Shirō's, Shiba, 180–81
Sloane, Hans, 23
Smith, Adam, 76, 112, 114, 118, 120–21, 124
Society of Friends, 1, 152
Sōseki, Natsume, 182–83
Stevenson, Margaret (Mrs.), 97
Stevenson, Margaret ("Polly"). *See* Hewson, Margaret, 24, 97
Stiles, Ezra, 4, 160
Stormont, Viscount, 86

Studies in Classic American Literature, 60–80
Sulzer, Johann Georg, 205

Temple, John, 106
Thayer, William Makepeace, 5
Thomson, Charles, 24
Tillets, Jean Jacques Leron des, 3
Tommasini, Antoinetta, 194–96
Tourtellot, Arthur Bernon, 12
Trent, William Peterfield, 7
Turgot, Anne-Robert-Jacques, Baron de l'Aulne, 3, 173–75
Twain, Mark, 6

Van Doren, Carl, 9–10
Van Zandt, James, 90
Vaughan, Benjamin, 19, 25, 29–31, 73–74, 160
Vergennes, Charles Gravier, Comte de, 84–87
Vicq-d'Azyr, Jacques Feliz, 175
View of the Causes and Consequences of the American Revolution, A, 2
Voltaire, 169–72

Washington, George, 93, 99–100, 185–86, 201–2
Wealth of Nations, 76, 114
Weber, Max, 7–8, 149
Wecter, Dixon, 8
Wedderburn, Alexander, 2, 11–12, 108
Weems, Mason Locke, 3–4
Weiss, Harry B., 6
Wentworth, Paul, 84
West, Benjamin, 24
Wharton, Samuel, 89
Whately, Thomas, 105
Whately, William, 106–7
Whatley, George, 114, 160
Whitefield, George, 100, 152
Wilcox, John, 23
Wilkes, John, 102
Williams, David, 160
Williams, William Carlos, 9
Woods, Leonard, 1, 3, 12
Wyndham, William, 23

Zahn, Christian Jakob, 203
Zimmerman, Johann Georg, 205